Japan, Korea and the 2002 World Cup

The soccer World Cup is unquestionably the biggest sporting event in the world, with an aggregate global audience of billions. This important new study examines the background to the 2002 World Cup finals, and explores the event's profound social, cultural, political and economic significance.

These are the first finals to be held in Asia, and the first to be co-hosted by two countries, Korea and Japan. This book brings together a team of international experts, including leading Japanese and Korean scholars, to assess the unparalleled impact of the event, and to provide a fascinating insight into 'the games behind the games'.

The book offers the first substantial English-language accounts of

- the development of professional football in Korea and Japan
- the political and diplomatic significance of the first co-hosted World Cup
- FIFA and the 'backstage' dealing behind the World Cup
- football as a global culture and its impact on 'traditional' East Asian structures.

Japan, Korea and the 2002 World Cup is essential reading for anybody looking to understand the power of sporting 'mega-events' and the increasingly complex relationship between sport and society. It is also an absorbing read for all serious fans of world football.

John Horne is Senior Lecturer in Sport and Leisure Studies at the University of Edinburgh. He has published widely on aspects of sport, leisure and popular culture in Japan, and is a co-author of *Understanding Sport*.

Wolfram Manzenreiter is Associate Professor at the Institute of East Asian Studies at Vienna University. His research focus is on sport, popular culture and the sociology of new media in Japan, and his recent publications include *The Social Construction of Japanese Alpinism*.

D0322409

Japan, Korea and the 2002 World Cup

Edited by John Horne and Wolfram Manzenreiter

London and New York

First published 2002
by Routledge
11 New Fetter Lane, London EC4P 4EE

Simultaneously published in the USA and Canada
by Routledge
29 West 35th Street, New York, NY 10001

Routledge is an imprint of the Taylor & Francis Group

© 2002 John Horne and Wolfram Manzenreiter

Typeset in Times by
M Rules
Printed and bound in Great Britain by MPG Books Ltd, Bodmin

British Library Cataloguing in Publication Data
A catalogue record for this book is available from the British Library

Library of Congress Cataloging in Publication Data
A catalog record for this book has been requested

ISBN 0–415–27562–8 (hbk)
ISBN 0–415–27563–6 (pbk)

Contents

State, civil society and popular resistance in football   **131**

9   **Japanese soccer fans: following the local and the national team**   **133**
     SHIMIZU SATOSHI

     Introduction – Japan's 'Man. United' – Violence and
     representation by Urawa Reds supporters – Making sense of
     soccer supporting, and the Match Day Program – On the
     Withered Lawn – Allez Japon! Japanese soccer supporters
     abroad – Ultra Nippon: travelling with the national team –
     Moment of resistance? – Alternative choices – Conclusion –
     References

10   **Another kick-off: the 2002 World Cup and soccer voluntary**
     groups as a new social movement   **147**
     YAMASHITA TAKAYUKI AND SAKA NATSUKO

     Introduction – Voluntary activities as a new social
     movement – The traditional Japanese social system of sport
     and soccer voluntary groups – The emergence of soccer
     voluntary groups – The present state of soccer voluntary
     groups – Starting soccer from barren land: the case of the
     2002 World Cup venue cities, Niigata and Oita – Conclusion –
     References

11   **The political economy of the World Cup in South Korea**   **162**
     AHN MIN-SEOK

     Introduction – Theoretical discussion – State and society in
     Korea – The World Cup and the state – The World Cup and
     civil society – Conclusion – References

PART IV
The 2002 World Cup as sports mega-event and sports media event   **175**

12   **Building mega-events: critical reflections on the 2002 World Cup**
     infrastructure   **177**
     NOGAWA HARUO AND MAMIYA TOSHIO

     Introduction: the World Cup is coming to town! – World Cup
     Fever I: the race to become an official World Cup venue –
     Let's spend the public money together! The World Cup as a

List of Illustrations

Figures

Tables

Contributors

Ahn Min-Seok is Professor of Sport Sociology in the Division of Sport and Leisure Studies, Chung-Ang University, South Korea. He has written extensively about sport in Korean society in Korean and other journals. His research interests include the politics and economy of sport, sport policy and Cultural Studies.

Derek Bleakley is currently Deputy Director of the Security Department of the Japan World Cup Organizing Committee (JAWOC). He was also a member of the Japan 2002 Bidding Committee. He was with the British Diplomatic Service from 1959 to 1993, serving as British Consul in Osaka between 1979 and 1983.

Oliver Butler is the editor of the football finance newsletter *Soccer Investor*. After living in Japan between 1991 and 1997, he returned to the UK to complete an MA in Japanese Studies, for which he submitted a thesis on the World Cup bidding process on which his chapter is based.

John Horne is Senior Lecturer in Sport and Leisure Studies at the University of Edinburgh. He has published several articles and book chapters on sport in Japan and is the co-author of *Understanding Sport* (1999) and co-editor of *Sport, Leisure and Social Relations* (1987).

Lee Jong-Young is a Professor in the Department of Sport and Leisure Studies at the Korean National University of Physical Education, Seoul. He is the Vice-President of the Korean Association for the Sociology of Sport and the association's journal editor. His research focuses on the sociological analysis of sport culture.

Mamiya Toshio is a former Professor in the Department of Sport Management at Juntendō University, Japan. He was the chief producer to run the Third World Cup Track and Field Championship. His major research interests are media sport and sport marketing.

Wolfram Manzenreiter is Associate Professor at the Institute of East Asian Studies at Vienna University. His research focus is on sport, popular culture and the sociology of new media in Japan. Recent publications include *The Social Construction of Japanese Alpinism: Culture, Ideology and Sports in Modern Mountaineering* (2000) and *Pachinko Monogatari: Explorations of Japan's Gambling Industry* (1998, published in German).

Gavan McCormack is a Professor in the Research School of Pacific and Asian Studies at the Australian National University, Canberra. He is the author, co-author and editor of numerous books on Japan, Korea and the history and politics of East Asia including *The Emptiness of Japanese Affluence* (2001).

Nogawa Haruo is a Professor in the Department of Sport Management at Juntendō University, Japan. He received his doctorate from Oregon State University in 1983. His major research interests are sport tourism and the secondary careers of professional athletes.

Leonid A. Petrov majored in the History of Afghanistan, Persian and Arabic at St Petersburg State University. After two years of military service with the Soviet Air Force, he studied Korean History, Korean, Japanese and Chinese. He was employed by Korean Airlines before becoming an interpreter for the national football team in 1994. Since 1996 he has been conducting postgraduate research into Korean history at the Australian National University, Canberra.

Saka Natsuko is a lecturer in sociology at Ritsumeikan University, Kyōto. She has conducted postgraduate research into the application of the ideas of Norbert Elias to the sociology of sport. She is also doing research into domestic violence.

Shimizu Satoshi is Associate Professor of Sociology of Sport and Body Culture Studies at the University of Tsukuba. He has researched the modernization of the body, baseball and soccer in Japanese cultural contexts. He is author of *Archaeology of Kōshien Baseball* (1998, published in Japanese).

John Sugden is Professor of Sociology of Sport at the University of Brighton. He is the author, co-author and co-editor of several publications on the political sociology of sport including *Sport in Divided Societies* (1999) and *Boxing and Society* (1996).

Alan Tomlinson is Professor of Sport and Leisure Cultures at the University of Brighton. He is the author, co-author, and co-editor of numerous studies in sport and leisure including *The Game's Up* (1999) and *FIFA and the Contest for World Football* (1998).

Yamashita Takayuki is Professor of Sociology at the College of Social Sciences, Ritsumeikan University, Kyōto. His current research interests include new social movements and voluntary activities, and British-based Cultural Studies.

Preface

In the production of collections such as this it is necessary to give due acknowledgement to various grant-giving bodies, institutions and individuals that have directly and indirectly assisted the various projects on which the book is based. For financial support we would like to thank the British Council (Kyoto Office, Japan), the British Academy, the National Museum of Ethnology (Minpaku) in Suita, the Council on East Asian Studies, Yale University, the Moray Foundation Trust, University of Edinburgh, the Carnegie Trust for the Universities of Scotland, the Travel Grant Fund for Short Term Research Projects of the Austrian Ministry of Science, Education and Culture, and the Japan Foundation.

For inviting us to present preliminary accounts of our research at different stages over the past eight years we would like to thank the Japan Society of Sport Sociology, the Korean Alliance for Health, Physical Education, Recreation and Dance, the Japan Anthropology Workshop, the International Sociology of Sport Association, the Korean Society for the Sociology of Sport and the 2nd International Convention of Asia Scholars.

In addition to the support we have received from libraries, faculty committees and departments in our own institutions – the University of Vienna and the University of Edinburgh – we would also like to mention the many staff, associates and friends at Yale University, Ritsumeikan University, and Tsukuba University who have helped us. Professor Bill Kelly facilitated the roundtable discussion at JAWS/Minpaku in 1999 and the 'Sport and Body Culture in Modern Japan' conference at Yale University in 2000 that enabled John and Wolfram to pursue in-depth discussions about this and other mutual interests in sport, leisure and popular culture in Japan. Professor Yamashita Takayuki enabled John to make his initial visit to Japan a few weeks before the J.League kicked-off and has been a constant source of support and encouragement ever since. Derek Bleakley, Deputy Director of Security at JAWOC, has, in a personal capacity, contributed his detailed knowledge of Japanese football to two of the chapters for which we are especially grateful. In addition, we must express our thanks to all the authors in this collection for their great contributions, their commitment and their timeliness. Simon Whitmore, editor of the Routledge Sport and Leisure Studies series, was supportive from the first moment he learned about this project, and generous enough to wait until it was finally done.

Of course, the biggest debt of gratitude is owed to our families, in particular to Delia, Gerda, Ingo, Lukas, Alison and Richard, and to our friends and pets who have had to rearrange their lifestyles and habits during weekends and evenings as the book was put together. We are also quite grateful to our supporters and various opponents at international table soccer tournaments. Even if they might not have deserved full credit, our final appreciation goes to the English and German national teams and their successful efforts to get through the qualifying stages. Some painful memories emerged during the qualification round, reminding us that the book is about more than just a game. However, the final outcome is to the utmost satisfaction of both editors, and anyway we know – it's only the result that counts. We could say the same about editing collections of articles.

We have asked our contributors to express monetary values in currencies with which they are most familiar and which are easily convertible – US dollars (US$); pounds sterling (GBP); Japanese yen (JPY); and Korean won (KRW). A billion, following American convention, is regarded here as one thousand million; hence a trillion is equivalent to a British billion. With most of Europe converting to the single Euro currency from January 2002, we are including a chart that shows the relative value of these five currencies at different stages of the build-up to the 2002 World Cup. In December 1989, the board of directors of the Korea Football Association decided to bid for the 2002 FIFA World Cup. One month earlier, the Japan Football Association had signalled to FIFA its interest in being a candidate for hosting the 2002 World Cup. October 1992 marks the half-way stage between the establishment of bidding committees for the 2002 FIFA World Cup in Japan (June 1991) and Korea (January 1994). On the last day of May 1996 the FIFA Executive Committee announced its decision to ask Korea and Japan to co-host the 2002 FIFA World Cup. On 15 November 2001(when this was drafted) all but one of the 32 places for the World Cup finals had been decided. To illustrate currency fluctuations over the past decade it may be worth noting that £1 was worth around Y230 in 1989, Y160 in 1996 and back to about Y230 in 1998; US$1 was worth about Y140 in 1989, Y100 in 1996 and back to about Y140 in 1998. Exchange rates in Table 0.1 have been obtained from the Foreign Currency Exchange Converter, provided by Pacific at the University of British Columbia, Vancouver, Canada <http://pacific.commerce.ubc.ca/xr/data.html>.

Table 0.1 Exchange rates

	US$	EUR	GBP	JPY	KRW
1 December 1989	1	–	0.64	143	675
1 October 1992	1	–	0.57	121	788
31 May 1996	1	–	0.65	108	789
15 November 2001	1	1.14	0.69	122	1278

As this book deals with sport, society and culture in non-Western societies, we felt obliged to pay attention to the phonetic particularities of their languages when transcribing names and words that are unfamiliar to most Western readers. We also follow local Asian convention in placing family names before personal names. Both rules do not work very well without exceptions. Strictly following the McCure–Reischauer and the modified Hepburn transcription systems would have facilitated our editorial work immensely, but in many instances people and places are internationally known by alternative transcriptions. Hence we have added alternative notations, where necessary. Otherwise we have kept to the principles of accuracy and consistency.

1 Global governance in world sport and the 2002 World Cup Korea/Japan

Wolfram Manzenreiter and John Horne

Make the game better, and take it to the world.
(FIFA's President Joseph S. Blatter's mission)

Introduction

For many football fans all over the world, time is structured in a four-year cycle that extends between the World Cup finals, football's biggest event. During the past four cycles football has emerged as the world's most salient game and dominant cultural form (Hare, 1999a). When the defending World Champions France kick off in the opening match in Seoul, capital of one of the co-hosting nations in May 2002, the undivided attention of the football world will be drawn again to Korea and Japan. Over a period of 30 days the 32 qualifying teams will compete for the title crown, watched by over two million spectators in the stadia and many thousand times more television viewers all over the world. Watching the World Cup proceed, football fans in Beijing, Brisbane, Bogota, Banjul, Baltimore, Berlin and most other places of the world will experience numerous moments of tension and excitement, dramatic scenes of victory and defeat, packaged and delivered to them by ever-more sophisticated media technologies and ever-increasing numbers of accredited media representatives. Attuned to the needs of local markets and the expectations of national audiences, the televised global event is repackaged in numerous versions of ready-made, localised, World Cups.

The way the global game is displayed has a lot to tell us about the way it is positioned in contemporary processes of globalisation and its significance for governance, economy and civil society. But who or what is in charge of determining the public image of football and the World Cup? Which actors and processes act authoritatively upon the way football is played, cheered in the stadia and consumed in front of television screens? As contributions to *Japan, Korea and the 2002 World Cup* were commissioned well in advance of the kick-off, the chapters in this volume do not deal with events at the actual World Cup finals. Rather, the collection is concerned with detailing the essential preliminaries on the way to fully understanding what is happening in

Seoul and Tokyo in the summer of 2002, including the spread of football to non-Western social formations and the political economy of contemporary sport. One illustration of the intricate nature, and sometimes sensitive path, towards the 2002 finals is revealed by the title of the book. Our title deliberately reverses the word order of Korea and Japan, officially stipulated by FIFA, as a provocative allusion to the power plays between host nations and supranational non-governmental sport organisations. By providing an in-depth and well-informed account of the history and development of football and its popular cultures in the host nations, and by analysing major institutional actors of sport and the media business, this book explicitly recognises that the World Cup is more than just a prominent sport tournament. In fact, as a 'mega-event' the World Cup is also a charismatic spectacle, a functional social ritual and a product of rational calculation (Roche, 2000, p. 7). It is a serious business as well as a public display of national achievements, and as a showcase of individual and collective excellence it also serves as a labour market for some of the best-paid salaried employees in the world. In dealing with 'the games behind the game', this book delivers its own, unique account of the 2002 World Cup.

A World Cup of superlatives

From a European point of view, the game of football has become dominated by the economics of football. Public attention circulates between the mind-boggling salaries of the top players, the widening gap between the less prominent and the ever-wealthier elite clubs and their stakeholders. While the latter are generating surplus income on the stock market and secondary media markets rather than at the ticket gate, the former clubs seem to be trapped in their own provinciality, cut off from the lucrative funds of broadcasting revenues that account for more than 80 per cent of Champions League income. Particularly since pay TV entered the stage in the mid-1990s, professionals' debates, as well as popular discourse, seem to be locked into discussing the business logic of media sport. This season's European Club Champion can expect to gross nearly twice the £40 million that all clubs participating in the first Champions League had to share (*The Sunday Times*, 9 September 2001). Not surprisingly, the winners of the last two tournaments are Europe's wealthiest teams. Manchester United and Bayern Munich not only dominate the national scene – on the pitch as well as in the media tabloids, in the ranks as well as in the balance sheets – but are also capable of attracting a worldwide following. The restructuring of the UEFA Champions League format in 1998, the reform of the football transfer system, and even some changes of football rules, have all been boosted by the sport's economic vitality and its insatiable demand for fresh capital. Football is a highly profitable business but, in order to remain so, a never-ceasing process of investment and re-investment is indispensable.

However, far from being the sole property of Europe, or the Western world, association football has become a truly worldwide phenomenon. To demonstrate the global scale of football interest, and probably also to legitimise its significance, the world football governing organisation FIFA initiated the 'Big Count', a survey of football participation, during the summer of 2000. According to numbers provided by FIFA's 204 national member organisations, 242,380,590 people are actively involved in playing the game (against 127,464 professional athletes), which is roughly 1 out of every 24 of the world's population. In re-occurring waves of a four-year cycle, the world is reminded by the sport's central event, the FIFA World Cup, of the fact that football certainly is the 'world's game'. Likewise, this tournament reveals that football is as much a spectacle and a commodity as it is a form of physical fitness and recreation. Following the 1994 World Cup finals in the United States it became clear just how much global interest had been generated by the sports event. Over 3.5 million football supporters attended the US tournament, more than 30 billion watched the games in front of TV screens, and 40 multinational corporations paid US$400 million in total to gain 'official product' status and guaranteed global advertising. Four years later the World Cup phenomenon took another leap forward at France'98: 190 countries competed in the qualifying stages to reach the 32 finalist positions – the largest number ever. According to FIFA numbers, 37 billion spectators followed the World Cup finals on television, and an estimated audience of 1.7 billion watched the host country, France, beat the defending champions, Brazil, in the final match – 'the biggest shared experience in human history'. Corporate sources contributed to more than 50 per cent of the French Organising Committee's £240 million turnover (Hare, 1999a, pp. 124–125). Not surprisingly, the 1998 World Cup has been described as the largest 'mass marketing of happiness' ever (Taylor, 1998).

And now it is the 2002 FIFA World Cup in Korea and Japan that promises to be an even larger spectacle on an epic scale. For the first time in history, FIFA decided to award the tournament to Asian hosts and to more than a single nation. This unprecedented, and to most observers downright surprising, move even forced FIFA to change its own regulations. As the contributions of Butler and Sugden and Tomlinson to this volume outline in greater detail, internal power struggles were at the root of the decision. It provoked the formation of a fragile alliance between the two East Asian states and their people whose relationship is still deeply tainted by memories of the Japanese annexation of the Korean peninsula in 1910 and the colonial oppression during parts of the first half of the twentieth century. As a consequence of the decline in the number of venues available to both parties involved in the involuntary partnership, a rising number of cities vied with each other for the chance to stage a number of games during the World Cup finals.

The result has been breathtaking: an estimated US$4.7 billion has been invested in sport facilities and equipment at the 20 designated venues. Out of 20 stadia, 18 are entirely new, representing the state of the art in sports–leisure multiplex architecture. The biggest starting field ever of 194 national teams battled out in 777 preliminaries to be seated among the remaining 29 finalists – France, as the reigning World Champions, and the host nations Japan and Korea, qualified automatically. FIFA granted the worldwide broadcasting rights to a private sport-marketing group for US$ 800 million, approximately a tenfold increase on what the international consortium of public service broadcasters had paid for the previous tournament. Two international broadcast centres in Seoul and Yokohama will be equipped with the most sophisticated video and audio transmission technologies, and the press centres in both countries are prepared to serve the needs of up to 16,000 accredited representatives of the media, a 1.5-fold increase since the previous World Cup in France 1998. No doubt, the coming tournament will consolidate similar large television audiences in about 200 countries. Experts believe, and the designated host broadcast company HBS (Host Broadcasting Services, owned by KirchMedia) hopes, that cumulative audience figures might reach 41 billion (HBS homepage). Such aggregate numbers clearly demand an in-depth study of the state of football in the host nations as well as on a global scale. If there is a sure bet to be made, the 2002 World Cup will generate huge profits for some of the key actors in the global media–sport–business alliance. It is an undecided issue yet, however, whether it will also turn out to be a lucrative enterprise for the local organisers, the venue cities and the economies of the host nations.

For us, the FIFA 2002 World Cup Korea/Japan is a highly welcome opportunity to introduce an international readership to a vibrant and varied, yet scarcely well known, football region on the edge of the Eurasian continent. While most football fans in the Western world are likely to be able to name some South or even North American football clubs or players, if asked to do so, probably hardly anyone will know the names of individual or corporate football powerhouses in Japan or Korea. Only recently has public and media awareness of them started to rise, particularly due to the nearing World Cup finals and the increasing presence of a handful of Japanese and Korean players on the rosters of some major European clubs. Despite the relatively early appearance of the Korean national team at the World Cup finals in 1954, and a longer history of professional football spanning nearly two decades, domestic football in Korea has remained in the limelight, overshadowed by the sparkling kick-off of Japan's J.League in 1993. Much of the public awareness in the West about Japan's new professional football league was due to the economic power of the new labour market that opened up in the Far East, providing a rich pre-retirement income source for ageing South American and European football stars. The business logic of the mass media and its obsession with novelty failed to pay tribute to the fact that even in Japan popular interest in football dated back to much earlier times. To provide an informative account of the development of professional football in both Korea and Japan is thus one of the other major ambitions of this collection.

Furthermore, we are particularly glad about the combination of co-hosting and the geopolitical framework of the event as it allows us to address some issues of crucial importance, including: centre–periphery relations related to governance in world sport; power relations between nation–states, supranational sport associations and the sport business; the media–sport–business connection; and the cultural production of ideologies essentially needed to cover the emergent fissures under the surface of the 'people's game'. These overlapping and intersecting key issues, that are at the core of sport and mega-sport events at the beginning of the new millennium, form a sometimes silent, sometimes more loudly spoken, subtext to the chapters of this volume. At the same time, while much of the research informing this collection is based on a more general inquiry into the theoretical presuppositions of sociological thinking when dealing with sport worlds in different cultural contexts, detailed treatment of this issue must be postponed to a future publication. However, we believe that our line-up of scholars from six different countries and at least that many academic fields, together with experts from inside the football business and sports administration, have contributed substantially to our overall objective of providing a concise, research- and experience-based, critical analysis of the social background to the 2002 FIFA World Cup, and the economic and political influences on world football and the broader diplomatic implications this event exerts on the East Asian region. The remainder of this introduction will briefly outline how these concerns are taken up in the rest of the volume.

The periphery on centre stage

A particularly intriguing aspect of governance in world football concerns centre–periphery relations that structure the allocation of power and wealth in late capitalist societies. Though not explicitly relating sport to globalisation, Rowe claims that sport must fulfil three preconditions in order to be successful as a product: it must have a popular base within communities; it must have a reliable governing body; and it must demonstrate itself to be attractive to the commercial trinity of sponsors, advertisers, and television (Rowe, 1995, p. 114). Even on a domestic level, these requirements are bound to evoke tensions between civil, commercial, and governmental actors who are involved in the production/consumption cycle of sport. Yet under the current neo-liberal influences of global capital accumulation and transnational marketing strategies, sport has become inextricably linked to agents, structures and processes of global capitalism (Wright, 1999).

This is the first time in history that FIFA has allowed the finals to be played in the football world periphery. Although the official FIFA emblem of two footballs imprinted with the map of the world depicts the Far East close to the centre where the two balls intersect, there can be no doubt that Asia is peripheral in terms of football power. The Asian continent is home to one-third of the world's population, and members of the Asian Football

Confederation (AFC), UEFA's counterpart in this region, account for more than 40 per cent of the 'Big Count's' football players. But in 2002 only two Asian teams were able to qualify together with the host nations, compared with thirteen fixed places for European nations with only half the number of, more or less, regular football players. There was a chance for Iran to go east in 2002 as the fifth Asian team, but it failed to qualify in the play-off against Ireland which became the fourteenth UEFA team. Asia's peripheral position is further expressed in terms of the number of football officials, professional players and achievements at previous World Cup finals. South Korea, which has a football population of 0.5 million (including 5,000 female players and 410 professionals), is heading for its fourth straight consecutive performance, but for Japan, which has 3.3 million players (20,000 women and 1,120 professionals), it is only their second appearance in the 'Theatre of the Great'. While Saudi Arabia travelled to the USA in 1994 and to France in 1998, China (7.2 million players, 40,000 women and 1,748 professionals) is making its debut at the 2002 World Cup finals, having managed, at long last, to travel the arduous road to the top with a wave of national enthusiasm sweeping through the People's Republic. Yet an Asian team has not reached the second stage of football's most prestigious tournament since 1966.

Peter Velappan, Secretary-General of the AFC and FIFA's Co-ordinating Director for the World Cup, called China's qualification a windfall for Japan and Korea. Already in 1990, half of the total television audience generated by the FIFA World Cup in Italy, were watching from Asia (Miller *et al.*, 2001, p. 64). Given the close geographic proximity and the participation of all three football powerhouses from the Far East, viewing rates in Asia are likely to increase even more. Even though close to the action as the crow flies, millions of Chinese fans are likely to watch their team via television as there is good reason to doubt that the authorities in Japan, and probably in Korea as well, will feel inclined to accede to Velappan's request to lift current visa restrictions for Chinese visitors to the two countries. Japan found it hard enough to relax the pre-travel tourist visa requirements for visitors from Korea, which is the only OECD country governed by this special measure, so it is likely that the administration's fear of uncontrolled illegal immigration from China will most likely prevent such a generous move.

Basically football in China, Japan and Korea shares a similar fate inherited from Europe's colonial past. The peripheral position of football in East Asia is due to the history of the world and its geopolitical structuration a century ago. In each of these countries football is in keen competition with other mass sports, but it hardly vies for the first rank. In China, football is supposedly the fourth or fifth most popular sport. In Korea and Japan, professional football is overshadowed by the overwhelming popular support for baseball and for the traditional wrestling sports of *ssireum* and *sumō*. Contrary to the Western experience, sports did not evolve gradually out of familiar folk traditions. Lumped together in the cultural backpack of

Western foreigners, modern sports were imported during the latter half of the nineteenth century, at a time when the geopolitics of imperialism had a rather downgrading impact on national consciousness in the Far East. Neither the consequences for local body cultures and leisure lifestyles are far from being exhaustively explained nor the concomitant processes of localisation. Whether one sees sport as a form of cultural imperialism or as a deliberate part of cultural domestication and emulation depends on the particular perspective of the individual author rather than on any commonly accepted understanding of the historic process of cultural flow (Manzenreiter, 1999a). Numerous studies have analysed the particular role of the nation–state and its institutional actors in adapting the new cultural practice for its own needs. Again, in contrast to the West, the firm grip of the state over the collective body is a characteristic feature of East Asian modern sport history that prevailed until recently even in Japan, undisputedly the most liberal of the three countries. In China, for example, legislation on tobacco promotion severely impacted upon revenues for the Chinese National Football League in 1999. After five years Philip Morris was forced to withdraw from sponsoring the former Marlboro League which was renamed in accordance with the new main sponsor as the Pepsi League (Holmes, 1999).

In contrast to post-socialist China, late capitalist Japan is accustomed to see liquor breweries Suntory and Kirin as official sponsors for football trophies or J.League stages. With revenues from tickets sales and broadcasting revenues decreasing, J.League clubs are increasingly dependent on corporate sponsorship. In the light of the economic recession, some clubs have even been considering a strategic partnership with Japan Tobacco, although the J.League's ethical mission prohibits such an alliance. During the World Cup, tobacco advertisements are banned from the stadia and smoking is restricted to specific areas, most likely far away from the television cameras. This is part of a campaign jointly conducted by FIFA and the World Health Organisation and a good example of FIFA exerting its influence upon the way the game, as well as its governing body, is presented to the world, namely, healthy, caring, and clean. However, FIFA's credibility may be somewhat undermined by its own declaration that beer, provided by official sponsor Budweiser in plastic cups, should be sold to spectators during the matches. After a series of violent incidents among football fans in South Korea, alcohol was completely banned in all stadia. Despite widespread concerns, including those expressed by the Japanese organisers, FIFA, acting for Budweiser, have enforced the company's entitlement to advertise and sell their product. This policy contrasts starkly with measures employed at European tournaments where alcohol bans within stadia, and the strict policing of sales outside stadia, have long been regarded as essential to crowd management. So strong were local regulations in France that Budweiser were unable to advertise during the 1998 World Cup and sold their on-the-pitchside sponsorship rights to electronics company Casio.

Dealing with football

So who determines how the World Cup is presented to the world audience? FIFA, football's commissioner that mixes with national governments and transnational corporations on equal footing, certainly is most influential in changing the rules of the game but it is highly dependent on the public support of host nations, funding from private enterprises, and the technological know-how of the media industry. Is it then the media content business, particularly the German media tycoon Leo Kirch, whose group possesses the worldwide broadcasting rights? While KirchMedia was able to demonstrate its power in lucrative deals with broadcasters all over the world (and some nervous European politicians as well), in some cases national laws have set strict limits on its negotiating power. Furthermore, the media agency relies heavily on its appeal to institutional investors and on the continuous demand of its customer base. The broadcasting companies, in turn, are constrained by national media laws, revenues generated from selling advertising time, and the vacillating interests of audiences. Television viewers have the power to stop the cycle as their collective decision to switch on and tune in is the cornerstone of the whole billion dollar sport industry. However, rather than turning off, the majority of sport viewers switch to matches where national interests are at stake, or where popular players or teams are shown in action. The power of individual club sides, however, is also very limited since it depends on many factors, which includes the strength of the opposition within the leagues with whom they compete. Sufficient to say, national regulations, corporate law, and commercial codes of conduct are no less influential than the rules of the game supervised by FIFA and the International Football Board (IFB).

Looking at structure and agency in the long and winding road to the kick-off on 31 May 2002, a number of competing interest groups and stakeholders come to the forefront. The prehistory of 2002 includes FIFA's internal, behind-the-curtain, power struggles, the bids for the designation of venue cities and training camps in Japan and Korea, sporadically erupting frictions between the host nations, and the common attempts to come to terms with the sudden collapse of FIFA's main marketing partner, ISMM/ISL in the spring of 2001. These incidents are all embedded within a complex set of sequential stages which are no less fascinating and thrilling than the preliminaries on the field. The Japan/Korea World Cup history began long before the previous FIFA president, the Brazilian João Havelange, declared in the late 1980s his intention to award the 2002 World Cup to an Asian host. In fact this public announcement heralded the third stage and the start of the most expensive World Cup bidding round ever, and the final stage was inaugurated with the decision of co-hosting and the subsequent formation of the two national organisation committees, KOWOC and JAWOC. Since the establishment of bidding committees, and most clearly in the installation of a government co-ordination board to facilitate security issues, working permits, visa and similar affairs, governmental involvement became clearly visible. Such was the leverage power of FIFA that it insisted on the designation of inter-ministerial delegates from both countries.

FIFA's role in ruling the people's game has already been systematically assessed by two contributors to this volume (Sugden and Tomlinson, 1998). Without reservation they approve of Simson and Jennings' (1992) observation that organisations such as the International Olympic Committee (IOC) or FIFA are part of the 'apex of a multi billion dollar global political economy' (Sugden and Tomlinson, 1999, p. 389). Therefore, they assessed FIFA both as a prime mover of transnational capitalism and as a bulwark against 'entrenched forms of imperialist domination' (1998, p. 228). For example, FIFA's Code of Conduct requires its corporate partners to observe basic labour laws, such as the abolition of forced or child labour, and to preserve the freedom of association and collective bargaining. Parties that infringe these provisions may have sanctions imposed, which can go as far as the withdrawal of FIFA licences. Although no case of sanctions is known, observing the rules pays off, as the international boycott against Nike for exploiting Third World labour has revealed. In positive terms, when Nike's biggest rival Adidas 'won' the last World Cup (Brazil was equipped by Nike, and the winning team, France by Adidas), Adidas' sales went up by 48 per cent. Months ahead of the finals, 'the other World Cup' (Hare, 1999b) had already been played in a friendly between Brazil and Germany, one of the other top teams on the long-term payroll of Adidas. This match was televised in two parallel live broadcasts, one for the German audience from a camera viewpoint that focused on the side where the Adidas stripes were visible, and another one for the international market from the opposite side showing Nike's advertisement boards. A replay of 'war of the boots' (Nike's Phil Knight) is scheduled for 2002. While the World Cup sponsor Adidas is also official supplier to the Japan Football Association (JFA) and the national squad, Nike, which also subcontracts part of its garment production to the South Korean textile industry, is officially sponsoring the Korean counterpart, the KFA.

Going back to the first stage of the road to the co-hosting decision may help us to better understand the inherent contradictions of capital accumulation and resistance to aspects of globalisation in sport. The groundwork of the inextricable link between sport, media and corporate business was prepared in the 1970s when Havelange took up office. It is well known that Havelange's installation in FIFA headquarters rested on the promise of expanding the game to the people of the peripheral world. Hence the choice of Asia as host can be seen as a strategic move delivering on an earlier promise. While this is the official FIFA version, alternative accounts (Ortner, 1987; Senda 1999; Taniguchi, 1999; Hirose, n.d.) allege that Havelange's successful candidacy, as well as the Spaniard Samaranch's move to the top of FIFA's sister organisation, the International Olympic Committee (IOC), owed much to ballot-rigging and behind-the scene-fixing.

The next stage along the way to the co-hosting decision was reached in the early 1980s when the traumatic experience of Montreal, the debt-ridden Olympic City of 1976, triggered world sport administrative bodies to explore new business realms. The involvement of the so-called 'Dark Emperor' of the sports world, Horst Dassler, head of the German–French sports garment producer Adidas, and the so-called 'Latin Mafia' was successful enough for all sides involved and laid the cornerstone for the sport–media–business triangle that transformed sport in the late twentieth century (Taniguchi, 1999, pp. 80, 81). Basic elements of the sales strategy, such as the idea of packaging, or the tri-partite business model of sponsorship rights, exclusive broadcasting rights and merchandising, were copied meticulously a decade later when Japan's professional football league was inaugurated (Ubukata, 1994, pp. 31–34). Given that Japan's largest advertisement agency Dentsū held a 49 per cent partnership in ISL (International Sports Culture and Leisure Management Service), Dassler's sport marketing arm, and the incorporated head and heart of world sport marketing, the implementation of this lucrative strategy was hardly surprising. The only surprise was that Dentsū's biggest rival at home, Hakuhōdō, was finally charged with devising the J.League's marketing concept. It is, however, an irony of history that FIFA's internal power struggles, that finally gave birth to the compromise of co-hosting, are at least partially attributable to the refinement of marketing techniques developed by former ISL managers. Setting up their own agency, TEAM and its flagship product, the Champions League, demonstrated to the European bloc inside FIFA how much more money could be squeezed out of broadcasters and sponsors. Additionally, it is worth noting that Japanese capital, inter-corporate networks and marketing know-how have been at centre stage of the commercialisation of world sport in the past twenty years. Japanese corporations, Matsushita, Ricoh and Plaza, for example, were part of the twelve official partners of the Olympic Programme between 1989 and 1992. In France in 1998 JVC, Canon and Fuji Film each paid US$30 million to be FIFA's corporate partners with all rights to use the FIFA emblems (Nufer, 1998, p. 5). In 2002, Canon declined the option of renewing their contract, but with Fuji Xerox refilling the slot of office equipment supplier, and NTT and Toshiba entering the board, five out of fifteen of the main sponsors of world football's greatest event are Japanese. In line with Coca-Cola and Gillette, both JVC and Fuji Film have been FIFA's Official Partners since corporate sponsorship entered world football two decades ago.

The politics of football

Transnational corporations and multinational non-governmental organisations have dominated the discussion above. To conclude that nation–states and their governmental actors are totally out of the game, however, would be misleading. Sports always have been used and misused by political actors for their specific purposes. Until today, the state in Japan and Korea has continued to play a seminal role in the administration and development of sport on various levels. The particular notion of strengthening the nation through training bodies has been at the heart of education policy in both countries for most of the twentieth century. As Ahn notes in this volume, both military regimes and democratic governments of the Republic of South Korea have implemented the same sport policy promoting national pride and identity. Also Kim (2000) observed the special treatment of top athletes in Korea and preference for a national appeasement policy that afforded higher investment in elite sports than in mass sports. Only recently, with the advance of consumer society in the 1980s, have governments become more aware of the economic power of sport and leisure-related investments. In Japan, an advisory council to the former Ministry of Industry and Trade declared sport to be a major growth machine of the twenty-first century. Issued long before the economic crisis of the 1990s terminated the Japanese leisure facility construction boom, the committee's final report, *Sport Vision 21*, indicated the still valid preferential policy of luring private enterprises into joint development projects (Seki, 1997, pp. 488–493).

The role of sports in domestic policy is just one of many ways of conceptualising how sports and politics interact. Given that sport mega-events are important elements in the orientation of nations to international or global society, as Roche argues (2000, p. 7), they offer points of reference for processes of change and modernisation in the collective memory and in the foreign policy of nation–states. According to Ahn, the central government is planning to use the 2002 World Cup as a catalyst to create popular harmony, system stability and to promote a neo-liberal hegemony in Korea. This differs considerably from the policy of the Fifth Republic towards the Seoul Olympics in 1988. Similar to the Tokyo Olympics in 1964 that heralded Japan's return to the international community of nation–states, the Seoul Olympics served to showcase economic and technological achievements to a world audience and, at the same time, to bridge the cleavages between conservative and progressive political blocs within their own population (Koh, 2001; Manzenreiter, 1999b).

As Butler's analysis of the bidding war shows, Japan's government was, initially at least, less interested in hosting the World Cup than the Korean. It certainly did not adopt the no-nonsense approach of the Koreans that secured the 1988 Olympics for Seoul (with 51 votes against 27 votes for the JOC's bid, Nagoya) and later procured half the World Cup. Media reaction in both countries to the co-hosting announcement reflected the different moods of the non-voluntary partners. Korea praised the acceptance of the bid as a clear victory, while Japan complained about anticipated diplomatic intricacies and the inevitable decrease in revenues (Ōno, 1996, p. 118). Throughout the 1990s, football in Japan has been a prime mover in regional development. As Horne and Bleakley's chapter discusses, the inauguration of the J.League is inextricably linked with economic restructuring policies, and the fostering of local identities as a counter-weapon against urban concentration and rural migration. The growth machine imagery is prominent in the national rhetoric on both sides of the Japan Sea. In March 2001, the Korean Ministry of Finance and Economy promised to develop a multi-faceted strategy to maximise the economic impact of the World Cup. The state-run Korean Development Institute predicted the creation of 350,000 jobs and an additional industrial output of US$8.82 billion, with a 22 per cent share going to the construction sector (Park, 2001). However, with the kick-off approaching, forecasts have got gloomier. According to the private Samsung Economic Research Institute, the World Cup will not generate the economic benefits that the Seoul Olympics did in 1988, unless there is a dramatic recovery in the global economy (Seo, 2001). Writing in November 2001, this likelihood is further off than ever.

It is interesting to note that the politicians' utopian dreams have found echoes in the writing of some social scientists in both countries (Lee, 2001; Maeda, 2001). Yamashita and Saka in this volume, however, warn against over-simplified visions of an emerging civil society as a third power between politics and economy. Doing fieldwork with some local activists in cities designated as venues for 2002 matches, they disclose a variety of motivations, interests and activities among the voluntary World Cup supporters. Nonetheless, even if the new volunteer movement is rather 'pre- and meta-political' in nature, the act of volunteering carries great social potential in Japan, and thus the volunteer groups in football may herald significant changes in the way society organises itself.

Pumping public money into the construction of huge sport stadia does not find unanimous consent, however. Sports venues are often utilised by dominant forces to articulate particular memories and 'a' version of the past rather than the plurality of inconsistent and contested meanings. Yet since the 1998 Winter Olympics in Nagano which failed to reproduce the atmosphere of the Tokyo Olympics and the mystical experience of national rebirth, negative sentiments against boosterism abound among many of the inhabitants of the debt-ridden prefectures. The unfulfilled promises of reviving the economy and reinstalling trust in the future have contributed to widespread pessimism and a dismissive stance against the construction of mega-sites for just a single occasion. However, the construction sector is at the heart of Japan's political economy, and growth machine ideologists are central actors in political parties, lobbying groups and non-governmental organisations. One prominent representative is the industrialist and real estate tycoon Tsutsumi Yoshiaki, one of the richest men in Japan and official member of many influential sports committees. Under his presidency, the Japan National Olympic Committee was turned into a professionally run sports agency, and it was probably his presidency of the Japan Ski Association that single-handedly drew the Morioka World Cup in 1994 and the Nagano Winter Olympics in 1998 to Japan. While the Nagano Olympics were reported to have generated a surplus income of 4.5 billion yen, the profits largely by-passed national tax-payers and the local population who were left standing in the rain with the hardly used bobsled 'Nagano Spiral' and the giant speed-skating venue M-Wave (*Asahi Shinbun*, 18 November 1998). Nogawa and Mamiya in this volume also draw a rather negative picture of the current state of public facility management in Japan. Unless sound management systems are established, and this seems not to be the case yet, they argue that many, if not all, of the World Cup stadia could remain as heavy burdens on local taxpayers and leave a negative heritage of the 2002 World Cup.

The tragic history of the two countries, concisely described and commented upon in McCormack's stimulating chapter, adds a particular twist to the way the World Cup has been used in foreign politics. On the one hand, bilateral relations started to improve, after South Korean President Kim Dae-Jung's 'sunshine policy' started to de-ice the frosty relationship with the former colonialist. In consequence, South Korea opened its doors to some aspects of Japanese popular culture, and both countries supported a successful rapprochement policy at the diplomatic level. On the other hand, as the very issue of co-hosting and the word order quarrel on tickets and application forms in early 2001 clearly indicated, both parties understood well that there was an opportunity to make effective use of the World Cup as moral leverage in diplomatic relations. For Japan, as Butler notes in this volume, 'co-hosting presented a means of re-orienting Japan's relations with South Korea toward the future without having to make the apologies and compensation that South Korea demanded as a prerequisite to such a development'. The word order issue is dealt with in detail later, yet while KOWOC insisted on maintaining the word order in strict compliance with the official title of the games, JAWOC appealed to a 'gentlemen's agreement' from 1996 that the order of the names could be revised when using Japanese script. Japan finally gave in to FIFA's mounting pressure and dropped the Japanese wording on application forms and tickets, thereby delaying the scheduled start of ticket sales (FAZ, 2001). JAWOC's reluctant attitude was perhaps related to the fear that the whole issue might have been manipulated by the politically ambitious KOWOC Co-chairman Chung Mong-Joon, who is also a member of the South Korean parliament, heir to Hyundai industries, FIFA Vice-president and a potential claimant for the South Korean presidential office which is up for election later in 2002.

Officially South Korea is keen to play down the disputes, separating the likes of the textbook issue from the hosting of the football event. The quarrel, over apparently minor matters, was symptomatic, however, of increasing tensions between the host nations. The Japanese policy of forced prostitution of Korean women during the Pacific (Second World) War, the history textbook issue and blunt right-wing jingoism among contemporary members of the Japanese political elite, all threatened to upset the short honeymoon period. The omnipresent Chung has always been quick to retaliate and criticise Japan for being insensitive to its former victims and for not doing enough to mend diplomatic ties. The claim that political disputes will not affect the World Cup is challenged by public opinion. Various opinion polls conducted in both countries since the co-hosting decision have revealed that the gap between Japan and its nearest neighbour can hardly be deeper. Hostile feelings (*kirai*) towards the other were more prominent among Koreans (65 per cent vs 17 per cent), though more than half of the Japanese sample said that they did not feel close to Korea (*shitashimi ga nai*). One out of three Japanese, but only every sixth Korean, expected an improvement of the atmosphere. Furthermore, the overwhelming majority in both countries explicitly stated no interest in active interaction with the other's cultural products (Lee, 1997, p. 146). If public sentiment remains as hostile in 2002, it will be impossible to realise the visit of Japanese Emperor Akihito to Seoul for the opening ceremony of the World Cup. Seoul and Japan have carefully presented the Emperor's visit as a sign of sealing a future-oriented relationship between the two neighbours, replacing the long-time bitterness. The Imperial Household Agency, however, has hurried to save face and proclaimed that older, more long-standing, invitations to the Emperor to visit the Netherlands make the historic visit very unlikely, anyway. As McCormack says, the co-hosting will either bring the two countries together or drive them further apart; it is impossible to know which it will be at this stage.

A third level of analysing the interaction of sport and politics is to look at the political uses to which non-governmental actors put sports. Some of the previously given examples could be repeated here as in many instances, office-holders fulfil multiple functions and it is far from being clear whether a statement has been made by the Member of Parliament or the representative of the NOC. Particularly insightful is the way FIFA emerges on the political platform. The anti-smoking alliance with the World Health Organisation is one example, another is the recent move to join the bandwagon of Western animal welfare activists and environmentalists. FIFA called on both World Cup co-hosts to change their culinary habits. Whale meat should be banned from Japan's menus, and South Korea was asked to stop its people mistreating and eating dogs, which is quite common among sections of the population, but also in other parts of the world. Back in 1988, South Korea banned restaurants from offering dog during the Olympics in order to enhance the country's international image, and if Chung is entitled to speak for the government, existing laws abolishing the mistreatment of animals will be enforced during the tournament.

FIFA is certainly aware of the importance of such occasions to enhance its own reputation as a political power. Caring for animals is a strong symbolic message. Probably even stronger is the message of caring for people, their health and welfare, and world peace. While North Korea still is a risk factor in the region, hardly anybody expects aggressive acts from the communist North to disrupt the games. Back in 1988, IOC President Samaranch was busily negotiating with members from the North Korean NOC to guarantee the peaceful procedure of the Games. In fact, the door to host at least a single match has been opened widely, though to date in vain, which has terminated any Nobel Peace Prize aspirations by FIFA. Football hooliganism, which was a major security issue in 1998 and most previous World Cups since the 1960s, might be thought of as only of minor importance in the Far East. In Japan hardly any football fans go on the rampage, in remarkable contrast to the tumultuous years of the immediate post-war period. Shimizu's first-hand account of a fan club vividly shows that their aggressive appearance and violent behaviour are mainly for show and are best understood in Goffmanian terms of acting or posing. The social appeasement policy of post-Olympic middle-class Japan was so successful, that Japan's Ultras have to mimic the subcultural behaviour of their European role models.

In South Korea, however, public security is less stable. When we visited Seoul in the summer of 2001, the English language TV network, serving the 37,000 American troops that are stationed in South Korea, warned us not to go downtown for two consecutive days as an unspecified demonstration was scheduled to happen during the weekend. Violent clashes between political protesters or labour unionists and the police forces occur frequently. Thus the Korean riot police are well prepared to cope with hooligans who are expected from Europe, if they actually travel as far as Cheju or Busan. A writer for the Japanese boulevard magazine *Shūkan Taishū* attributed to the Japanese special police forces the same uselessness as the Japanese army in equally 'lacking experience in combat'. In case the police fail to reassure their own people, shopkeepers in Japan can take out a special insurance policy against hooligan damage that runs a month before the first game and a week after the last game in each city. CNN reported that Nisshin Fire & Marine had developed this unusual product in response to requests by store owners in Yokohama, site of the final match. Although both Japan and Korea have insurance companies as official suppliers, Nisshin is not one of them. To improve on tactics for the unexpected, the Metropolitan Police Agencies in Seoul and Tokyo invited British police experts to assist with training in spring 2001. The *Asahi Shinbun* published a photograph of some dozen members of the riot police squad, dressed up as fanatic soccer hooligans, waving little Union Jack flags. From the picture it looks as though the officers had a good time, although they got soaked to the skin as real water cannons chased them all over the place (a disused gas works rather than a football stadium). The British Embassy in Tokyo was less amused and demanded an apology for the unfortunate use of a symbol of hooliganism (*The Independent*, April 2001).

Japan's police forces might have been less merry after 11 September 2001 when a less visible yet much more violent threat to the finals appeared. The terrorist attack on the World Trade Center seriously changed the way the finals will be staged. Both countries hurried to declare that they were going to impose tighter security measures in one of the biggest police operations ever mounted. With the heavy reliance on air travel, it is planned to tighten security at airports and immigration procedures, and to increase security personnel, including armed forces, and the establishment of no-fly zones over the stadia. The situation became even more earnest, when USA and China qualified. Japan finally boosted its security budget by 25 per cent to US$18.5

million. Yet this is only a small part of the US$270 million IOC President Rogge announced for security issues during the Winter Olympics held in Salt Lake City three months earlier. It is a very tiny amount if compared with the incredible amounts that are at stake in the worst case scenario: cancellation, and it serves well to demonstrate a particular facet of the interdependency of transnational capital and sports.

Cancelling the World Cup would imply massive claims for damages from broadcasting companies and corporate sponsors that have invested their co-operation with FIFA. Furthermore, the loss of scheduled revenues would endanger FIFA's reliability as well as the execution of most of its operations. Therefore, the World Cup in France was insured for US$391 million, including coverage against cancellation, advertising losses, television rights and spectator injury (Kaplan, 1998). Four years later FIFA, taking into account the increase in television rights, and dangers deriving from natural disasters and political instability, was ready to pay as much as US$16.7 million for an all-risks policy and coverage of US$700 million against loss of revenues and the like. This lucrative deal was sealed with the German insurance group Albingia that had insured all World Cups since 1974. Albeit rather small in international comparison, Albingia always had managed to benefit from its traditionally good connections with the world of sports – since 1921 Albingia had insured the German national team – and its relations to Erich Himmelseher. A German broker and insurer, Himmelseher specialised in sport events and was given the FIFA award of merit in 2000 because of his achievements in making the World Cup a financial success for the first time in 1974 and paving the way for FIFA's prosperity.

Yet the risk of total damage to the 2002 World Cup is too high for any single insurance company. To recoup losses from a worst case scenario would require, under current terms, the premium of roughly forty World Cup insurances, or 160 years. Therefore, usually a consortium of some dozen insurers and re-insurers share risk and revenues. This policy may have changed after AXA Colonia, a fast-growing international insurance group, took over the majority of Albingia shares from the British parent company Guardian Royal Exchange. Then suddenly AXA Colonia terminated the insurance contract, due to huge net losses imposed by the WTC attack. FIFA reacted with talks and threats of legal action, while the world was left in suspense about whether the World Cup was to take place at all (Croft and Hunt, 2001). Tensions eased after two weeks with FIFA's announcement of a new cancellation insurance contract. The new partner was found in US-based National Indemnity, a subsidiary of another old acquaintance, the investment group Berkshire Hathaway, that was chiefly involved in the former insurance deal by underwriting the bonds FIFA issued in order to defray costs. While details of the new premium or whether the arrangement included cover against terrorism were not released immediately, FIFA was eager to stress that the terms of the new policy did not allow it to be terminated by the insurer.

Two weeks later, FIFA officials expressed their confidence that the threat of terrorism was being dealt with by Korea and Japan to their utmost satisfaction. Praising these countries as the safest places in the world, Vice-president Mattarese assured the world that the governments would do everything necessary to ensure a safe World Cup for everybody (Walker, 2001b). According to various media sources, Mattarese elegantly added that 'responsibility for people's safety is for the two governments, not FIFA. The issue is not only stadium security, but venue security and national security' (Himmer, 2001). Unfortunately he did not elaborate whether this assertion also conceded the right to terminate the World Cup, if in the interest of public security, to national sovereignty.

Uniting the nations, unifying the nation: the work of ideologies

Since 11 September 2001 FIFA President Blatter has sedulously spread the message that the games will go on, predicting a return soon to 'a, if not peaceful, an understandable situation amongst the people in this world'. With reference to the mediating power of 'the game of the people' that may contribute to a 'better understanding between the people', he gave an account of football that 'has no boundaries in race and religion, in cultural differences, the rich and the poor' (Walker, 2001a). Whatever Blatter actually wanted to say, the condensed quotation taken from the media contains core elements of the rhetorical language used to disguise the inherent contradictions and tensions in world football. Thus it does not matter whether the FIFA official, the newspaper writer, or his or her editor is responsible for the reproduction of such simple-minded stereotypes. It is sufficient to note the crucial role of the media in transmitting the imagery of a democratic, autochthonous and unifying sport.

Sport always was of particular appeal to the media industry because it is cheap to produce and attracts huge audiences. Modern sport and the mass media developed simultaneously out of the common desire for growth resources, i.e. capital and audiences, and mutually propelled each other's growth. Far from being an exception to the rule, Japanese regional and national newspapers emerged as major sponsors (and beneficiaries) of sport events during the early twentieth century. Publishers estimated highly the promotional value of sport and sports events as sales machines to boost publicity and circulation figures. The diffusion of all other modern mass media was introduced and accelerated by the appeal of sport as well which is still today a vital element of the sport–media nexus. With the progress of digitalisation technology, media corporations increasingly see sport as a context to enhance their customer base and to sell new kinds of ever-diversified services. In the Japanese market, the 2002 World Cup clearly has the function of increasing subscription rates to digital television. For this purpose, SKY PerfecTV, Japan's largest digital broadcasting service and part of Rupert Murdoch's News Corporation group, outbid a Japanese consortium consisting of public and private broadcasters, for the rights to cover all the 2002 matches. The other networks are only entitled to transmit forty-two of the sixty-four games. Other fields of cutting edge media technology that might be displayed at the 2002 World Cup include Internet broadcasting, new pre-mium-based services provided by FIFA's youngest official sponsor, Yahoo!, and state-of-the-art computer graphics, perhaps even in virtual advertising that FIFA in principle acknowledged in late 1999 (Sone, 2000, p. 7).

The fascination of media sport is partially rooted in the elimination of spatial distances and time differences, as the mediated events occur in an artificial, virtual, framework of space and time. A second factor of central importance is the role of the mass media in community building and identity construction. Cheering the local team in away matches or supporting the national team in international encounters became possible with the develop-ment of more efficient transmission technologies. However, in order to promote the deeply solitary activity of media consumption towards the col-lective experience of solidarity, new narrative techniques and modes of reference had to be devised, a meta-language capable of expressing two con-tradictory messages: unity and difference.

This is most evident in the view that sports bring people of different nations and peoples closer together. The ideology of international peace and harmony in sports, however, hardly corresponds with the reality of the media coverage of sport. Either incapable or unwilling to confront audiences with the chauvinist and sometimes bluntly racist conceptions of otherness that are abundant in great parts of the population, media sport inevitably tends to enforce prejudicial stereotypes, particularly if national pride and the display of achievement are at stake. In both Japan and Korea, interest in football is highest when the nation is represented. The J.League, for example, faced a steady decline in public support when the first boom was over. The decrease of spectators in the bleachers was accompanied by the ongoing decline of viewing rates, until a critical borderline was reached. In 2000, live broadcast-ing was nearly completely banned from the prime time of public national television and left to either pay TV or the local broadcasters. Yet when the national team is on the telly, viewer rates tend to rise well above average. In fact, some of the highest viewer rates of the past twenty-five years have been achieved during the transmission of international football matches. In Korea, club football is of comparatively low standing. Yet national games, that have occasionally reached up to 70 per cent of the people, are more than just a game, as Lee explains in this volume. During the colonial period, football was a social catalyst because it provided one of the rare occasions where Korea usually triumphed over Japan. The consciousness of being Asia's football powerhouse is still prevalent among large parts of the population. For many Koreans, losing against the former colonialist was a worse and more humili-ating experience than the harsh regulations imposed by the International Monetary Fund during the economic crisis of 1997–98.

Shimizu who travelled with Japanese football fans to France in 1998 and Hong Kong also stresses the role of the media in reproducing nationalist stances and behaviour. The display of the national symbols always attracted high media interest, probably because of the unsolved domestic dispute over the legitimate usage of the *hinomaru* flag and the anthem *kimigayo*. Yet long before the Japanese Diet finally adopted the flag and the anthem as national symbols in August 1999, Japanese supporters were seen in stadia all over the country (and the football world) avidly waving huge flags and singing the anthem. Shimizu would argue again that such behaviour also is part of a devised strategy to attract the interest of the media, and consequently, to make it into the media. Sometimes, however, people act differently from what is expected. Hostile sentiments ironically might be less prominent among football fans than the average population, and it seems that they may be of minor importance on the pitch where the former power relations have evened out recently. With more and more Koreans playing in the J.League, and recently Japanese also playing for K-League teams, both the media of Japan and of Korea have begun to produce more sympathetic pictures of the 'other'. When South Korea hosted Japan in Seoul on 3 November 1997, Korean supporters unrolled a banner imprinted with the message 'Let's go to France together'. Four years later, when neither Japan nor Korea had to qualify, direct competitions became rare. A unique encounter happened in early 2001, when Tokyo Broadcasting System (TBS) celebrated its fiftieth anniversary. The Tokyo-based broadcaster sponsored a football match ('Accenture Soccer Dream') that paired a world all-stars selection and a joint Japan–Korea team.

The assertion of the media in actively steering the image of the nation cannot pass unchallenged, because of the sense of ambiguity about what the nation is. In Korea, the question of what it is, is of course deeply tainted by history. The fragmentation of the Korean people into two divided states is a major source of ambiguity as public opinion regards North and South as one nation with a common past, one language and a monolithic culture. At the same time, conservative and progressive forces quarrel about the legitimate representation of the Korean state. This debate is fuelled by differing views on the authoritarian and military governments, on the communist threat and on the economic developments achieved under liberal democracy (Chang, 2001, pp. 75–78). The claim of a monolithic culture, however, can easily be repudiated when the manifold encounters and exchanges with China are taken into account. Japan shares with Korea the widespread popular belief of being a monolithic people with a unique past and culture. That at least three migration waves of people with distinct ethnic origins have contributed to the early formation of the Japanese people is usually excluded from dominant conceptions of the national and cultural identity, and so is the issue of foreigners currently living in Japan.

The largest number of foreigners permanently residing in Japan is of Korean origin. Most of them are second- or third-generation Koreans who were born and bred in Japan but kept their Korean nationality either through personal choice or the inconsistencies of Japan's immigration system. Japan's harsh citizenship laws made it extremely difficult for them to obtain Japanese citizenship while maintaining their cultural identity. The exclusion policy, a kind of inverse assimilation policy, is also extended to the fields of sports. Korean students enrolled at one of the more than 150 private Korean schools were systematically banned from all interschool tournaments until a policy shift in 1991 led to the gradual opening of leagues and tournaments.

Institutionalised inequality was reinforced in 1999 when the J.League was close to reaching bottom. Fading popularity led to decrease in revenues, while the expenditures hardly changed. The biggest drain on club resources was the wage bill, which accounted for at least half of the clubs' expenses. The average annual salary for foreign players jumped from US$317,000 (1993) to 631,200 in 1994 and 834,500 in 1997. By comparison, the Japanese average staggered around the US$227,000 mark. Some clubs kept big and expensive squads that sent several franchises to the brink of bankruptcy. In order to help the debt-ridden clubs out of the red, the Japan Football Federation introduced a salary cap system in 1998, limiting the number of players any club was allowed to have in a certain wage category. In addition, the number of foreigners was reduced to five per team, only three of whom can play at any one time. The JFA, however, was not amused when one of its prefectural branches applied the new regulations even to elementary school football tournaments. All attempts to ask for more flexibility, 'after all, this concerns pre-teenage children of a different ethnic origin, not international soccer stars being transferred from AC Milan', were in vain, as the Osaka Prefectural Football Association said it was merely abiding by the JFA rules (Hadfield, 2000).

Whether this system really was devised to curtail the wage spiral deserves questioning. For the JFA, as well as for its Korean counterpart, maintaining face at the 2002 World Cup has always had strict priority. The discriminatory policy inevitably reduced the chances of Korean residents in Japan getting on the roster as they were directly competing against the foreign star players for a small number of places. On the contrary, Japanese players' chances to be listed on the roster increased, and valuable match experience, needed to raise standards, could be gained. The long-term effects, however, are no less doubtful than the practice of naturalising foreign star players.

In the case of Brazilian-born Lopes, the usually long-winded processes of Japan's bureaucracy proved to be miraculously fast. Having played in Japan for a decade and proven to be one of the most powerful strikers in the 1997 season, he was naturalised in the same year. The application procedure lasted for only eight months which is considerably faster than the average of one to one and a half years (Chiba *et al.*, 2001, p. 215). Months before the 2002 World Cup, Japan's fortunes took another turn for the better when Brazilian-born striker Alex from Shimizu S-Pulse secured Japanese citizenship. As in the case of Lopes, the new Japanese citizen had to wait a mere eight months to become naturalised (*Mainichi Shinbun*, 12 November 2001).

Whose people's game?

Next to ethnic discrimination, gender discrimination is the most eye-catching rupture in the ideology of the 'people's game' as it reveals the highly gendered nature of football. Football, along with virtually all other team sports, has long been popularly imagined as a sport for male competitors played for the enjoyment of male fans. Participating opportunities for girls have been extremely limited in Japan until recently. Female players were allowed to register with the JFA from 1979. The 1980s witnessed a spectacular increase in popularity, partly due to the proliferation of regional leagues and national championships and partly due to the successes of the women's national team that stood in sharp contrast to the failures of the male national team. With the financial support of large industrial firms, the L-League (the Japan Ladies' Soccer League) was finally inaugurated in 1989. Players as well as managers were 'corporate amateurs', Japan's characteristic type of semi-professionals on the pay-roll of a club's parent company.

However, as one anthropologist who came to Japan to coach a women's football team and to conduct research for her PhD, noted, women's progress in the field of sport in Japan has been contained within a more general discourse. First, it is 'inherently comparative in its logic' and, second, it is 'rooted in a firm belief that the world of competitive sport is naturally and irreversibly first and foremost the domain of male and natural masculinity' (Edwards, 2000). Looking at Japan's junior and senior high schools where football is most popular, only twenty girls teams were counted in 1997, compared with a total of 7,000 boys clubs. Female students thus were mainly conceded the role of managers whose duties primarily consist of serving food and drinks to the players, washing the kit, cleaning up and keeping the scores (Nogawa and Maeda, 1999, p. 227). No wonder that the inferiority of women in football is easily reproduced. Similarly, the ongoing recession has forced many companies to reconsider their spending on corporate welfare and marketing which have been traditionally the two rationales for supporting corporate sport. Cutting down expenditures hit the L-League harder than the male J.League, which is, at least in theory and in comparison, less dependent on corporate sponsorship. Despite the relative strength of the women's national team, the L-League has not been a commercial success, attracting no more than 1,000 spectators to an average match which is usually free of charge. With a few exceptions – the USA, Italy and possibly England – women's football all over the world is in a similar state, and so the future of the semi-professional football league in Japan is in doubt.

Both live attendances and television audiences are much higher in the world of male football, which has been referred to as a realm of hyper-masculinity. As Hargreaves has noted, the media constitute one of the prime sites for the reproduction of gender divisions. Men figure much more than women as participants and even more so as media-sport professionals, writers and academics in all sport-related fields (1986, p. 151). However, in recent years, motivated by the desire to produce greater fan support and increase revenues, football teams and associations around the world have taken a closer look at the make-up of their fan constituencies. With the imperative of attracting customers wherever they can be found, women were targeted. At the same time, women started to claim their rights as part of the mediated sports spectacles. The result, far from equal time representation or being a 'uni-sex televisual culture' (Rowe, 1995, p. 151), is the strategic spectacularisation and sexualisation of screen sport. In Japan, marketing specialists attempted to reverse the traditional relationship between the female body and male gaze. As spectatorship surveys during the first rounds of the J.League clearly have shown, the concept worked out well. Opening new spaces of consumption for new consumer groups was one of the most cogent explanations for the sudden success of the J.League in 1993. The recent 'Nakata-Boom' also underlines the particular importance of turning the male players into a commodity for a young and wealthy female audience. For the first time in Asian history, it seems that a generation of women has emerged which is in the position to define dominant concepts of masculinity and to impose role models on their male contemporaries. Of course, this does not imply the rise of a new kind of civil society where women can exercise hegemonic power. Yet it suggests that, at least in the realm of consumption, lifestyles and popular culture, the football World Cup will have a lasting impact on society.

Conclusion

In a very illuminating study Maurice Roche outlines a political sociology and social theory of 'mega-events', that is, 'large-scale cultural (including commercial and sporting) events which have a dramatic character, mass popular appeal and international significance' (2000, p. 1). His research posed two questions: what were the main personal and interpersonal meanings attributable to mega-events at the end of the twentieth century, and what was the social significance of mega-events going to be in the twenty-first century? To do justice to these questions, and in studying globalisation, identities and sports mega-events in the late modern world, requires a combination of research methods, multidisciplinary studies and multicultural research teams. Like Roche we argue that mega-events operate as the 'hubs' and 'switches' by which the global is translated into the local at individual and institutional levels. This involves not simply charting an unfolding process of sports development, but recognising that it is a process composed of differently located resistances, negotiations and struggles over alternative futures. This volume of essays on the 2002 World Cup aims to demonstrate that the beginnings of adequate answers to questions about the relevance of sporting mega-events for personal identity and for the governance of world sport as an integral part of global society, are only to be found in detailed analyses of civil societies, states and economies, as well as the institutions of sport.

References

Asahi Shinbun (1998) 'Nagano struggles with money-losing Olympic venues', 18 November.

Chang Yun-Shik (2001) 'Two faces of Korean nationalism and South Korean democracy', in Whang Soon-He (ed.) *Nationalism, Sports, and Body Culture in the Twentieth Century*, Tsukuba: Tsukuba University, Institute of Social Sciences, pp. 69–82.

Chiba Naoki, Ebihara Osamu and Morino Shinji (2001) 'Globalization, naturalization and identity: the case of borderless elite athletes in Japan', *International Review for the Sociology of Sport*, 36, 2: 203–221.

Croft, Jane and Hunt, Ben (2001) 'Axa terminates insurance for 2002 World Cup', *Financial Times*, 12 October (online: <http://news.ft.com>).

Edwards, Elise (2000) 'Gender lessons on the field: the philosophy and practice of coaching the female athlete in contemporary Japan', unpublished paper delivered at the international conference 'Sports and Body Culture in Japan', New Haven, Yale University, 31 March–1 April.

FAZ/*Frankfurter Allgemeine Zeitung* (2001) 'Die WM-Gastgeber streiten über ein Logo' [World Cup hosts quarrel over logo], 17 January.

Hadfield, Peter (2000) 'Primary school soccer tainted by racism', *South China Morning Post* 17 May (online: <www.scmp.com>).

Hare, Geoff (1999a) 'Buying and selling the World Cup', in Hugh Dauncey and Geoff Hare (eds) *France and the 1998 World Cup*, London: Frank Cass, pp. 121–142.

Hare, Geoff (1999b) '"Get your kit on for the lads": Adidas versus Nike, the other World Cup', *Sociology of Sport Online*, vol. 2, no. 2 (online: <http://www.brunel.ac.uk/depts/sps/sosol/v2i2a1.htm>). (Accessed 14 November, 2000.)

Hargreaves, John (1986) *Sport, Power and Culture*, Oxford: Blackwell Publishers.

Himmer, Alastair (2001) 'FIFA gives thumbs-up to Japan's World Cup venues', *Yahoo! Sports Singapore*. (online: <http://uk.sports.yahoo.com/011108/80/ceuoq.html>). (Accessed 8 November 2001.)

Hirose Ichirō (n.d.) 'Kindai (modan) to supōtsu' [Modernity and sport], first published in *Gekkan Nyū Media*. (online: <http://home.att.ne.jp/blue/supportista/series/hirose/hirose_modern1.tml>). (Accessed 7 November 2001.)

Holmes, Carol (1999) 'Cash cow on its last breath', *Adweek Asia*, 9147.

Kaplan, Daniel (1998) 'FIFA takes new approach to insure future World Cups', *Nashville Business Magazine*, Print Edition, 3 July.

Kim Hye-Ja (2000) 'Mō hitotsu no Kōshien' [The other Kōshien], in Hirai Hajime (ed.) *Supōtsu de yomu Ajia*, Kyōto: Sekai Shisō Sha, pp. 133–152.

Koh Byung-Chul (2001) 'Sports and politics in the two Koreas', in Whang Soon-He (ed.) *Nationalism, Sports, and Body Culture in the Twentieth Century*, Tsukuba: Tsukuba University, Institute of Social Sciences, pp. 85–94.

Lee Hong-Goo (2001) 'The effect of 2002 FIFA World Cup event on the development of local community', in Koh Eunha *et al.* (eds) *Sociology of Sport and New Global Order: Bridging Perspectives and Crossing Boundaries. Proceedings of the 1st World Congress of Sociology of Sport, Seoul July 20–24*, Seoul: Organizing Committee for the 1st World Congress of Sociology of Sport, pp. 195–200.

Lee Jong-Young (1997) 'Wārudo kappu kyōsai to Kankoku shakai. Kokusai kankei ni dono yō na eikyō o motarasu no ka' [Co-hosting and Korean society. Questioning the influence on international relations], in Nihon Supōtsu Shakai

Gakkai (ed.) *Henyō suru gendai shakai to supōtsu.* Kyōto: Sekai Shisō Sha, pp 138–147.

Maeda Hiroko (2001) 'Wārudo Kappu Nihon kokunai kaisaichi no kitai to chiketto no dōkō' [Expectations of World Cup venues in Japan and ticket sales], in Nihon Supōtsu Shakai Gakkai Dai 10 Kai Daikai Jikkō Iinkai (ed.) *Nihon Supōtsu Shakai Gakkai Dai 10 Kai Daikai. Shōrokushū.* Tsukuba: Tsukuba Daigaku Taiiku Kagakukei Supōtsu Shakaigaku Kenkūshitsu, pp. 60–61.

Mainichi Shinbun (2001) 'National soccer squad bolstered as Alex secures citizenship', 12 November.

Manzenreiter, Wolfram (1999a) 'Some considerations on the institutionalization of modern sport in Japan', *Romanian Journal of Japanese Studies*, 1, pp. 139–150. (online: <http://www.opensys.ro/rjjs/manzenreiter/>).

Manzenreiter, Wolfram (1999b) 'Breitensport in Japan: Infrastruktur, Institutionen, Ideologien' [Mass sports in Japan], in Hannelore Eisenhofer-Halim, Peter Pörtner and Holger Wöhlbier (eds) *Facetten des modernen Japans*, Frankfurt: Peter Lang, pp. 261–286.

Miller, Toby *et al.* (2001) *Globalization and Sport: Playing the World*, London: Sage.

Nogawa Haruo and Maeda Hiroko (1999): 'The Japanese dream: soccer culture towards the new millennium', in Gary Armstrong and Richard Giulianotti (eds) *Football Cultures and Identities*, Houndmills: Macmillan, pp. 223–233.

Nufer, Gerd (1998) *Event Sponsoring. Am Beispiel der Fußball-Weltmeisterschaft 1998 in Frankreich*, (online: <http://www.uni-tuebingen.de/uni/w04/DiskBeitraege/a5a.pdf.>). (Accessed 25 October 2001.)

Ōno Akira (1996) *Gendai supōtsu no hyōron. Supōtsu hōdō saishinsen kara no repōto* [Contemporary sport critique from the frontline of sports media], Tokyo: Taishūkan Shoten.

Ortner, Helmut (1987) *Das Geschäft mit dem Sport* [Sport business], Rastatt: Moewig.

Park Yoon-Bae (2001) 'Construction sector enjoying largest benefit from 2002 World Cup boom', *Korea Times*, 4 June.

Roche, Maurice (2000) *Mega-Events and Modernity*, London: Routledge.

Rowe, David (1995) *Popular Cultures: Rock Music, Sport and the Politics of Pleasure*, London: Sage.

Seki Harunami (1997) *Sengo Nihon no supōtsu seisaku. Sono kōzō to tenkai* [Sport policy in post-war Japan], Tokyo: Taishūkan Shoten.

Senda Toshio (1999) 'Terebi to supōtsu to no aijōgeki' [The romance of television and sport], *Gendai Supōtsu Hyōron*, 1, pp. 64–79.

Seo Jee-Yeon (2001) 'World Cup may not stimulate economy', *Korea Times*, 5 October.

Simson, Viv and Jennings, Andrew (1992) *The Lords of the Rings: Power, Money and Drugs in the Modern Olympics*, London: Simon & Schuster.

Sone Toshirō (2000) 'Supōtsu chūdan to bācharu kōkoku. Kasō genjitsu wa doko made yurusareru ka' [Sports relays and virtual advertisements: limits to the use of virtual reality], *Hōsō Kenkyū to Chōsa*, 4: 2–13.

Sugden, John and Tomlinson, Alan (1998) *FIFA and the Contest for World Football*, Cambridge: Polity Press.

Sugden, John and Tomlinson, Alan (1999) 'Digging the dirt and staying clean: retrieving the investigative tradition for a critical sociology of sport', *International Review for the Sociology of Sport*, 34, 4: 385–397.

Taniguchi Gentarō (1999): 'Horusuto Dasurā no senryaku' [Dassler's strategy], *Gendai Supōtsu Hyōron* 1, pp. 80–93.

Taylor, Ian (1998) *The New Economics of World Football: Contradictory Aspects of Contemporary Football*, unpublished paper presented at 'Football, National Identities and the World Cup', a FIFA conference, Paris, 5 July 1998.

Ubutaka Yukio (1994) *J.riigu no keizaigaku* [The economics of the J.League], Tokyo: Asahi Shinbun Sha.

Walker, Jeremy (2001a) 'Blatter upbeat on World Cup', *Asahi Shinbun online*, 11 October.

Walker, Jeremy (2001b) 'FIFA lauds safety of host countries', *Asahi Shinbun online*, 9 November.

Wright, George (1999) 'The impact of globalisation', *New Political Economy*, 4, 2: 268–272.

Part I

Politics, football and football politics

2 Things more important than football?

Japan, Korea and the 2002 World Cup

Gavan McCormack

Introduction

The World Cup is sport, spectacle, politics, and economics, and all of these entwined. In 2002, when it is contested for the first time in East Asia, the world can expect the best of sport – since that is what the World Cup is about wherever it is held – and some grand spectacle, with something of the flair shown by Japan in 1964 and Korea in 1988 with their respective Olympic Games. But the politics and economics are another matter. This chapter concentrates on those aspects.

The 2002 World Cup is the joint production of two countries that have barely cooperated on anything ever before. They only 'normalised' their diplomatic and political relations in 1965, after thirty-five years of colonial domination by Japan of Korea (1910–45) and twenty years of frozen antagonism that followed the liquidation of the Japanese empire, and they are still in the process of trying to 'normalise' cultural, people-to-people relations. As the World Cup finals approach, relations between the two countries drastically deteriorate. The co-hosting will either bring them together or drive them further apart; it is impossible to know which it will be.

The well-known Korean scholar, Chong-Sik Lee, introduces his book on the Japan–Korea relationship by saying:

> [A]lthough Japanese and Koreans can form lasting friendships and working relationships at the individual level, there is no sense of genuine friendship between the two peoples at the collective or societal level. Most Japanese are disdainful and contemptuous of Korea, do not wish to understand and are insensitive toward the feeling of Koreans, and simply do not wish to be involved with anything related to Korea, unless, of course, there are specific reasons for doing so.
>
> The Koreans, for their part, admire the Japanese ability to organize and accomplish important objectives, but this is also a cause for apprehension, since Japan once dominated Korea and imposed a harsh rule over the Koreans. Not only are the Japanese unrepentant, but also many are proud of their 'accomplishments' in Korea. They do not understand

the feelings of the Koreans and have no interest in doing so. The Japanese are indeed 'economic animals' to the Koreans; and the only interest Japan has in Korea is to aggrandize itself by exploiting whatever opportunity Korea provides.

(Lee, 1985, pp. 1–2)

This World Cup will feature necessary cooperation between the co-hosts – it could not be conducted without it – but it will also be characterised by fierce and consuming struggle between them. Both are determined to out-perform the other on the field, in the streets and public squares, before the global audience, to show a more sophisticated, open, modern face and a richer, traditional culture to the world. Visitors and viewers around the world will constitute a kind of global jury to assess their performance. Perhaps the best result to be hoped for from this contest might be that the two sides learn to respect and like each other somewhat better. In that event, whatever the outcome on the field, it will have been well worth it. But the other outcome – of distrust and hostility that spills over with unforeseen consequences for the Cup's sport and spectacle – remains a possibility.

The two countries are geographically close, separated at their closest point by about 200 kilometres of water, about five times the distance that divides Britain from France or twice that between Ireland and Wales, but it is a relative proximity that preserves distance. Tied through history by the most intimate links of culture and language, they remain divided by a gulf whose depth is in almost inverse proportion to its narrowness. The two countries are sometimes seen as the Britain and Ireland of East Asia, and the analogy has some force in the sense of the combination of physical closeness with temperamental, emotional and spiritual distance.

Perhaps it is the very similarity, the closeness in historical, cultural and linguistic terms, which makes Japan and Korea so insistent on difference from the other. From ancient times continental influences flowed from continent to archipelago – religious, political, philosophical, linguistic, with the inhabitants of the archipelago (who gradually became the people known as 'Japanese') torn between appreciation and fear of assimilation. Downplaying any debt to other cultures and peoples, they insisted on their absolute difference from them, imagining their own origins in terms of descent from the gods rather than the more likely, but mundane, arrival in stages from the continent, and came to believe themselves to be superior, unique, and destined to rule over other peoples. It was a myth that helped to forge and maintain a distinctive identity and culture, but which in modern times has made for great difficulty in conceiving of any common 'Asian' identity or in building an East Asian community on anything like European lines. Even today, many Japanese believe that Japan is unique and superior, and that Asia is a place to go for holidays, to invest money, or to manufacture goods. That ambiguity has long been a prominent theme in Japan's relations with its Asian continental neighbours.

As the rest of the world begins to make tentative moves towards transcending nationalism, in Japan since the 1990s neo-nationalist sentiment has risen and stresses again the themes of separateness, purity, and the superiority of Japan. In Korea, alone in Asia except for Taiwan, nationalism remains still unfulfilled, the country divided. Taiwan's status does indeed remain anomalous, but a replication of the Korean situation in China would require something like a division of the country at the Yangzi River into two separate states. For Korea the pain of the twentieth century, both the first half of colonial subjugation and the second half of division, divided by the horrors of war, is seen as deeply rooted in the Japanese intervention that began the process, and the bitterness of the memory of the twentieth century is compounded by the deeper historical memory of the immense wave of Japanese violence that swept their country in the late sixteenth century, leaving scars no less deep in the national memory than on the landscape. As the Irish remember Cromwell, whose name is synonymous with aggression, in their history Koreans remember Hideyoshi, Cromwell's near contemporary. To understand the gulf that divides the national sentiment of Korea and Japan to this day, the history of the relationship, especially in the traumatic sixteenth and twentieth centuries, has to be briefly recounted.

War and memory

Medieval Japan experienced a long period of violence and civil war, that culminated in the late sixteenth-century victory of the coalition of forces led by the warlord (to give him a modern designation), Toyotomi Hideyoshi. Victorious, Hideyoshi proceeded to demilitarise the country, seizing swords and other weapons and melting them down. But the turmoil had its own momentum, for which mere stability was no satisfaction. Having pacified Japan, he therefore resolved to conquer China. His ambition was nothing less than the creation of a new world order.

Korea was then a highly cultivated independent kingdom, closely tied to the (Chinese) Ming court and committed to the Confucian moral and political world order centred in Peking. When it refused to recognise and defer to him, Hideyoshi launched a war against it. His forces, around 160,000 men, armed with modern (matchlock) firearms and seasoned from generations of warfare, wrought havoc across the southern provinces of the country, beginning in 1592 and not finally withdrawing until 1598, after suffering major defeats on land and at sea. During this war, Hideyoshi rewarded his commanders in proportion to the number of enemy they could show they had slaughtered. The noses of those killed, pickled in barrels, were despatched back to Japan, where they were duly counted and rewards meted out accordingly. His men were assigned quotas – three Korean noses for each Japanese soldier – and civilian noses, or the noses of women, children and old people, were counted along with those of Korean soldiers and sailors. Various counts point to a figure between 100,000 and 200,000 noses being brought back from Korea to Japan, several tens of thousands of which were later buried in front of the Great Buddha hall at Hōkōji Temple in Kyoto, where to this day the '*Mimizuka*' (literally 'Ear Mound', by some quirk of historical memory) remains, a place now partially swallowed by suburbs (McCormack, 2001b, *passim*).

Throughout Japanese history till very recent decades this burial mound was a celebrated place of pilgrimage, a monument to Hideyoshi's triumphs and his clemency (for having given the defeated enemy a Buddhist repose). Elsewhere too the exploits of the Japanese war on Korea are celebrated, as those of British forces despatched to Ireland in the seventeenth century are commemorated in Northern Ireland. At Fujisaki Shrine in Kumamoto in Kyushu, the autumn festival is known as '*Boshita-sai*', short for '*Chōsen o horoboshita*' (or 'the laying waste of Korea'). In Korea, by contrast, the devastation wrought by Hideyoshi's forces is remembered across the countryside, and Admiral Yi Sun-Shin, who decisively defeated the Japanese at sea, is honoured as one of the greatest Korean heroes of all time.

Korean culture in the late sixteenth century was in many, perhaps most respects (save warfare), more developed than Japan's. Consequently it was not just noses that Hideyoshi and his commanders plundered. The living were also seized in large numbers, most famous being the potters, whose descendants even now, after fourteen or so generations, still retain a distinctive identity and remember their Korean origins. With them they brought back to Japan doctors, printers, artisans in wood and metal, paper makers, scroll makers, painters, dyers, weavers and spinners, garden designers and experts, and scholars, along with printing presses, the 'high tech' items of their time, many cultural treasures and, perhaps the greatest prize, Korea's young women. How many of them were seized is impossible to know, but an estimate of between 50,000 and 60,000, in a total figure of at least 100,000 Koreans transported to Japan has been suggested in various scholarly accounts. Other Koreans were sold as slaves, or exchanged for guns, silk, or other prized foreign goods, whether directly or via third country slave traders, to many countries (ibid.).

After the Japanese withdrawal from Korea, the adoption of a policy of national isolation ushered in two centuries of peace in Japan. However, from the seventeenth century to the nineteenth century there was no debate in Japan on this Korean war, no regrets save over it having ended in defeat and withdrawal. Hideyoshi came to be eulogised as the quintessential Japanese commoner who rose from the ranks, and modern Japan from the nineteenth century revived both his dreams of continental empire and his ruthless methods of accomplishing them.

Japan was the first in nineteenth-century Asia to adapt successfully to the modern world, and modernity meant military power and colonial expansion. From 1910 to 1945 it established colonial control over Korea, renamed Chōsen. Japanese colonialism was in some respects a positive force. The population grew, and modernisation and industrialisation went ahead. Order prevailed, and a huge social and economic transformation took place (Lone and McCormack, 1993, *passim*). However, what is remembered first by Koreans is not the modernisation but the humiliation, the crushing of Korea's nationalist resistance, and the imposition of policies and practices designed to incorporate, assimilate, and thereby extinguish Korea as a separate political, national identity. Japanese state religion Shintō was imposed on Korea, along with the cult of Japan's emperor and his imperial ancestors as gods. Koreans were forced to adopt Japanese names and Japanese as the official language, which meant that speaking Korean was punished. 'Love the country' (i.e. Japan) days were instituted in schools, shrines to the Japanese imperial family gods were turned into focal points in all towns, flag wavings and recitals of Japanese imperial rescripts were instituted. Ultimately, as the system of total mobilisation was adopted from 1942, around a million young Korean men were mobilised to work in the mines and construction sites in Japan, and quite a few thousands went directly into low-ranking positions in the Japanese military itself, while tens of thousands of young Korean women, most of them between the ages of sixteen and nineteen, were mobilised as 'comfort women' to sexually service the Imperial Japanese Army (Yoshimi, 2001; Tanaka, 2001).

In Korea, there is no Auschwitz or Dachau, no Nanjing or Harbin, but the independence of the Korean kingdom was extinguished in 1910 and Korea was destroyed as 'a national group'. The attempt to extinguish Korea as a separate identity, culture and state, crushing its history and memory, traditions and religion, and appropriating its language, its people's names, and many of its bodies, especially those of its youth, was not considered criminal by the tribunal that the Allies convened in Tokyo between 1946 and 1948 to try Japanese war crimes. As other nations were being born, the Korean nation was thus extinguished, and the world paid little heed. 15 August 1945, the day of Japan's defeat, is celebrated in Korea as the day of liberation, and An Chung-Kun, the patriot who in 1909 assassinated the Japanese regent, is commemorated in both South and North Korea as a national hero, while in Japan he is reviled as a terrorist. The psychological wounds of all this do not easily heal. Japan and Korea remember their past very differently. History is an extremely sensitive subject.

Struggling to become 'normal'

The Japan–Korea rapprochement that was accomplished in 1965 was confined to diplomatic and economic relations between states. Absent was the dimension of forgiveness, mutual understanding and respect at the people's level, and recognition of the suffering of countless individual victims. The issues remained unresolved, postponed for a half century, commonly forgotten in Japan while constituting a deep memory in Korea.

For long thereafter Japan–Korea cooperation meant cooperation by the authorities in shoring up the Cold War anti-communist and anti-democratic regime in South Korea. At its worst, it included cooperation in the abduction from Japan of the then democratic leader, Kim Dae-Jung, in a 1973 incident from which he barely escaped with his life. It was 1987 before South Korea could finally throw off the yoke of successive military dictatorships. In 1997 Kim Dae-Jung was elected president, and in 2000 he was awarded the Nobel Prize for Peace.

During the Cold War, Japan paid little attention to its identity, content with its subordinate position within the US global and economic strategy and concentrating on economic growth. In the region as a whole, a historical consensus about the meaning of Japanese imperialism and militarism emerged, but in Japan itself the ideology of the war lived on, not strongly asserted, but not denied or overcome either. Unlike Germany, where war responsibility was taken very seriously by the German parliament, courts and public opinion, and thousands of former Nazis were tried and convicted of war crimes, in Japan such issues were set aside, and the insistence on the *justness* of the war remained a strong current in public life. From the 1990s, however, with the Cold War ended, growth and expansion turned to slump and long forgotten or shelved issues came to the surface. As internationalisation and globalisation proceeded, so, in contrapuntal tension, did the insistence on national 'identity'. Between the desire to forge closer post-Cold War links with neighbouring countries and the desire to reassert deeply embedded notions of Japanese identity as unique and superior, there is an irreconcilable contradiction on which Japanese diplomacy continues to founder.

In the 1990s, long-frozen issues had at last to be faced. On the one hand, high-level official apologies – including a formal resolution in the national Diet – began to issue from Tokyo, and a few lines of text were inserted into history books dealing with Japanese crimes such as the massacre at Nanjing and the widespread system of military sexual slavery. On the other hand, however, a fierce opposition emerged. From high state officials, political parties and various social groups came the riposte that the war was virtuous, even sacred, and that no apologies were due, that the textbooks should not deal with the dark matters of war but should uplift and imbue people with pride; they should teach *'correct'* history (McCormack, 2000, pp. 55–73; 2001a, pp. xvii–xx).

The project to create a 'bright' history and a 'proud' Japanese identity by return to the certainties of an earlier time, in symbol, rhetoric, and educational policy, attracted powerful sponsorship and support. In 1999, following a vigorous campaign by neo-nationalist groups, the central symbols of the pre-war empire, its flag and anthem, were restored as officially sanctioned national symbols, and schools throughout the country were ordered to construct standardised school rituals around them, symbols which to Japan's neighbours were the symbols of aggression and atrocity. Teachers and students who pleaded a constitutional right to freedom of conscience and resisted the process were punished. Prime Minister Mori declared his high regard for the institutions and values of Japan's militarist past (the 'national polity' or *kokutai* and the Meiji emperor's Education Rescript), and, most controversially, in a speech on 15 May 2000 declared that 'Japan is a country of the gods, with the emperor at its centre'. It would be hard to imagine a more bizarre, end-of-century spectacle than this: fifty-five years after the end of the war, Japan's Prime Minister thus declaring, and doing so before a gathering of Shintō believers, Japan's special place as 'a country of the gods', thus articulating the precise racist and exclusionary formula of Japanese identity of the official ideology of 1930s' and 1940s' fascist Japan (McCormack, 2001a, p. xvi). Not surprisingly, alarm bells rang in Seoul and Beijing.

In January 2000 Constitutional Research Councils were set up and formal deliberations opened in both houses of the Diet. The 'Bright Japan' agenda, backed by powerful corporate and media forces, has considerable momentum and backing, pushing the debate in the direction of institutional change designed to construct a 'proud' Japan, with a 'correct' history, the emperor restored to a central role both in its past and its future, individual human rights subjected to limitations and conditions, and state prerogatives expanded (Hook and McCormack, 2001, *passim*).

It is not surprising that those who watch these events unfolding from a perspective of Seoul (or Beijing) do so nervously. The uniqueness that Japan insists on as a 'land of the gods centred on the emperor', superior and distinct, is analogous to the ideology of 'ethnic cleansing' elsewhere in the world and to the demagogic and anti-foreign views of neo-nationalist politicians such as or Jörg Haider in Austria and Jean-Marie Le Pen in France. A cooperative and harmonious twenty-first-century Asian commonwealth such as Korea's Kim is committed to construct is unlikely to be advanced so long as Japanese identity is defined in such terms. There is a deeper issue at stake here than 'mere' Japan–Korea relations or football.

While Japan under Obuchi, Mori and Koizumi in 1998–2001 thus became embroiled in fierce domestic disputes over identity and history, South Korea gained confidence under a leader whose moral stature was second only to that of Nelson Mandela. Kim directed his presidency towards attempting to resolve the national question, by a 'sunshine' policy, designed to help bring North Korea in from the cold of diplomatic isolation and persistent economic crisis, and to 'normalise' relations with Japan and build a new framework of regional peace, security, and cooperation. To that end he gave priority to trying to accomplish 'normalisation' in the broad sense. When he became president, the relationship with Japan was still far from 'normal'. Korea was the one country in Asia (and one of the few in the world) where Japanese cars were not to be seen, films viewed, songs heard, novels and magazines bought and sold. Opinion surveys regularly showed that each country was among the least popular in the other.

Making a formal visit to Japan in 1998, Kim Dae-Jung was the soul of magnanimity, saying little of the past, the many Korean grievances, and making clear his readiness to 'let bygones be bygones'. He did not pursue the mysterious circumstances of his own abduction from Tokyo two and a half decades earlier, nor did he seek any compensation on war-related matters, including the so-called 'military comfort women' issue. Instead he adopted a fresh, forward-looking approach centring on future cooperation. In the joint declaration Japanese Prime Minister Obuchi reflected on and apologised for the damage and agony inflicted by Japan on the Korean people during its colonial rule and voiced the 'deepest remorse and heartfelt apology', while President Kim expressed his resolve to 'get over the unfortunate history and strive to nurture a future-oriented relationship based on a spirit of reconciliation and neighbourly cooperation'. As part of the 'Action Plan' for a bilateral partnership for the twenty-first century, a complex of cultural and student exchanges and working holidays was agreed and the Korean ban on Japanese culture (including music, drama, cartoons and video games) was to be lifted by degrees, with full opening to be accomplished by the time of the 2002 World Cup. It was indeed a historic agreement, and those associated with the organisation of the World Cup took heart from it.

However, the issues continued to rage in Japan, especially after the advent of the Koizumi government in April 2001. The new Prime Minister declared his commitment to revision of the constitution and his resolve to worship at Yasukuni shrine (the Shintō shrine where Japan's war dead, including war criminals are honoured, and a focal point of the emperor-centred cult of pre-war Japan). A second major issue was his refusal to amend passages of a new school textbook that was seen in Korea and China as particularly offensive because of the way it glossed over Japanese aggression. The history text in question had been produced by a group of neo-nationalist scholars committed to 'proud', 'pure', and 'correct' history, and determined that Japan should move away from what they refer to as its 'masochistic' view of history, i.e. the view that Japan was 'guilty' for either the war itself or for the way it was prosecuted. The text became an overnight best seller when released generally in Japan (half a million copies in a couple of months). In Korea it was seen as 'inflammatory'. When the Japanese Ministry of Education approved it for adoption in schools the South Korean government immediately protested, demanding thirty-five specific changes (on matters ranging from ancient Korea–Japan relations to more recent history). On 9 July the Japanese government notified Seoul that it would not intervene to order the corrections sought. Seoul was shocked, seeing Tokyo as conniving in the distortion of history and the defence of wartime atrocities, in effect, as having repudiated the 1998 agreement (and an earlier, 1982, Japanese government pledge to ensure that false and offensive history education would not be allowed). After Kim Dae-Jung had gone further than any previous Korean leader in attempting reconciliation with Japan, this was a heavy blow. Describing the response as 'intolerable', Kim went on: 'Japan has an obligation to teach its people the truth and we have a right to demand it' (Hwang, 2001b). Demonstrators stormed the Japanese embassy in Seoul, burning Japanese flags and calling for a boycott of Japanese goods.

On 18 July 2001, Korea's National Assembly voted *unanimously* to review all relations with Japan. Defence talks were cancelled, twin-town relationships abandoned, school visits (to Japan) suspended, and legislators proposed a motion to block Japan's efforts to gain membership of the UN Security Council. Korea might not be able to force Japan to change its history texts, but it accused Japan of 'immorality and wrongdoing'(Hwang, 2000a) and planned to exact revenge by shaming it on the international stage, broadcasting accusations against Japan of 'distorting' its history at every international forum possible. It was to start (said the Korean Ministry of Foreign Affairs) at a UN conference against racism in South Africa beginning 31 August 2001. Then it would continue at the United Nations General Assembly, where from September the Korean Minister of Foreign Affairs, Han Seung-Soo, would become president, and at a major UNESCO conference in October. Seoul also announced that a list, initially comprising twenty-five names, had been prepared of Japanese war criminals to whom admission to Korea would henceforth be denied. It promised that more names would be added in due course. A proposal was also aired in the National Assembly that in future Korea begin referring officially to the Japanese emperor (*tennō*, or *ch'onhwang* in Korean) as 'king of Japan' (*kokuō* or *kugwang* in Korean), a seemingly innocuous play with words, but actually a step which would, by relativising it, raise profound questions about the nature of the Japanese institution and be seen by Japanese nationalists as an insufferable insult. Chung Mong-Joon, chair of KOWOC, the Korean organising committee of the 2002 World Cup, was surely not exaggerating when he said these steps would 'inevitably undermine the image of the World Cup' (Agence France Presse, 2001).

With the bilateral atmosphere extremely heated from the textbook issue, on 13 August 2001, the Japanese Prime Minister Koizumi brushed aside the objections of neighbouring countries and proceeded to worship at Yasukuni shrine. Yasukuni is the Shintō religious institution devoted to honouring those throughout modern Japan's history who have died in the service of the emperor (who is also the high priest of Shintō). In pre-war and wartime Japan, it played a central role in generating the ideology of chauvinism and militarism. Despite his protestations of sorrow over the pain and suffering Japan had caused the region, Koizumi's visit to the shrine was nevertheless insult added to the injury caused by the textbook issue. His statement that 'the peace and prosperity we [Japan] enjoy today was built on the sacrifice of the war dead', as if the Japanese dead were valiant national heroes instead of members of a brutal force engaged in criminal actions, added fuel to the anger of the response (Tanaka, 2001, pp. 30–33).

In Korea the visit was seen as 'the decisive signal of [Japan's] resurrection of hard-line nationalism' (Lee, 2001). Demonstrations broke out in Seoul and Pusan (Busan), Hong Kong and Beijing. Japanese flags were burned, and Pyongyang joined in issuing words of harsh denunciation. Twenty young Korean men ceremonially chopped off their little fingers and sent them to the

Japanese embassy in protest. Korean Vice Foreign Minister Choi Sung-Hong summoned the Japanese ambassador to make a formal protest in which he said, 'It is deeply regrettable that Prime Minister Koizumi paid respects at Yasukuni shrine, which is a symbol of Japanese militarism, in defiance of the South Korean government's repeated expressions of concern.' He added that the Japanese government should have a correct sense of history and respect the feelings of the ROK public (*The Australian*, 2001b). The Korean government backed a suit launched in the Japanese courts to demand the removal of the names of more than 21,000 Koreans who fought in the Japanese armed forces from the list of those worshipped at Yasukuni (*The Australian*, 2001a).

Speaking at a nationally televised 15 August meeting to commemorate the fifty-sixth anniversary of Korea's liberation from Japan, Kim Dae-Jung said that the South Korean people 'earnestly hope that Korea–Japan relations run on a right course on the basis of a firm historical consciousness'. He went on:

> Many conscientious Japanese citizens watched with apprehension the distortion of history and their prime minister's paying tribute at the controversial war shrine . . . To our disappointment, however, some people in Japan are attempting to distort history, casting dark clouds over Korea-Japan relations again . . . How can we make good friends with people who try to forget and ignore the many pains they inflicted on us? How can we deal with them in the future with any degree of trust? Those are questions that we have about the Japanese.
>
> (*Japan Times*, 2001)

It was as severe a comment as had ever been made by a Korean leader about Japan. Thunderclouds were visibly gathering over the World Cup. They were partially dispersed, however, when the particular school text to which such objection had been taken in Korea (and China) was rejected by 99 per cent of Japan's school district boards, after a vigorous mobilisation of citizen's groups who basically agreed with Kim (Struck and Togo, 2001). It was an encouraging, but scarcely decisive outcome. What it showed was that Japan was divided, and although Japan's leaders, from the highest level, were reverting to the myths of Japan's pristine, superior, non-Asian identity, many ordinary Japanese people took strong exception to their narrow, chauvinist message. Numbers of Japanese tourists to Korea continued to hit new record levels, large numbers of them now young women rather than the ill-famed, all-male sex tour groups of the past. Kim Dae-Jung might have more allies in Japan than he feared, and the reactionary, neo-nationalist forces more bark than bite.

Money

The World Cup may be described as 'the biggest sporting event in history' (*Daily Yomiuri Online*). In France in 1998 it was watched by 2.7 million spectators and a worldwide audience of about 40 billion people, many more than the Olympic Games. Like the Olympics, it combines immensity of scale with national pride and destiny. In both host countries the political economy of sport, resort, and construction is closely linked, and has come under increasing challenge for its carelessness of conventional economics, its steady pumping up of the public debt, damage to the environment, and reliance on political protection. The Japanese 'construction state', which reached a climax in the resort development frenzy of the late 1980s, eventually brought the national economy to the brink of bankruptcy (McCormack, 2001c, pp. 11–12). In Korea, while negative attention focused on Japan's past, its development path and political economy, including its problematic construction sector, tended to be seen in positive light. For both countries, the questions are the same: what is the cost and who will pay it; what are the profits and who will get them?

Kim Dae-Jung spoke of the Cup as 'a chance [for Korea] to make the country prosper diplomatically, economically and culturally, in sectors like tourism and science' (*Korea Now*, 2001, p. 40). The official estimate of visitors for the Cup was put at 350,000. The Korean Development Institute estimated direct and indirect economic benefits at 11.6 trillion won (US$8.5 billion) and 240,000 jobs (O, 2001). In Japan, the Dentsū Institute of Human Studies estimates even greater economic benefits of two trillion yen (US$25 billion). But despite these bullish projections, whether the Cup would indeed pay for itself is moot.

Both countries have committed substantial resources to the Cup. In Korea a special law was passed to cover the extraordinary mobilisation required, and ten completely new stadia were built, costing just under two trillion won (US$1.5 billion). The cost in Japan was at least as much (60 billion yen for International Stadium Yokohama, 54 billion yen for Sapporo Dome and 25 billion yen for Oita's 'Big Eye' Stadium) (Osumi, 2001, p. 3). Many – if not all – host cities will carry forward substantial debts, while being uncertain about the long-term viability of the elaborate structures they will be left with. One well-known commentator estimates that each stadium needs six matches to break even, but because of the divided country hosting arrangement gets only three (ibid.).

To cope with this problem, some cities were striving to design and build stadia that would also be multi-purpose structures. On Korea's Jeju (Cheju) Island, the Jeju World Cup Stadium had been leased in advance to an American corporation for fifty years from the end of the Cup, at an initial rent of US$500,000 per year, rising in 2003 to US$1.5 million. This stadium would therefore, according to Korean soccer's chief, Chung Mong-Joon, produce an income equivalent to that of twenty golf courses (Yi, 2001). Such optimism was the exception rather than the rule. In Japan's Saitama, a prefectural government official lamented that he thought it would be impossible ever to get local finances back into the black. At Oita, one organiser of a local campaign *against* the Cup remarked that the local stadium's 40,000 seats might expect to be filled 'once a year at most'. He therefore described it as 'a luxurious and wasteful public works project' (Yi, 2001). Cities that already had a strong international image and infrastructure, such as Yokohama, could expect to gain most. Even there, however, the Yokohama-based Hamagin Research Institute reckoned that the economy of the city might expect a boost of about 25.7 billion yen, significantly less than the 31.6 billion generated when the Yokohama BayStars won the baseball Japan Series in 1998. The example of cities such as Nagano, host city of the 1998 Winter Olympics, which went deeply into the red to construct the facilities and is sliding deeper into it because of the continuing costs of running and maintaining them, is not encouraging.

There is of course an element of competition between the co-host countries as to how their facilities will impress visitors. But this competition will be more intense in the area of transport and communications, as well as in the ineffable area of national symbol and image. In terms of air transport facilities, visitors can make direct comparisons and the contest for hearts and minds – and via them, pockets – will be intense. Korea has staked much on using the Cup to make its case for Inchŏn (Incheon) as North-East Asia's new international 'hub' airport, against Japan's Narita and Kansai. It is an 'off the field' contest which will be fought throughout the Cup.

The new Incheon International Airport, 50 kilometres west of Seoul, aspires to become the major 'hub' airport for the whole of Asia, prising a substantial amount of business away from Japan's two major airports (*Asahi Shinbun*, 2001). Constructed on reclaimed tidal wetlands, with two 4,000-metre runways, and two more to be constructed in the coming decade, it will operate on a round-the-clock basis, with no noise restrictions. With direct connections to nineteen airports in Japan, and with forty-three cities of over one million in population in a three- to five-hour flight radius, it expects an initial load of 27 million passengers per year (the equal of Japan's Narita Airport in 2000) and plans to accommodate a steady increase to 100 million in due course. Given the notorious inconvenience of Japan's major airport at Narita (65 kilometres north of Tokyo), still incomplete and originally a bureaucratic imposition enforced in the teeth of decades of fierce local opposition, and the relatively greater cost and inconvenience also of the Kansai International Airport at Osaka (which labours under mounting debt and is said to be slowly sinking into the sea), the idea of encouraging Japanese passengers to start connecting at Incheon for their international flights might be not unrealistic. It depends, of course, on how well it works and how good a reputation it can build.

Conclusion

The contest over hosting the World Cup 2002 was bitterly fought and only resolved in May 1996 at the last minute, and in the face of resentment on both sides, by the co-hosting agreement. In Korea in particular only a tiny section of people favoured the co-hosting formula, and many believed the outcome was the result of high-level IOC manoeuvring to save Japan from the embarrassment of inevitable defeat in the deciding vote (*Asahi Shinbun*, 1996). As part of the compromise hammered out, the official title was settled as '2002 FIFA World Cup Korea/Japan', with the opening match to be played in Korea and the final in Japan. Early in 2002, however, a dispute broke out over the Japanese decision to use the formula 'Japan-Korea' in Japanese language materials. Korea protested, and FIFA upheld the protest. The dispute was eventually settled by agreement that the Japanese wording need not mention the countries at all.

Skirmishes of this kind reflected the ongoing tension and rivalry, and in the summer of 2001, as the row over history and memory between the two countries spread, threatened to escalate unpredictably. Nothing could be more evocative of the problems faced by the Cup than Korean president Kim's August 2001 statement: 'How can we make good friends with people who try to forget the many pains they have caused us? How can we deal with them in the future with any degree of trust?' Yet on both sides, as the friction escalated, there was continuing evidence of an unprecedented level of trust and cooperation at the grassroots and between citizens groups. When the Korean railways announced that Japanese announcements on the Pusan–Seoul express would be suspended as part of the retaliation over the textbook dispute, the public response in Korea was plain that this was going too far. After just one day the broadcasts were resumed (Han, 2001; Im, 2001).

In the 2002 World Cup, the world will converge on the stadia of the two countries. Many matches will be played, reputations and fame made and lost. But the host countries are playing for greater stakes than sporting glory. Relations between the two countries are historically over-burdened, and that history will impinge on all their dealings as co-hosts. How their teams perform in relation to each other will be of prime concern to both. If the Korean stadium can come to life in rejoicing over a Japanese victory, and likewise the Japanese stadia celebrate Korean victories as their own, that would have a significance far greater than any outcome in the final. The odds on such an outcome are long, but the outcome of the great game of history is as difficult to predict as is the outcome of the great game of football.

References

Agence France Presse (2001) 'South Korea seeks books revenge by shaming Japan', 13 July <http://www.nautilus.org/napsnet/dr/0107/Jul13.html> (Accessed 14 August 2001.)

Asahi Shinbun (1996) 'Kyūten no ura ni Nihon no ketsudan' [Japanese resolve behind sudden shift], 1 June.

Asahi Shinbun (2001) 'Kenshō – Nihon no kyōi? Kyodai-na genkan?' [Study – Will huge gateway prove threat to Japan?], 30 March.

Daily Yomiuri Online (2001) 'Kickoff on the horizon', <http://www.yomiuri.co.jp.> (Accessed 31 May 2001.)

Han Soo-San (2001) 'Radical reactions don't speak for all S. Koreans', *Asahi Shinbun Online* <http://www.asahi.com.> (Accessed 24 August 2001.)

Hook, Glenn and McCormack, Gavan (2001) *Japan's Contested Constitution*, London: Routledge.

Hwang Jang-Jin (2001a) 'Seoul set to deny entry for Japanese cultural goods', *Korea Herald*, 12 July.

Hwang Jang-Jin (2001b) 'President warns of tough action over Japan's "intolerable" behavior', *Korea Herald*, 20 August.

Im Hyŏn-Jin (2001) '2002 nyŏn wŏldk'ŏp ŏttŏkke ch'ilul-gŏiniga? Munhwa ch'ukje rosŏ hanil hyŏpnyŏk' [How to run the 2002 World Cup – Korea–Japan co-operation as a cultural festival], unpublished paper delivered at Seoul National University.

Japan Times (2001) 'South Korean leader warns Yasukuni is clouding ties', 16 August.

Korea Now (2001) 'World Cup runneth over', 16 June, pp. 40–44.

Lee Chi-Dong (2001) 'Angry protests against Japan replace joy of Liberation Day', *Korea Herald*, 14 August.

Lee, Chong-Sik (1985) *Japan and Korea: The Political Dimension*, Stanford, CA: Hoover Institution Press, Stanford University.

Lone, Stewart and McCormack, Gavan (1993) *Korea since 1850*, Melbourne: Longman Cheshire, and New York: St Martin's Press.

McCormack, Gavan (2000) 'The Japanese movement to "correct" history', in Laura Hein and Mark Selden (eds) *Censoring History: Citizenship and Memory in Japan, Germany and the United States*, New York: M.E. Sharpe, pp. 55–73.

McCormack, Gavan (2001a) *The Emptiness of Japanese Affluence*, second revised edition, New York: M. E. Sharpe.

McCormack, Gavan (2001b) 'Reflections on modern Japanese history in the context of the concept of "genocide"', *Occasional Papers in Japanese Studies* (of the Edwin O. Reischauer Institute of Japanese Studies, Harvard University), No. 2001–01, July.

McCormack, Gavan (2001c) 'Japan's construction state lies in ruins', *Australian Financial Review*, 'Review' section, pp. 11–12.

O Yun-Hyŏn (2001) 'Yokohama-nun k'onssŏtŭjang Sŭgwĭp'o-nun yonghwagwan-ŭro' [A concert-hall for Yokohama and a movie theatre for Sŭgwĭp'o], *Sisa Jŏnŏl*, 16 February.

Osumi Yoshiyuki (2001) '[Comment]', *The Nikkei Weekly*, 9 July, p. 3.

Struck, Doug and Shigehiko Togo (2001) 'Japanese schools rejecting textbook', *Washington Post*, 15 August.

Tanaka Nobumasa (2001) 'Seiji no Yasukuni' [Yasukuni as politics], *Shūkan Kinyōbi*, 10 August, pp. 30–33.

Tanaka Yuki (2001) *Japan's Comfort Women: Sexual Slavery and Prostitution during World War II and the U.S. Occupation*, London: Routledge.

The Australian (2001a) 'Korean spirits captive to Japan war amnesia', 18 July.

The Australian (2001b) 'Fiery protests at Koizumi homage', 15 August.

Yi Mun-Je (2001) 'Kyŏnggijang/ch'ukkujang-e K'ondo'ga-itta' [World Cup soccer complex to become condominium], *Sisa Jŏnŏl*, 28 February.

Yoshimi Yoshiaki (2001) *Comfort Women: Sexual Slavery in the Japanese Military during World War II*, New York: Columbia Press.

3   Getting the games
Japan, South Korea and the co-hosted World Cup

Oliver Butler

Introduction

The decision by FIFA to award the 2002 World Cup to both Korea and Japan was an unprecedented one. Never before had two countries been asked to jointly stage a football tournament and this was the largest and richest football tournament in the world. This chapter will analyse the developments that led to this decision. The final result, that the two countries would co-host the tournament, reflected the extraordinary circumstances that surrounded the bidding by the two countries. These circumstances involved not only an intertwining of governmental politics and sport but politics within soccer's organising body, the Fédération Internationale de Football Association (FIFA).

Football, by the very nature of its popularity, has always been one of the most convenient sports for serving political aims. With the best footballing countries in the world gathering to compete every four years, the World Cup is the premier footballing competition. Through successful performances of national teams it provides a reliable platform for displays of national capability and the instilling of national pride. The extra revenue which the World Cup generates through the increase in commercial interest in the competition provides what Dominique Moisi (1998) calls 'a perfect illustration of the contradictions inherent in the present era'. Football, Moisi says, 'constitutes a bridge between our past and our future, demonstrating the vitality of the former – that is, nationalism – and the inescapable nature of the second – that is, globalisation in its new capitalist form'. Nevertheless, until 1996 the World Cup had managed to stay relatively free of politicisation when compared with the only other sports mega-event of comparable size, the Summer Olympics.

With the increase in the popularity of football and the commercial potential it offers, to host a World Cup final has become an attractive proposition. Possible television audiences of over 30 billion people have generated high levels of sponsorship and have made hosting the event an opportunity to generate massive profits. The World Cup provides a means for economic development as it 'delivers a rationale for revitalising the communication and civic infrastructures of primary sites [of World Cup games]' (Sugden and Tomlinson, 1998, p. 100). The media coverage provides a spotlight on the country and thus a chance to establish national prestige and recognition. Furthermore, automatic qualification to the finals for the host country's national team generates opportunities for the expression of national pride.

Global games and regional ambitions

Japan and South Korea had reasons for wanting to host the World Cup beyond these. For Japan, the World Cup was the ultimate objective of a process which began with the formation of the J. League, the professional football league, in 1993. The World Cup would provide a boost to the popularity of football in Japan, which was still competing with baseball to be the most popular sport, and thus maintain the momentum initiated by the J. League and the massive investment it required. Hosting the World Cup had also been seen as part of a process to promote new patterns of sport and leisure involvement in Japan as economic growth and the work ethic had declined relatively. Furthermore, there was a sense of regional pride in that football's world governing body, FIFA, had long intimated that the 2002 World Cup would be held in Asia and so Japan, having led the region economically, inevitably wanted to lead Asia in this particular sporting field.

For South Korea, on the other hand, intra-regional competition was paramount, exacerbated by the competition that South Korea felt with Japan in particular. Such competition had been manifested mainly in economic success, but also in sport and sporting events, especially football, the most popular sport in Korea and the sport which had become 'a mean [sic] of resistance to Japanese rule' (Lee, 1997) during the occupation. The success of the bid by Seoul for the 1988 Olympics over Japanese competition and the success of the Games themselves gave South Korea cause for hope and expectation of the benefits of hosting the World Cup. There also lay personal political ambitions in any moves for bidding. The president of the Korean Football Association, Chung Mong-Joon, was a national politician in the Diet and was seen as a possible future candidate for President. Success in the bidding for the World Cup would be a good launch-pad for Chung's presidential ambitions.

The success of each country's bids can perhaps be traced back to the formation of their bidding committees. The Korean bidding committee (KOBID) had a very strong political streak running through it, that was not only limited to Chung, who took the post of vice-chairman. Chairman of the committee was Lee Hong-Koo, then Deputy Prime Minister and head of the New Korea Party. He was also head of the government's unification committee and despite the funeral of Kim Il-Sung at the same time deemed a reception for the Korean bid after the 1994 World Cup final in the USA to be a more pressing matter! Chung also filled many committee posts with men from the Korean Foreign Ministry and enlisted the help of Korean embassy staff. A KOBID secretary was placed in the embassies of each country of the twenty-one members of the FIFA Executive Committee who would decide the host. Other posts were filled by business leaders – Chung himself was the heir to the Hyundai *chaebol* (conglomerate) and President of Hyundai Heavy Industries – and the successor to Lee as Chairman of KOBID, Koo Pyong-Hwoi, was Chairman of the Lucky Goldstar *chaebol* and President of the Korean Board of Trade.

The World Cup Japanese Bidding Committee (JBC) was, on the other hand, mainly composed of the executive of the Japan Football Association (JFA). Its leaders, such as Naganuma Ken (JFA Chairman), Okano Shun-ichiro (bidding committee chairman) were successful ex-footballers who had since worked in business before entering the JFA. With struggling English, compared with the personnel appointed in KOBID, they were mere 'salary-men'. Only in response to the political appointees in KOBID, did Japan appoint the former Prime Minister, Miyazawa Kiichi, as their honorary chairman.

The difference between these bids was evident in the level of government support. Despite only launching their bid long after the Japanese, KOBID easily obtained the government approval required by FIFA for all bids. President Kim Young-Sam met the executive members of FIFA, went jogging every day with a '2002 World Cup' T-shirt and cap and took Chung with him on his tour of European countries. The Ministry of Foreign Affairs meanwhile produced and distributed promotional brochures. The Japanese bidding committee, in contrast, despite requesting government approval in 1992 only received it a week before the FIFA deadline for official bids at the end of February 1995.

The nature of the two countries' bidding also presented a strong contrast. The Korean bid played heavily on two political elements. One was the World Cup acting as a 'catalyst for peace' (Sugden and Tomlinson, 1998, p. 118) on the Korean peninsula. The Secretary-general of KOBID, General Song Young-Shik, argued, '[h]osting the World Cup can play a role in facilitating the reunification process' (ibid.). The organisers of the Seoul Olympics had also flirted with the idea of trying to use the Games to unite the two Koreas but this had been after Seoul had been decided as host city. North Korean intransigence prevented any sharing of events. At every opportunity, KOBID promoted the unification ideal, even using North Korean border incursions to highlight the issue. This can be seen as an attempt to woo FIFA members with the temptation of potential diplomatic powers – it was well known that João Havelange, the FIFA president, wanted the Nobel Peace Prize – and with an eye on Chung's own political ambitions. In fact, the North Korean issue had more of a negative impact, especially on the Europeans. A formal offer to the North Koreans was never made while a tentative North Korean offer in January 1996 was deemed to have been the work of reformists within Pyongyang who had since been purged.

The second political aspect to the Korean bid was the use of the Japanese occupation of Korea from 1910 to 1945. This occupation had been brutal. Koreans were forced to change their names to Japanese names as the ruling powers sought to surpress the identity of the Korean nation. The occupation still remained a major barrier in relations between the two countries as Koreans accused the Japanese of failing to atone for the brutality imposed. Chung regularly used the Japanese occupation to discredit the Japanese bid: 'The Japanese occupation of Asia was the most barbarous and brutal in the history of humanity. It should acknowledge that image and stop trying to spoil our bid' (Calvin, 1995, p. 39). KOBID pamphlets were also distributed explaining the history of Korean football, making great reference to the Japanese occupation and its repression.

Japan sought, instead, to concentrate their bid on the country's infrastructure, its political stability and its high technology. While such issues were comparatively better than in South Korea and could be seen as a hint at Korean 'backwardness' compared with Japan, direct comparison was never proffered. The only political element to the Japanese bid was the inclusion of Hiroshima as one of the cities that would host matches. The 'city of peace' was, however, never put at the forefront of the Japanese bid. Furthermore, Japan refused to comment on the Korean statements and continued to emphasise the sporting and technological, and not political, nature of its bid.

FIFA's own power struggles

The contents of the two countries' bids, however, were to become irrelevant in the battle for power that was simultaneously developing within FIFA. FIFA had been ruled since 1974 by its president, João Havelange. During this time he had overseen a massive expansion in the game of football, especially its commercial side. In order to finance the plans to expand football which had won him election to president in 1974, Havelange brought in the involvement of multinational corporations, such as Coca-Cola and Adidas. The growth in the popularity of football and its commercial use created an industry that was, by the mid-1990s, generating US$225 billion per annum. As the organisation in charge of football, therefore, FIFA held a great deal of power. In 1974, Havelange had wrested control of FIFA from the organisation in charge of European football, UEFA, by leading a Third World challenge whereby the football associations of South America teamed up with the football associations of the Third World nations that had emerged in the 1970s. Havelange had won the election in 1974 by promising such nations a greater share of the spoils of football and when in power used the untapped commercial potential of football to finance and fulfil his promises.

In the 1990s, UEFA and its president Lennart Johansson saw the octogenarian FIFA President as on his way out: 'The time comes when you reach an age when you don't understand that it's time to climb down from the throne. We in Europe think it's time for him [Havelange] to go. He's 81 years old'

(Haydon, 1996). This challenge 'was testimony to the determination of Europe to wrestle back control of the world game' (Sugden and Tomlinson, 1997, p. 24). FIFA was formally a democratic institution accountable to its members and congress, but Havelange had, since his election, run FIFA as his own personal fiefdom. With the FIFA General Secretary, Sepp Blatter, alongside running football's 'civil service', Havelange was able to control FIFA through a combination of patronage and fear, allocating positions on committees to his supporters. While FIFA officially worked for the 'good of the game', as its power spread, it began to serve the aspirations of its own members rather than the objectives for which it was established.

However, by the mid-1990s, the growing discontent among nations not favoured by such patronage had spread beyond Europe and was beginning to be aired where it had not been before. In 1994, African nations, unhappy at African candidates for hosting the World Cup being defeated on two consecutive occasions, proposed at the FIFA Congress a rotation of the World Cup around the continents. This proposal failed, but it demonstrated to Europe that there was dissent elsewhere even if it was limited to proposals at FIFA's congress.

Johansson had failed with an attempt to challenge Havelange for the FIFA presidency in 1994. Havelange, in response to this challenge, carried out a purge of his potential opponents in the FIFA committees. This worked, however, in UEFA's favour as it disenchanted other FIFA members outside Europe. With the election of Korean Football Association (KFA) President, Chung Mong-Joon to the FIFA Executive Committee (ExCom), this provided a chance for UEFA to work against Havelange. Chung's election to the FIFA ExCom seat for the Asian Football Confederation (AFC) provided a foretaste of the competition between Japan and Korea for the World Cup. Despite being only recently elected to the presidency of the Korean FA, Chung was able to beat the Japanese candidate, Murata Tadao, who had held the advantage in terms of contacts and experience. This was done not only by a more efficient campaign enlisting help from Hyundai workers but also, it is alleged, the buying of votes. Japan's political inexperience was also in evidence. A failure to read the votes kept Murata in the contest when a withdrawal could have transferred his two votes to the Kuwaiti candidate, Sheikh Ahmad Fahad, who in the end lost by one vote.

With Chung in the FIFA ExCom, the Korean bid had the distinct advantage that it was guaranteed one vote in the committee which decided the World Cup host and through Chung it was able to gauge and lobby the votes of the ExCom members more effectively. For UEFA, Chung provided a dissenting voice on ExCom which would not alienate non-European members. As a result, Chung and the Europeans worked closely together to serve their own ends. Between 1994 and 1996 Chung became one of the most critical voices in ExCom with regard to the working of FIFA and Havelange. Chung attacked Havelange's visit to Nigeria when its government was executing dissidents and his criticism of the way in which FIFA decided the allocation of television rights for the World Cup mirrored UEFA's call for democratisation and transparency in FIFA's workings. In return, UEFA aided the Korean bid. The Korean bidding document for the 2002 World Cup impressed with its details on the potential finances and distribution of funds. It also pledged to donate its profits back to the development of football worldwide. Only later did it become apparent that these figures and plans closely resembled those put forward by UEFA in its proposals to improve World Cup revenues.

The decision of the host for the 2002 World Cup was developing along the lines of a FIFA–UEFA axis. A vote for Japan was seen as a vote for Havelange. He had openly favoured the Japanese bid and he was closely linked with the media company, International Sports & Leisure (ISL), with whom World Cup TV rights had hitherto been concluded and in which the Japanese advertising giant, Dentsū, once had held 49 per cent of shares. Support for South Korea represented a challenge to Havelange and his manner of rule, and support for UEFA's reforms. Japan, if it was aware of this development, still maintained its trust in Havelange and his ability to deliver his promises. Yet his strength was diminishing. Ill health robbed him of his infamous vitality in lobbying for support, while his actions were becoming eccentric and were beginning to alienate his supporters. His attempt to bring forward the World Cup decision date from 1 June 1996 to the end of 1995 was seen as favouring the Japanese and was thwarted by an alliance engineered by Chung and UEFA in the ExCom.

This was the first sign for Japan that European support for its bid was being threatened. It had hitherto believed that Europe, the origin of democracy and individual freedom, would allow its members on ExCom to vote freely. However, the football confederations, while autonomous from FIFA, had grown more powerful and UEFA in its challenge against Havelange sought loyalty from its members on the ExCom. Japanese attempts to lobby support from the African confederation (CAF) comprised sponsored football schools in various African countries. While grateful for such help, CAF members on ExCom realised the power struggle within FIFA was more important for their future. While Havelange had done much to help the development of football in Africa, Europe had become a major source of income for Africa with the transfer of many African footballers to European clubs. The UEFA proposals for more power to the confederations and more World Cup money to national associations were attractive.

Japan was witnessing its support slipping away with only the three South American votes on the ExCom guaranteed. Nevertheless, it refused to distance itself from Havelange, believing right up until the last moment that he was capable of delivering a majority for Japan. Nor did it seek to address the issue of the anti-Havelange vote. Attempts were made to separate the World Cup vote and the anti-Havelange issues with the Europeans, but they were futile as the Japanese were seen as too close to Havelange. Success for Japan meant success for Havelange who might seek to use this success to strengthen his position further and undermine those who challenged him. This lack of support for Japan's bid was not necessarily translated into support for South Korea. The Europeans realised the importance of Japanese money to football. Japanese companies were prominent sponsors of European football competitions. They realised that victory for South Korea for reasons of the FIFA power struggle could deal a crushing blow to the fledgling J. League and Japanese interest in football. If Japan and South Korea were to share the World Cup hosting it would still deal a blow to Havelange's prestige without Japan or South Korea suffering a severe defeat.

Furthermore, it could be seen as establishing a precedent. UEFA had already decided that Belgium and Holland would co-host its European Championships in 2000 and there was talk of the four Scandinavian countries of Denmark, Norway, Sweden (Johansson's native land) and Finland proposing a joint bid for the 2006 World Cup. Takeuchi Hiroshi believes it was with this in mind that the FIFA inspection committee sent to check the candidatures of Japan and Korea in November 1995 reported no great difference between the nature of the two bids, when in fact there was, and recommended consideration of co-hosting. Horst Schmidt, the head of the inspection committee, was closely linked to UEFA General Secretary Gerhard Aigner and the German management of TEAM, UEFA's marketing consultants, who drew up the UEFA proposals for reforming FIFA. For other FIFA ExCom members, co-hosting also proved attractive. For the Asian Football Confederation it would end a bitter contest between two of its members, guarantee an Asian World Cup and possibly win Asia increased representation at the World Cup from four to five nations.

In general, the expansion of the World Cup had restricted the number of nations that could play sole host to such a large event. Like the Scandinavian countries, co-hosting presented an opportunity for confederations like the Central American to submit bids from countries that would not have considered it before. For some members of FIFA's ExCom co-hosting was also a convenient means of avoiding declaring outright opposition to their patron Havelange. The bitterness and intensity of the contest provided a convenient reason to call for co-hosting. These calls started in mid-1995 from the Asian Football Confederation and UEFA members and were echoed by some Japanese and Korean politicians. South Korea was taking a conciliatory stance, saying that if FIFA decreed it, it would consider co-hosting. This policy was following domestic political pressure, but this flexibility was also winning political points for the bid.

In the case of South Korea, it appears that the reason for pressure for co-hosting was a government decision in 1994 that the country was not able to stage the finals alone. Takeuchi quotes a FIFA expert on Asia saying that the Korean government decided long before the decision, possibly two years before, that the investment required to construct 16 stadia for the finals if it was to be the sole host was excessive. Investment for five stadia was possible and so it was decided that the ultimate goal was to co-host with Japan. Certainly while such news has never been disclosed, it appears to be confirmed by the fact that a possible Mexican candidature for 2002 withdrew in early 1995 when informed by the Koreans of the co-hosting plan and by the fact that Korean suggestions for co-hosting never met any form of protest from the local governments where the 16 sites were planned and of whom many would have lost much investment if co-hosting took place. Of course, such plans could not be revealed before the decision by the FIFA ExCom as the disclosure of insufficient infrastructure would jeopardise the Korean bid and favour Japan. Therefore, a pretence of campaigning for sole hosting or a joint bid with North Korea was maintained, while at the same time appearing flexible to the idea of co-hosting but not too flexible in case co-hosting was not approved.

Japan, in following Havelange's line of rejection of co-hosting that it was not in the FIFA Statutes and therefore was not at all feasible, appeared, on the other hand, inflexible and stubborn. The Japanese stance continued until the last moment in part because the bidding committee believed, 'naively' according to Alan Tomlinson (Interview with author in Brighton, 13 August 1998), that Havelange would still prevail and in part because of an inherent sporting nature of 'fair play'.

Throughout the bidding process, the Japanese bidding committee members had referred to the bidding contest in terms of a sporting contest. 'The World Cup bid competition has become like an actual soccer game. And the team that loses passion to win will lose the game' (De Bellis, 1996), stated Ogura Junji, JBC general secretary. Okano Shun-ichiro, when asked about possible repercussions on the competition, replied:

> It is inevitable that in a sporting contest there is a winner and a loser. But, should it be that because of this the opponents' mutual hatred increase? I, personally, believe that after the contest opponents who have tried his best attain a deeper understanding of each other.
>
> (Takeuchi, 1996, p. 83)

While such words can be dismissed as empty rhetoric for public consumption, it must not be forgotten that most of the committee members came from a high-profile sporting background. Takeuchi also mentions how the Japanese refrained from lobbying activities of which the legality was in doubt, even when in fact there was no FIFA regulation on lobbying, and how the bidding committee's conduct was praised by FIFA members. On the other hand, the Korean campaign was labelled 'dirty' and was tainted with rumours of vote-buying. The Japanese did not realise that in the contest for power within FIFA, FIFA rules would become irrelevant.

Pressure from the past

It was at this stage that external pressure from outside the world of football and FIFA also played a major part in convincing the JBC to compromise its stance. Initial pressure to maintain the sole host bid had come from the fifteen local governments who had donated around 235 million yen each to host the finals and who did not want to be omitted as a result of co-hosting. Such feelings were inevitably echoed at the Ministry of Education, the ministry in charge of sport and funding for its facilities and most closely connected with the JBC. But, there had also grown from around 1994 pressure from Japanese politicians for the two nations to co-host. This came not only from those politicians in the Japan-Korea Parliamentary Alliance, but also from within the Ministry of Foreign Affairs (MOFA). MOFA naturally seeks positive diplomatic relations with other countries. However, Japanese relations with South Korea had from the time of official bidding taken a strong downturn that was affecting and in turn being affected by the bidding competition.

Japanese relations with Korea have been complex and full of emotion with present-day ties shaped by the Japanese colonial occupation from 1910 to 1945. The brutal treatment of Koreans by the Japanese during the occupation, the issue of compensation for Korean women used as sex slaves by the Japanese Imperial Army during World War II ('comfort women'), and the treatment of Koreans living in Japan as a result of the occupation, had all affected relations adversely. But, in the 1990s it was hoped that with growing Korean diplomacy throughout the world, a democratically elected civilian president in Kim Young-Sam from 1993 and deepening economic ties, the two countries would improve relations. This seemed to be confirmed as President Kim visited Japan in 1994 and talked of a 'future-oriented' economic relationship and did not blame the trade imbalance between the two countries on Japan. Yet, partly as a result of unfortunate timing, partly due to undiplomatic remarks by senior Japanese politicians, Japan's historical legacy was to re-introduce itself at the forefront of relations between the two.

The bids reached full speed in 1995, the fiftieth anniversary of the end of World War II and of Korean freedom from the Japanese occupation. Therefore it was inevitable that Japan's past re-emerged in Korean politics, highlighted by the symbolic start of demolition of the National Central Museum in Seoul, the former residence of the Japanese Governor General. While the anniversary brought an apologetic statement from the Japanese Prime Minister, Murayama Tomiichi, that went beyond previous statements, the positive effect was cancelled out by various inflammatory remarks made by Japanese politicians around the time concerning the Japanese occupation and how it had been valid and had done some good for Korea. Such statements angered Korea greatly and tension between the two countries heightened. But South Korea was also voluntarily raising the issue of the past. President Kim stated in both a Japanese, and then an American, newspaper that Japan was responsible for the division of the Korean peninsula and was hindering its reunification. Then, South Korea used its acquisition of a seat on the United Nations Security Council to raise the issue of compensation for comfort women.

Tensions had been heightened in early 1996 with the dispute over possession of the island of Takeshima (Tokdo in Korean). Tensions were fuelled to
the extent that a scheduled visit of Japanese politicians to Seoul was cancelled
as they would not be welcome. While in a meeting shortly after, President
Kim and Japanese Prime Minister Hashimoto Ryūtarō agreed to start talks
on the dispute, tensions continued to simmer in part due to the intensification
in the World Cup bidding competition as the day of the decision approached.
Japanese embassy officials in Seoul even warned Japanese nationals in South
Korea to be on their guard should Japan's bid prove victorious.

Co-hosting the 2002 World Cup was therefore seen by many Japanese
politicians as first of all extinguishing these tensions but also as having a positive effect on Japan's international role by Japan's foreign policy-makers.
Co-hosting presented a means of re-orienting Japan's relations with South
Korea towards the future without having to make the apologies and compensation that South Korea demanded as a prerequisite to such a
development and that they were loath to give, since it was a sign of weakness
and might hurt national pride. With many Japanese regarding their bid as
greatly superior and, prior to May 1996, likely to win, a 'sporting' gesture
such as sharing the hosting would gain Japan moral authority and improve its
international reputation in much the same way as apologies and compensation measures would. Furthermore, from a basic economic viewpoint, by
sharing the benefits of the World Cup this would also maintain the economic
hierarchy of the two countries whereas South Korea sole hosting might have
brought it closer to Japan.

It was this pressure that JBC honorary chairman and former Prime
Minister, Miyazawa Kiichi, brought to the JBC camp a day before the decision day, when the JBC had also learnt that its bid could be defeated.
Miyazawa was instrumental in pressuring the JBC members into agreeing to
co-hosting and in a secret meeting with Lee Hong-Koo, also honorary chairman of KOBID and a former Prime Minister, on 30 May 1996 they sealed the
deal to co-host. So, when Havelange, faced with a large majority of ExCom
members in support of co-hosting and pressured by close friends to support
co-hosting, asked Japan to consider it, the decision had in effect already been
made. Japan, faced with political pressure from home and fearing a straight
vote might spell victory for South Korea, relented and accepted co-hosting,
albeit very reluctantly.

The decision to share the hosting of the 2002 World Cup between Japan
and South Korea was accompanied by various statements justifying how the
decision was, in the words of UEFA Chairman, Lennart Johansson, 'in the
spirit of peace and the interest of the game' (Associated Press, 1996).
Politicians from both countries stated how the decision would usher in a new
chapter in relations between the countries. Such platitudes sought to mask the
divisions and tensions that had in fact inspired the decision and so there was
widespread scepticism that such a decision made rather for the considerations
of FIFA's internal politics than bilateral relations between Japan and South

Korea could have such a positive diplomatic effect. On top of this was a sense of disappointment in both countries at the failure to win the right to host outright.

Competitive hosting for the good of the games

Nevertheless, it appears that the co-hosting of the 2002 World Cup has had a positive effect on bilateral relations and will continue to do so. There were initial fears that the decision to co-host had not ended the competition, but rather merely transferred it to within the framework of co-hosting, which had become 'competitive hosting'. This seemed to be the attitude of the South Korean camp. First, they were quick to interpret the 'draw' of co-hosting as in fact a victory for them. Then South Korea football officials sought to 'win' the negotiation of various aspects of the World Cup. This was carried out in a fashion not too dissimilar from the way they contested the right to host. J. League chairman, Kawabuchi Saburō, in comments about the negotiations between FIFA, Japan and South Korea, explained how Japan acceded to Korea's demands of the title of 'Korea-Japan 2002 World Cup' – as Korea came before Japan in French, the official language of FIFA, rather than in English. This was despite the fact that FIFA had declared Japan's name was to come first and for the country to host the final. Chung declared this decision as a victory to his national media.

Chung had also mischievously suggested beforehand a football match between the two countries to decide the location of the final match. When it was decided that the opening ceremony was to be held in Seoul, a Korean television station interpreted it as an opportunity for the nation to demonstrate its cultural superiority to the world before Japan could start its hosting of matches.

However, such sense of competition eased off as the work towards the hosting of the tournament progressed. The formation of a triumvirate in the 2002 Planning Group, made up of Japan, South Korea and FIFA has complemented the bilateral co-operation that has taken place and maintains order, avoiding unnecessary competition. Indeed, members of the two local organising committees have complained about FIFA's lack of leadership and the fact that it is lagging behind the level of co-operation taking place between the committees.

Beyond football: the future of Japanese–Korean relations

FIFA's decision to share the finals has put responsibility on the two nations to successfully co-host, establishing a rule for co-operation, even if the uniqueness of co-hosting has meant rewriting the hosting rules. A sporting event of such or even similar size has never been co-hosted between countries before, so it is difficult to evaluate what sort of effect such an event will have on the diplomatic relations between the two countries. While some will see possible competition between the two over how successfully they host their share of the finals, the criteria for relative success or failure are difficult to discern and so it will likely not become a prominent issue. In terms of each national team representing national prestige and an encounter of the two as a source of conflict, the two teams will be drawn in different groups and must progress to a stage of the finals neither has ever reached in order to meet. Therefore, it is likely that the national team will provide a source of national pride but not in a confrontational sense with regard to the other host nation.

Indeed, as co-hosting is now undisputed and neither country for the sake of national pride can afford to back out, the two countries must work with each other to ensure the finals' success. Indeed, it has been suggested that the economic downturn in South Korea in 1997 forced Japan to subsidise the construction of some stadia in South Korea (although the Koreans fiercely denied this report). The organisation required to host such an event will necessitate a level of co-operation that is unprecedented between the two countries. The logistics of co-hosting the World Cup has forced co-operation between Seoul and Tokyo to improve ties before the finals take place. Co-hosting will generate travel between Japan and South Korea by teams, supporters and media of all nationalities, which requires government co-operation on security, visas, and telecommunications among other things.

As it is common for the head of state to attend the opening ceremony, negotiation is necessary to lay the groundwork for the visit of the Japanese Emperor to South Korea for the opening ceremony, with a prior visit deemed likely to defuse any tension. Therefore, co-operation at the level of national football associations has been reciprocated by co-operation at a political and governmental level to facilitate these issues. This has been followed up by South Korean government actions which can be interpreted as settling past issues and complementing the future-oriented policy statements. A committee has been established to lay down the guidelines for the opening up of Korea to Japanese culture while the Korean government's decision to compensate 'comfort women' has been accompanied by suggestions that it will no longer ask the Japanese government for compensation.

All these events have been seen as linked to the co-hosting. But, while the South Korean government has explicitly stated that Japan's ability to 'face up to its past wrongdoings' is a prerequisite to the issues of cultural exchange, an Imperial visit to South Korea and the successful co-hosting of the 2002 World Cup, Japan has yet to make any such concessions or promises to do so without seemingly any adverse effect so far. An example of this development is the intense row over the adoption of a textbook in Japanese schools that fails to portray the Japanese actions in Asia during the Second World War as an act of atrocity. Despite fierce opposition from South Korea, the new government of the right-leaning Prime Minister Koizumi Junichirō failed to back down. Several times the hosting of the World Cup was brought into question by Korean lawmakers over the issue, but eventually it remained.

The World Cup has encouraged the two countries to realise that strengthened cultural ties are necessary before the finals take place. Until now, there has been criticism that relations between the two countries have been restricted to a political level, with a cycle of good relations spoiled by Japanese politicians' remarks followed by their apologies.

However, the fear remains that while all this progress has been made so far, and will be made in relations between Japan and South Korea in preparation for the joint hosting of the 2002 World Cup, when the finals are over and the 'circus has left town', it is not certain whether this will be accompanied by a similar departure of incentive in maintaining good bilateral relations or whether the progress achieved has a degree of permanency or has set in motion a process which cannot be halted or reversed. Similar fears have been raised over events which have been held where the spotlight of the world on that event caused the hosts to adopt favourable behaviour which deviated from previous policy. Many major sporting events have forced the host nations' rulers into some form of 'amnesty' during the event which has ended with the end of competition, but the 1988 Seoul Olympics demonstrated how permanent reform can be made as a result of the event. It remains to be seen whether the Japanese and South Korean governments will strive to achieve similar permanency to the improvement in their countries' relations.

References

Associated Press (1996) 'Soccer truce', *Associated Press Report*, 1 June.

Calvin, Michael (1995) 'Havelange's powerbase is challenged by Korean bid', *Daily Telegraph*, 29 September, p. 39.

De Bellis, John (1996) 'Japan plugging away at World Cup promotion', (online: <http://www.iac.co.jp/~ecs/soccer/wcup.html>).

Haydon, Simon (1996) 'Soccer – UEFA boss says time for Havelange to go', Reuters, 14 November.

Lee Jong-Young (1997) 'Wārudo kappu kyōsai to Kankoku shakai' [World-Cup co-hosting and Korean society], in Nihon Supōtsu Shakai Gakkai (ed.) *Henyō suru gendai shakai to supōtsu*. Kyōto: Sekai Shisō Sha, pp. 80–91.

Moisi, Dominique (1998) 'The globe as a football', *Financial Times*, 6 July, p. 20.

Sugden, John and Tomlinson, Alan (1997) 'Global power struggles in world football: FIFA and UEFA, 1954–74, and their legacy', *The International Journal of the History of Sport*, 14, 2 (August): 1–25.

Sugden, John and Tomlinson, Alan (1998) *FIFA and the Contest for World Football: Who Rules the Peoples' Game?*, Cambridge: Polity Press.

Takeuchi Hiroshi (1996) *2002 nen no fea purē. Nikkan kyōsai to FIFA no seijiryokugaku* [Fair play 2002. Japan–Korea's co-hosting and a study of FIFA's power politics], Tokyo: Kyōdō Tsūshin Sha.

4 International power struggles in the governance of world football

The 2002 and 2006 World Cup bidding wars

John Sugden and Alan Tomlinson

Introduction: staging international sporting events

In the context of debates concerning England's bid to host the 2006 football World Cup, talk of a bid to stage a London Olympics, and concern over an English national stadium to replace Wembley, a Select Committee of the UK Parliament's Department of Culture, Media and Sport began to examine the staging of international sports events in the late 1990s. One of us presented an appendix to the minutes of evidence of this committee a year before the outcome of the bidding process for the 2006 football World Cup:

> the staging of international sporting events has been based upon a mixture of political, cultural and economic motives . . . The international sporting event is a vehicle for television companies/broadcasters to reach global markets, and for multinational capital to strut its wares in exclusive mediaspace. The benefits for communities, regions and single nations have been grossly exaggerated, the problems and potential pitfalls veiled by the hyperbole of political boosterism and economic opportunism.
>
> (Tomlinson, 1999, p. 279)

Although the Committee's Fourth Report of Session 1998–99 adjudged the England 2006 bid to have been 'well conceived, well managed and well executed', with support from the government described as 'exemplary', the English bid was always doomed. Any close reading of the nature of the bidding process for events of this scale would have produced a more realistically framed campaign and bid.

In written evidence to a later House of Commons Select Committee investigating the staging of international events, the parliamentary committee was reminded that the Sydney Olympic Games had been received rapturously by media, sports organisers, politicians and the public. With dramatic gains in the medal ranking for Great Britain, in comparison to its 1996 showing in Atlanta, a momentum was building to support a London Olympic bid. What fuels such initiatives?

Australia celebrated what was recurrently claimed as 'the biggest peace-time event in the world' in a series of welcomes to its global audience and its hundreds of thousands of visitors. In three ways, staging the Olympic spectacle can be seen as beneficial. It profiles modernity, showcases excellence, and boosts the tourism/visitor economy. But on closer scrutiny, the benefits of the events look less certain. It is of course too soon to say this about the Sydney Games, but the charter flights hardly keep Seoul and Calgary (Winter Games, 1988) full of sports-mad tourists or other visitors. Barcelona showcased itself in 1992, but would be a world tourist city anyway. And Atlanta suffered, if anything, in self-esteem with its less than impressive staging of the 1996 Summer Olympics.

Before a London bid for the Olympics is considered, the reality behind the three main sorts of claim made for the benefits of staging the Games should be reviewed. London is very much a world city on every kind of visitor agenda, without a new Wembley or a Millennium Dome.

(Tomlinson, 2001a, p. 59)

Two other potential benefits are also claimed for the staging of these events – 'the intangible yet felt and real sense of national identity and pride that a nation or city might feel in hosting such events, and the infrastructural benefits (the transport and communications infrastructure for instance, as in Barcelona)' (Tomlinson, 2001b, p. 292). There are spectacular examples where some of these benefits are indeed demonstrable, as in Barcelona in 1992. There are many other examples where any discussion of the projected benefits is, after the event, far from welcomed. Only one year after the climax of the Olympic Games in Sydney, there was much debate as to the usefulness of the Olympic Park, where Stadium Australia is host to very few large-scale capacity-drawing events. It is not the logic of rational decision-making that dictates the outcome of bidding processes, nor the strength or merit of individual cases. As one of us also commented to the House of Commons committee:

[It] is a level of international *football realpolitik* that determines the outcome of bidding processes for events such as the football World Cup, and it is a valid question to pose whether this is at all compatible with any aspirations to operate ethically in international relations and foreign policy, particularly as the England 2006 bid was perhaps the most explicitly political initiative of its kind to date.

(ibid., pp. 58–59)

The outcome of the bidding war to stage the 2002 World Cup dramatically revealed the nature of that process. As a prelude to a re-evaluation of the 2006 bidding outcome, it is illuminating to revisit the Japan–Korea co-hosting decision.

Japan versus Korea

It was a little over six months before the FIFA executive committee was to make its decision on who would host the 2002 World Cup finals. For years the Japanese had felt that the decision was in the bag, and a self-assured confidence came over their big reception at the Sandton Sun, Johannesburg, held at the tail end of the African Cup of Nations in January 1996. Sir Bobby Charlton was on display, plugging the bid. Jim Trecker, PR at USA '94 and US football nut, spoke in upbeat fashion about the Japanese qualities. A video relayed the views of football luminaries that if the Japanese did something they would do it well, and offered glimpses of a virtual football spectacle that might be doing some things too well for some of us. How could the bid fail? Hadn't the FIFA president, Havelange, favoured the Japanese all along? Wasn't the South Korean bid – as we all *really* knew – paper-thin? Maybe. But the in-house politics of the FIFA family hierarchy would develop in ways that were to give the Japanese business-led bid a rude shock, as the more explicitly political-led bid of the South Koreans powered towards the finishing post as the bidding process drew to a close. Critical to this was the profile and impact of Dr Chung Mong-Joon. Immaculately groomed, jet-black hair, tall, lean and trim for his early middle age, you knew when Chung was around, surrounded by minders as he swept through the palm trees of the Sheraton lobby in Abu Dhabi. For Chung, the Korean FA was an apprenticeship for bigger things – like heading Hyundai heavy industries, sitting in the national parliament, and profiling his country in world sports politics.

FIFA Vice-President David Will recalled the race between Morocco and France for the prize of staging the 1998 Finals: 'that was bad enough, the pressures on that were terrible', but this was nothing compared with the pressure that mounted during 1996, as FIFA prepared to select the host for the 2002 Finals. As Japan and (the Republic of) Korea moved towards the decision date, the competitors followed the French example of a last-ditch assault on the motivations and appetites of key FIFA personnel. As Will recalls in an interview with the authors in his Brechin home:

> This was so dramatic, this one, this was just unbelievable . . . It was ridiculous. I, about January of this year, I approached them. I said to Japan and Korea: 'Now, I am not coming to any more receptions, I am not accepting any more gifts.' The stuff was arriving at the door here, and of course, what do you do? The postman delivers it. It's just ridiculous. The only thing that was missing was the cash in a plain brown envelope, you know, it was unbelievable. And I am not accepting invitations to Japan or Korea, this is not out of discourtesy, I am stopping. And I know that most of the Europeans did the same. They just stopped.

The UEFA President Lennart Johansson was one of those Europeans. Asked to confirm that FIFA's executive committee had endured bribery attempts by nations seeking to host the 2002 World Cup, Johansson told us, 'Yes, there were no limits. A bottle of whisky, a camera or a computer, everything was permissible', adding that he had been sent a computer that he returned.

FIFA executive committee member Dr Michel D'Hooghe, of Belgium, talking to us in his office at the Belgian FA's base at the former Heysel Stadium, described how hotel rooms were garlanded with flowers, and a lobbyist from one of the bidding countries even appeared in the seat next to him on a flight from Brussels to Prague, to take the opportunity to talk with him for the duration of the flight. 'Could this be a coincidence?', he asked in a fashion that needed no answer. We responded with a non-committal shrug, separated from Dr D'Hooghe by a magnificent circular green pot, inscribed by the Korean Dr Chung, proffering his best wishes to FIFA executive committee member Dr Hooghe's association. It's hard to do the arithmetic accurately – we've put the questions to the Koreans and the Japanese, but the face-to-face ones are politely and coldly deflected, the e-mails not reciprocated – but estimates reckon that US$100 million were spent by Korea and Japan in their bidding campaigns.

Asia had long been seen as the venue for the 2002 World Cup, for to stage the first finals ever to be staged outside of Europe and the Americas was seen as an unprecedented boost to Asian football. No serious candidate was available from Africa, so in many ways the staging of the finals by an Asian country would be a dramatic gesture by FIFA, fulfilling Havelange's pledge to raise the profile of the game in a continent in which playing standards were certainly improving, but whose teams were not yet as effectively competitive as were a number of national sides from the African continent. With no system in place or established precedent for a coordinated bid from single confederations, there was nothing to stop any number of national bids for the staging and hosting role. From the late 1980s onwards, the escalating scale of the bids from South Korea and Japan was to dominate FIFA and World Cup politics, culminating in the decision that the two rivals should co-host the event. The way in which this decision was reached expressed the deep-rooted and simmering tensions between FIFA and the European federation, and the positioning and implicit campaigning of potential successors to Havelange.

In his inimitable style Havelange had led the Japanese to believe that the World Cup finals were within his individual gift. An Asian venue was very much in his thinking as early as 1986, when he gave an interview to the Swiss magazine *Sport*. Havelange reaffirmed the principle of the regular rotation of the finals in Europe and America up until 1994, but 'expressed the wish' that the 'finals in 2002 should be held in China'. In the autumn of 1987 Havelange travelled to Beijing, for further preliminary discussions with China's sports leaders. His encouragement of a Chinese bid was also linked to his belief – as experienced IOC member and catalyst for other South and Central American IOC committee members – that China would be awarded the Summer Olympic Games for the year 2000: 'Anyone who can organize Olympic Games is no doubt capable of hosting the Finals of Soccer's World Cup' (Sugden and Tomlinson, 1998a, p. 113).

Meanwhile, as the Chinese dwelt upon Havelange's overtures, Japan and South Korea expressed their interest in developing bids, at a meeting of the Asian confederation. FIFA's General Secretary Blatter, heir apparent to Havelange's presidency, had visited South Korea's soccer facilities earlier in the year, and the aggressive and uncompromising tone of the South Korean bid was set from the start of the campaign. A Summer Olympics the following year in Seoul was presented by the Koreans as a perfect illustration of the nation's abilities to stage such events, and the Korean press mobilised against the other potential bidders: China's low standard of living would bar it from meeting FIFA's financial criteria and Japan's main sport, baseball, would obstruct any Japanese plans to stage the world soccer finals during the base-ball season. An effectively staged 1988 Olympic Games, and the concentration by the Chinese upon their bid for the 2000 Olympics, boosted Korean confi-dence in the race for the 2002 World Cup. By the summer of 1990 Havelange could tell the Xinhua press agency (speaking during Italia '90 in Rome) that as well as Korea, additional candidates for the finals were Japan, Saudi Arabia, China and Malaysia. Asian football standards were improving, he stated, and would be close to those of Europe and South America by 2000: an Asian venue was therefore ideal for 2002. This was the classic Havelange and Samaranch tactic, talking up the candidates to stoke the fires of rivalry.

At the same time, Havelange erected a huge barrier against the Korean case, by saying that the reunification of the two Koreas should be a pre-requisite for any successful Korean bid. A couple of years later, in a press conference in Rio de Janeiro in November 1992, the FIFA President described Japan and South Africa as the 'most promising candidates' for the finals of 2002 and 2006 respectively. During the World Under-17 Championships staged in Japan in 1993, Havelange consistently gave the impression to the Japanese that they were the firm favourites: 'People he talked to in Japan gained the impression that it is also Havelange's aim to award the first World Cup of the third millennium to Japan', reported the gossip-monger of world sports politics, *Sport Intern*. Reservations remained over the lack of English-speaking expertise in Japan, and the rising costs of accommodation and transport, but there was no doubt that Japan was the favourite for 2002, and, perhaps too complacently, saw itself as exactly that.

Two critical, interrelated, developments were to change this, and, for a year or two at least, to alter world football politics and to take the gift of the World Cup from the fiefdom of Havelange. For a while, up to the succession to the presidency of Blatter, new influences and alliances swayed FIFA and its decisions. One was the transformation of FIFA's own committee practices, with more committee members – clustering around the burly truck magnate Swede, Johansson – willing to openly challenge Havelange. The other was the accession of the Korean, Chung, to the Asian confederation's vice-presiden-tial place on FIFA's executive committee.

Chung's father, Chung Ju-Yung, head of Hyundai, was the real leader of the successful Olympic bid, and five years after the Seoul Olympics made an unsuccessful bid for the presidency of the country. Chung the Younger was coming into the FIFA boardroom with an agenda of his own, way beyond FIFA's fixture list. Bound up with these developments was the determination of the Europeans not to be outflanked when the time came to contest the FIFA presidency. The success of South Korea in forcing Havelange's hand and levering the decision that the event would be co-hosted illustrates the power of combined political and economic interests in sport's global governance (see Butler this volume; Sugden and Tomlinson, 1998a, Chapter 5; Sugden and Tomlinson, 1999a, Chapter 8 for further details of the 2002 decision).

The race for 2006

Brussels is an engaging mix of the old and the new. At one end of the Boulevard Adolphe Max, itself littered with seedy sex shops and *chambres privées*, lies Place de la Bourse, one of the city's gathering points, and a focus for riot police when football fans in Euro 2000 were getting out of hand. At the other end is a concrete wasteland of ugly buildings, among which lies the Sheraton Hotel, a shrine to the glamour and opulence of post-war reconstruction. The hotel was the base for the team from England campaigning to win the right to host the 2006 World Cup. A mournfully resigned Tony Banks, assigned to the bid by the New Labour government, would soon be conceding that the arrest of 800 or so England fans just before the England–Germany game at Charleroi 'hasn't done us any good at all'. Things were 'looking bleak indeed, with last week's images', he concluded.

England 2006 boss Alec McGivan was claiming that things were still looking good before the Charleroi problems and the media's saturation coverage of the outburst of fan trouble and its accompanying worldwide publicity. It would be important, he pleaded, for FIFA to hear reassurances from the British government's Home Secretary, and from Prime Minister Blair, on tougher measures to deal with the hooligans. Tony Blair has usually backed winners in his career, and he wasn't about to back the wrong horse. Banks and McGivan were sounding more and more like a background chorus. As we had consistently noted (see Sugden and Tomlinson, 1998b), the England 2006 bid was dead long before Charleroi.

England's bid to host the World Cup finals in 2006 was an ill-conceived, badly led and embarrassingly inept campaign. It wasted at least £10 million, including a big chunk of lottery – i.e. public – money and confirmed what many of us knew already: while the national team was bad on the field, in the corridors of power of world football, England's football administrators were worse.

The bungling began in the late 1980s when the English FA, led by Bert Millichip, was desperate to restore some prestige to the national game in the post-Heysel and post- Hillsborough period: a time when England's club sides had been subjected to a humiliating exclusion from all European competitions, and football hooliganism had been given the shaming, universal nickname of 'the English disease'. It was in this unlikely context that the FA decided to mount a bid to host Euro'96.

Lennart Johansson, UEFA's Swedish President, was sympathetic to the English cause and used his good relations with the influential Germans to broker a deal whereby they would back England's bid for Euro'96 if the English would reciprocate by giving Germany a free run at World Cup 2006. Without German support Bert Millichip knew that England's bid for Euro'96 would fail, and so at the time was happy to shake on the deal. While nothing was in writing, the powerful inner circle of European football administrators was privy to the arrangement.

According to the FA, Euro'96 was an outstanding, hooligan-free, success (although there are many who remember the half-empty grounds, the xenophobia of the English national press, and the violence unleashed against German fans and tourists after Germany knocked the hosts out) – so much so that, as soon as Millichip got his knighthood and retired, in 1997, much to the astonishment of the German FA and UEFA hierarchy, the new regime at the FA decided to launch a bid to host World Cup 2006. As a prominent element in its 1997 election manifesto, New Labour also got in on the act, pledging to do all that it could to secure the rights to the staging of international sports events.

If this piece of undignified back stabbing by the English was bad, worse was to follow. Lennart Johansson, frustrated with the undemocratic, unaccountable, and dictatorial style of leadership given to FIFA by its long self-serving Brazilian president, João Havelange, decided to make a challenge for the world body's leadership in 1998.[1] Acutely aware of the potential for major skulduggery in elections of this kind, Johansson persuaded almost all of UEFA's fifty plus members to sign a declaration pledging their support for him in the1998 election. The English FA signed up to this deal, but with just a day or two left before the vote at the FIFA Congress in Paris, it held a press conference, announcing that support for Johansson had been exchanged for its backing for FIFA's insider candidate Sepp Blatter, Havelange's protégé and nominated successor. This not only gave Blatter an extra vote and reduced Johansson's yield, but it also gave an excuse to other countries, particularly former British colonies, to shift their allegiances to a man who, like Havelange a quarter of a century earlier, had travelled the length and breadth of Africa and Asia making lavish promises in the quest for votes.

England's shameful volte-face was another bad miscalculation by the 2006 campaign team. England 2006 knew that Johansson was privy to the gentleman's agreement and knew that he felt honour-bound to back the German candidacy. With Johansson as FIFA President the English felt that their bid would be doomed. Blatter duly won the Paris election amidst a cry of protests including allegations of bribery and corruption that were never proven, but were believed by those close to the proceedings.

It is beyond doubt that much of Blatter's support came from Africa and that in order to garner that support he offered the Africans, among other things, FIFA's biggest prize – the World Cup finals in 2006. With Johansson at FIFA's helm England's bid would have had little chance, with Blatter in charge it had no chance. Thus, even before the campaign was seriously under-way, England 2006 had managed to alienate the most powerful men in the European confederation, and helped to elect a FIFA President who was oath-bound to promote an African country as host for the 2006 competition.

Then we have 'Lancastergate' – the FA's clumsy dirty tricks operation through which it tried to parachute the then FA Chairman Keith Wiseman into the FIFA Executive. When Bert Millichip retired, the English FA was left with absolutely nobody on any of the important FIFA or UEFA committees, and was thus incapable of engaging in the insider wheeling and dealing that was essential in the pursuit of hosting such things as World or European championships.

Most people believe that FIFA control the rules of football. They are wrong. This is the job of the IFB, a body that has been in existence for well over one hundred years. Originally its membership was restricted to the 'home' football associations of England, Wales, Ireland and Scotland. The formation of the IFB preceded the foundation of FIFA in 1904 by almost two decades, and for some time the two bodies competed as guardians of the world game. Eventually a compromise was reached in the late 1920s, whereby the IFB retained its jurisdiction over rules and all other matters were dealt with by FIFA. In addition, four FIFA members would match the home countries' four voting members. Also, and crucial to this story, the home countries would, on re-entering FIFA just after the Second World War, always have a UK representative as a member of the FIFA Executive Committee.

The UK representative to FIFA is cycled around England, Scotland, Northern Ireland and Wales every four years. During England's 2006 campaign the representative was Scotland's David Will. Led by Graham Kelly, the English FA sought to oust Will and install (English) FA chair Keith Wiseman in his place. To achieve this the FA sought to persuade the Welsh and the Northern Irish to accept millions of pounds in 'football development aid' in return for signing a letter that withdrew support for David Will as the UK representative, pledging instead support for England's Wiseman. The Welsh went for the deal, but, to their credit, the Northern Irish rejected it out of hand. When the Welsh FA came looking for their money, the deal – unap-proved by any FA committee – was exposed and Kelly and Wiseman tramped inevitably towards resignation.

Of course there was no official FIFA inquiry. David Will had been a forth-right champion of Lennart Johansson and fierce in his opposition to Blatter. There would have been few tears shed in Blatter's entourage if Will had been deposed from the FIFA Executive, by fair means or foul. There are even sug-gestions that the whole thing was Blatter's idea! Either way, once more, all for the sake of 2006, the English and their fabled reputation for fair play suffered public ridicule.

Oozing with self-congratulatory nostalgia, (new) Wembley, the 'home of football', and the 'world's oldest football competition', the FA Cup, were at the centre of England's 2006 campaign propaganda. Led to believe that a redeveloped Wembley Stadium could also be used as an athletics facility and serve as the proposed venue for bids for the World Athletics Championships and the 2012 Olympic Games, the government agreed to contribute £120 million from the National Lottery. As it turned out, it soon became clear that transforming Wembley from a football to an athletics venue would be both costly and time-consuming. Worse still, once the temporary running track had been installed, the stadium's capacity would be reduced from 80,000 to 67,000, falling short of the IOC's (International Olympic Committee) minimum requirements for the Olympic Games.

There followed an acrimonious public argument involving the Wembley development team (WNSL), the FA, England 2006, Sport England, UK Athletics and various government ministers, including the then Culture Secretary, Chris Smith, and the new Sports Minister, Kate Hoey. In the end the idea of a dual facility was abandoned and UK athletics was left looking for new funding and another greenfield site on which to build an athletics stadium. This only made any sense if England won the right to host the World Cup in 2006, but the manner through which the development of the new national stadium took place was a public scandal that further undermined the credibility of the English case, particularly as all of this took place at the time when FIFA's inspection team was assessing the relative merits of the rival bids.

Not satisfied with making a mess of the national stadium, the mandarins behind the England 2006 machine decided to tamper with another national institution – the FA Cup. FIFA's newly elected president, Sepp Blatter, was determined to extend FIFA's (and his own) power by moving into club football. He spearheaded the introduction of yet another club competition whereby the strongest club sides in FIFA's six continental confederations would meet annually and compete in a round-robin tournament. The inaugural event was held in December 1999 in Brazil and, as the then European champions, Manchester United were invited to represent Europe.

The ABMU (Anybody But Manchester United) brigade argue that a pleasant mid-winter break on the beaches of Rio suited Manchester United down to the ground, gave them an unfair advantage, and helped them to go on to win the Premiership with a record number of points in the 1999–2000 season. In truth, it is highly likely that Sir Alex Ferguson did not want to take his treble-winning side to what many pundits agreed was a worthless tournament. It is certain that he did not want to add more competitive games to an already congested fixture list. Despite the fact that Blatter himself had said that attendance at the tournament would have no bearing upon who would be the eventual hosts of World Cup 2006, England's 2006 campaigners believed that it would. Furthermore they knew that if Manchester United did not go, then the German team whom they had defeated in the 1999 Champions' League Final, Bayern Munich, would go in their place, enhancing Germany's own profile at a crucial phase in the 2006 bid.

Backed by the government – which at this stage still thought that the bid stood a chance and so was keen to stay on the bandwagon – England 2006 together with the FA persuaded United to go to Brazil in return for an agreement whereby they, the holders, were not required to play in that season's FA Cup. As it turned out, Manchester United performed poorly on the field and lost most of their games. They fared even worse off the pitch, avoiding the media whenever possible and generally snubbing the Brazilian public, thus losing any potential PR benefits that they might have gained for England 2006 by turning up in the first place.

Just when you think that things can't get much worse, Tony Banks resigned as Sports Minister and was appointed Special Envoy to the Bid, joining an already lacklustre team. England 2006 was fronted by Sir Bobby Charlton, Sir Geoff Hurst, and (occasionally) Gary Lineker, who were all rewarded handsomely for their globe-trotting efforts on England's behalf. They may be legends in England, but hardly household names in the rest of the world. Charlton, who received the most global exposure, may have been one of England's greatest ever players, but today he is legendary only for his almost total lack of charisma. Similarly, Hurst is no chat show host, and neither man has been able to make much impact on the lucrative media-pundit circuit. Lineker has achieved the latter, but outside of England, he is not recognised as one of the world's greatest sports diplomats. These grey front men were backed by a yes-ministerly civil service of ex-public school and Foreign Office flunkies led by Alec McGivan, who knew where they were at garden parties on embassy lawns, but were lost in the Machiavellian political corridors of world football.

Measured up against the 'Kaiser', Franz Beckenbauer, the suave, slick-suited, multi-lingual spokesman for the German bid, himself a World Cup winner as both player and manager, a front stage entourage that included recent superstars like Jürgen Klinnsman, plus German supermodel Claudia Schiffer, and a backroom staff that had powerful friends at the heart of UEFA, Banks and his team looked comprehensively out of their league.

In May 1999 the twenty-four members of the FIFA Executive were flown to London, put up in the best hotels in suites costing up to £1,000 a night. They were treated regally with a reception at 10 Downing Street, shopping at Harrods, tickets to top West End shows, and, of course, VIP tickets to the FA Cup Final at Wembley. When the technical team arrived to do the inspection, its members were compensated with more of the same including receptions at Prince Charles's home, Highgrove, and at Hampton Court Palace.

Despite such largesse, less than a month before the 2006 vote, the technical inspection team's report was published and England was ranked third behind Germany and South Africa. Sir Bobby Charlton declared the findings 'an insult'. Tony Banks called them 'ludicrous, laughable'. And for once we believe Banks was correct. It is widely accepted in football circles that the Premiership's network of modern stadia is among the best in the world and, with a redeveloped Wembley, in terms of playing facilities, media technologies, tourist capacity and related communications, England's case, in terms of existing infrastructure, could be seen as the strongest.

Germany's was a virtual bid, in as much as the country's existing football infrastructure was dated and in much need of significant upgrading which the German bid promised to do only if Germany was awarded the tournament. With the exception of Soweto's FNB Stadium (Soccer City) South Africa's bid was based almost entirely on apartheid-era rugby facilities, with huge problems associated with communications and accommodation yet to be resolved.

Banks and McGivan finally got the message and went on an aggressive offensive, accusing both UEFA and FIFA of conspiring against England. They were of course right, but refused to accept that the whole England 2006 strategy had encouraged such conspiring. Whatever the truth, insulting the voters moments before the election eradicated even the slenderest of chances that England would prevail.

The predictable 'hooligans abroad' Charleroi episode during Euro 2000 did, however, provide the England 2006 team with a convenient smoke screen under which to creep away, blaming unruly fans for the bid's failure. But, even before the first plastic chair was thrown, the England bid was long dead in the water. Even with the might of Foreign Office support, England 2006 was a lost cause. Lacking absentee frontman Gary Lineker – on a hefty retainer, but usually too media-busy to turn up for international duty – the bidding team of seconded Foreign Office veterans, promotional and political operators such as McGivan, faithful figureheads such as Sir Bobby Charlton, and *parvenu* dignitaries such as New Labour ennobled Sir Geoff Hurst, dashed around the world smiling at FIFAfolk, all to no avail. England's bid showed all the symptoms of an empire on the wane. Like Keegan's team at Euro 2000, it was all puff and bluster up front, clumsy and self-deluding at its core, aging and not up to it at the back.

Throughout, the tone of England's campaign won few friends. It was seen to be arrogant, imperious and negative. The blend of neo-imperial and New Labour arrogance in the bid irritated and sometimes infuriated key players in the power games of FIFA's executive, such as Chuck Blazer of the North and Central American Federation, CONCACAF. Champions League mastermind, Jürgen Lenz, of crack Swiss agency TEAM, considered the bid to be aggressive and alienating. There was widespread indifference and sometimes hostility towards the bid, particularly in the way that it dismissed South Africa's prospects and amplified a moral panic about crime and political instability in the former colony. Most outside of the rival bidding camps agreed that while South Africa would have to overcome a number of infrastructural and social problems, it was the most deserving. At a certain point, once it became obvious that England stood no chance, the England FA's bid should have been withdrawn, and it should have pledged economic and political support for South Africa's bid. This might have tipped the scales in South Africa's favour, and given England and perhaps even the UK the moral high ground from which to make an earnest and honest bid to host the event in 2010. Instead, the champagne flowed and the band played on as the English marched head on into the final humiliation in Zurich.

The world media like to deny or at least marginalise the skulduggery and *realpolitik* of the international power struggles around world sports and the most sought-after sport mega-events. Thus the world media, rather than probe the politics of international diplomacy and deal-making in the world economy, found it easier to point to individuals. In this the media come close to portraying the world of sport politics as a series of interpersonal battles. Thus one man, the 78-year-old New Zealander, Charles Dempsey, was vilified in the world press when Germany won the FIFA executive decision for 2006 by a single vote. Dempsey had voted for England, and not registered a vote for anyone in the next round after England's elimination. He had left to fly back to his Oceania base, claiming, in his own words, that he was confident that the FIFA committee's vote would secure the decision for South Africa. But South Africa was a vote short of gaining a 12–12 outcome in the vote, a tied outcome that would have to have been broken by the casting vote of the committee chair, President Blatter. Blatter fumed across the world media, that he would have cast this for South Africa. If Dempsey had recast his vote, Blatter would have been able to gift the tournament to the African confederation, thus paying off some of the debts that he'd accumulated on the way to his electoral victory in 1998. Dempsey became FIFA's, the world media's, and especially the South African's whipping boy and scapegoat in the media backlash after the German victory. Nobody talked about the two Middle East votes that were lost to the South African bid. It was easier to doorstep Dempsey and chase rentaquote politicians in New Zealand and Australia, than ask how other forces beyond the savvy of Kaiser Franz Beckenbauer and the glamour of model Claudia Schiffer could clear the path for a German triumph.

Wherever you were in the world for the few days after the 2006 decision, you could see the haunted and hunted face of Dempsey dominating news items in the print and broadcast media. 'A right Charlie!' bawled *The Sun*, screaming in its caption to a flustered looking Dempsey: 'This old git made a fool out of football' (Saturday, 8 July 2000, p. 68). Dempsey was hounded throughout the weekend. 'A donkey's vote – South Africans livid at Dempsey's faux pas', reported the Saturday edition of the *Newcastle Herald* in New South Wales. It was still the main sport story on the Monday: 'Fall on the sword – Dempsey told to avoid the sack by resigning' (10 July 2000, p. 62). Vivek Chaudhary in *The Guardian* (Sport, Saturday, 8 July 2000, p. 6) labelled Dempsey as 'the man who killed an African dream'. Dempsey was widely assumed to have reneged on an Oceania decision to back South Africa should the Federation's preferred candidate, England, be eliminated. Dempsey has denied such allegations, reiterating his claim that Oceania never passed any resolution of commitment to South Africa after the elimination of England. In September 2000 in Brisbane and Sydney, he was cocooned in the bosom of the FIFA family gathered to enjoy the Olympic football tournament. On one sunny Sunday morning, leaving the Novotel in Brisbane in his FIFA car, to fit in a spot of golf with his wife Annie, he bumped into Issa Hayatou, President of the African Federation. Befitting the FIFA rhetoric of family, loyalty and interdependence, the two men embraced. Hayatou, suave in light but immaculate lounge suit. Dempsey, in baggy khaki neo-imperialist shorts and casual shirt – 'Ah, Charley', spluttered the man whose continent was said to have lost World Cup 2006 at the hands of Dempsey, 'your Guinness, where's your Guinness'? As ever, FIFA knew that continuing to look after your own was the surest way of continuing to keep the skeletons securely locked in their own cupboard.

But there was another story. 'Deutschland AG' is the nickname for the whole of Germany conceived as one large company, with all Germans as shareholders. As the day of the vote was approaching several new business deals with Asian countries were announced, worth several billion marks. The Federal Security Council of Germany gave permission, on the 28 June just a few days before the 2006 vote, to deliver 1,200 bazookas to Saudi Arabia. Deals were put in place to aid troubled Korean car manufacturer Hyundai, family business of FIFA executive committee member Chung. A sponsor of the German FA, Bayer bought South Korean plastic manufacturers, Sewon Enterprises. Chemical giant, BASF announced investments worth 800 million marks in South Korea up to the year 2003. Bayer also announced huge investments in Thailand, home of FIFA executive member Worawi Makudi, known for his sideline in Daimler dealerships in the expanding Asian market: the polycarbonate production in the Map Ta Phut plant would be tripled on the basis of this investment. Not all of these connections could guarantee votes for Germany. But on the inside, it was known that key votes coming Germany's way did come from the delegates from Saudi Arabia and Qatar, if not Korea. Charley Dempsey whispered darkly, in a corner of FIFA's hotel in Brisbane, that there was much to tell on this story, but that FIFA politics were now more dangerous than ever, and it might be too risky to tell it. And Charley would still want the privileges of ambassadorial status or family retainer at FIFA events.

Conclusion

There remains much ferreting and investigative work still to be done to account for the outcome of recent World Cup bidding wars. But such work must recognise that this story is not one of individual personalities – in the 2006 case, Beckenbauer versus Charlton, Tony Banks versus Claudia Schiffer. Or even of the big players, like South Korean Chung in getting Korea so successfully into the picture for the 2002 bid. That's surface stuff. The votes of the twenty-four individuals on FIFA's executive committee are cast not according to any logic of rational organisational life, or in starstruck spontaneity, but within a framing context of a complex international politics and a persistently influential geo-political historical legacy. These international power struggles can be adequately understood only if the historical, the political and the sociological contexts are recognised as one and the same thing, in a post-colonial global network of business, politics and sport, and the struggles for power that are at the heart of world sport's governance (Sugden and Tomlinson, 1998a; Sugden, 2002; Sugden and Tomlinson, 2002). And, to end on a methodological note, such struggles must be scrutinised and studied on the basis of a sceptical fieldwork strategy and investigative method (Sugden and Tomlinson, 1999b), in which some of the conventional rules of social scientific method are cast aside in favour of a realistic recognition of how these international networks carry out their tasks.

Acknowledgements

As our solipsistic list of references shows, this chapter reworks a number of our earlier analyses. It also draws upon pieces commissioned by *When Saturday Comes*.

We have presented versions of the chapter at a workshop of the British Sociological Association Sociology of Sport Study Group at the University Of Ulster (February, 2001), and at the First World Congress of the Sociology of Sport in Seoul, Korea (July, 2001). We are grateful to the Chelsea School, University of Brighton, for support for the Ulster event; and to UK Sport's International Conference Committee for Supporting John Sugden's attendance at the Seoul/Korea conference.

Note

1 For the election of its presidents, FIFA operates a one country one vote secret ballot system in which the value of one of the organisation's longest established members – say, France – is worth no more or no less than that of one of its newest members – say, Palestine. On the surface this may look very democratic. In practice it is wide open to corruption as it encourages football's wannabe global tyrants to circumnavigate the globe, attempting to garner support by whatever means in some of the world's poorest countries. Havelange demonstrated this to devastating effect when he first took the FIFA presidency from Europe to South America when he crushed England's Stanley Rous in 1974 largely on the back of African votes.

References

Sugden, John (2002) 'Network football', in John Sugden and Alan Tomlinson (eds) *Power Games: Theory and Method for a Critical Sociology of Sport*, London: Routledge.

Sugden, John and Tomlinson, Alan (1998a) *FIFA and the Contest for World Football: Who Rules the Peoples' Game?*, Cambridge: Polity Press.

Sugden, John and Tomlinson, Alan (1998b) 'Fifa's World Cup wars', *New Statesman*, 1 May, pp. 38–39.

Sugden, John and Tomlinson, Alan (1999a) *Great Balls of Fire: How Big Money is Hijacking World Football*, Edinburgh: Mainstream Publishing.

Sugden, John and Tomlinson, Alan (1999b) 'Digging the dirt and staying clean: retrieving the investigative tradition for a critical sociology of sport', *International Review for the Sociology of Sport*, 34, 4: 385–397.

Sugden, John and Tomlinson, Alan (2002) 'Theory and method for a critical sociology of sport', in John Sugden and Alan Tomlinson (eds) *Power Games: A Critical Sociology of Sport*, London: Routledge.

Tomlinson, Alan (1999) 'Memorandum submitted by Professor Alan Tomlinson – appendix 44', *Staging International Sporting Events Volume III, Appendices to the Minutes of Evidence*, Fourth Report of House of Commons Culture, Media and Sport Committee, Session 1998–99, pp. 278–279.

Tomlinson, Alan (2001a) 'Memorandum submitted by Professor Alan Tomlinson', *Staging International Sporting Events Volume II, Minutes of Evidence and Appendices to the Minutes of Evidence*, Third Report of House of Commons Culture, Media and Sport Committee, Session 2000–1, pp. 58–59.

Tomlinson, Alan (2001b) 'Supplementary memorandum submitted by Professor Alan Tomlinson', *Staging International Sporting Events Volume II, Minutes of Evidence and Appendices to the Minutes of Evidence*, Third Report of House of Commons Culture, Media and Sport Committee, Session 2000–1, pp. 291–293.

Part II
Football in Korea and Japan

5 The development of football in Korea

Lee Jong-Young

Introduction

The Korean people are extremely proud of their long and unique history that extends for at least five thousand years. The historical record of Korea dates back to 2333 BC, and Koreans have a traditional calendar system called *dangi*, which counts the years starting from this period. According to the system, the year 2001 marks *dangi* 4334 (Lee, 1973). This calendar system is still used to deliberately express Korean nationalism in some instances.

Throughout their long history, the Korean people have been known to play ball games similar to the modern game of football. Historical records show that *ch'ukku* (Kim, 1988) which is similar to modern football, was imported from China and became a popular sport played by the nobility and soldiers during the Samguk or Shilla era (BC 57–AD 935). In *ch'ukku* players kicked a ball made of rice straw with one of the aims to keep the ball in the air (Lee, 1987). Some commentators have argued that Korea's emergence as a leading, if no longer number one, footballing nation among the Asian countries was attributable to this long history of playing *ch'ukku*.

The development of modern sport in Korea

In order to situate the development of football in Korea more clearly it is important to briefly outline the development of modern sport in Korea. The growth of modern sport in Korea paralleled the modernization, or more accurately westernization, process of Korea. As most modern sports originated in western countries, they were first introduced and developed in close relationship with the social, economic and political development of Korea. Arguably the most important event in the early modernization of Korea was the period of Japanese colonial rule in Korea during the period from 1910 to 1945. It is useful to organize our discussion of social developments in Korea using the temporal division of pre-, during, and post-Japanese rule.

Pre-Japanese colonization

In 1876, Chosŏn (Chosun; the last royal regime in Korea) opened the Pusan (Busan) harbour to western countries (Lee, 2000). Following the opening of the Pusan harbour, several other ports were made accessible and western culture was introduced in areas such as education, religion, economics, sports, and games. However, during this early stage of modernization, Korean people were very cautious and selective in accepting western culture since they felt that they were being forced to open their country under the threatening presence of the western powers at the time.

A pro-western, or pro-modern, campaign took place in 1884 (Kwak *et al.*, 1994), and the introduction of western culture, including modern sports, accelerated. The first successful introduction of western ideas and institutions was in education. Christian missionaries built schools in Korea and as these schools introduced western curricula, modern sports were also introduced. Gymnastics was first introduced in 1895, followed by track and field, association football, baseball, basketball, tennis, ice skating, swimming, and cycling (Korea Sports Council, 1990). The first sports clubs and associations appeared in Korea around this time. One of the more popular clubs belonged to the Seoul Young Men's Christian Association (YMCA). The YMCA sports club introduced different sports to Korea, and held sports meetings and competitions at various levels (Lee, 2000).

During Japanese rule

With the signing of an agreement between Korea and Japan in 1905, which effectively made Korea a protectorate of Japan, and the Treaty of Annexation in 1910, the Japanese were able to act as colonial rulers in Korea for most of the first half of the twentieth century. In fact, there were three phases of Japanese colonial rule. The first from 1910 to 1919 was a period of subjugation and repression, the second from 1920 to 1931 saw greater accommodation between the Japanese and Koreans, and the third, from 1931 until August 1945, was a period of heightened 'Japanization' and industrialization (Nahm, 1996, pp. 223ff.). During the first of these phases the Korean people's favourable attitude towards foreign cultures rapidly decreased with growing concern about losing their country's sovereignty, and nationalistic sentiment prevailed in Korea (Kwak *et al.*, 1994). Patriotic Koreans and their friends built a few secondary schools. In these nationalistic schools, students engaged in rigorous physical drills to develop fitness and a strong mentality (Lee, 2000). Sports were seen as a way of expressing Koreans' anti-Japanese feelings. Koreans used sports events to show Korean nationalistic sentiment and resistance to the Japanese, often by hanging out national flags not only on the sports field but in front of their houses as well. This is succinctly shown in a newspaper report about school sports days in 1910 (from a Hangsung newspaper, possibly *Maeil Shinbo* (*The Daily News*, 17 March 1910, p. 2): 'Each household held out the national flag to celebrate the sports day of the Jesuit Middle School in Pyongyang the other day. Today, every house again held out the national flag to celebrate the sports day of Daesung School.'

After the Japanese took over the Korean educational system there were radical changes in the curricula at all school levels. The terms of school years for elementary and secondary schools were shortened and subjects that promoted national identity, ethics, nationalism and the like were eliminated from the curriculum (Lee, 2000). The rigorous drills exercised in some schools to promote nationalistic patriotism were replaced with modern gymnastics and sports. In this way, modern sports were practised and spread throughout the nation.

The poor condition of Korean society at the time did not allow the majority of the population to participate in sports in their own time. Therefore, student participation in modern sports and physical education was central to the development of modern sports in Korea. Players for competitive sports were produced almost exclusively through the educational system, and this trend continued until very recently, when recreational sport participation finally caught up with the progress of physical education (Ministry of Culture and Tourism, 1998).

Student athletes were treated well since they were regarded as valuable assets of their school. This superiority allowed the student athletes to take liberties with school regulations, and delinquent behaviour like drinking, smoking, and violence were often tolerated or ignored (Kwak *et al.*, 1994). Student athletes were allowed to meet lower academic requirements or sometimes exempted from schoolwork totally. Those behavioural trends of student athletes which originated in this period have continued until recent times in Korean society.

After the start of a nationwide anti-Japanese resistance movement on 1 March 1919, the Japanese authorities reduced the level of control in supervising and surveilling the Korean people. This change in policy facilitated a nationalistic movement in sports activities. Korean nationalists were able to use various sports events and competitions as a means of bringing people together in order to heighten their national cohesion and confirm their patriotism (Lee, 2000). At the games, Korean people cheered especially when their players were competing against Japanese players, dearly wanting victory over Japanese teams and athletes. Defeating Japanese sports teams was analogous to defeating the ruling oppressive Japanese government. These nationalistic sentiments were rooted very deep during this era and have remained to this day, so that when Korean sports players or teams compete against Japanese ones, the only outcome of the game that any Korean can think of is victory over Japan.

Post-Japanese rule

Korea faced most drastic social and political changes after liberation from Japan in 1945. Korea was divided into two in 1948 with a democratic republican government in the south and a communist government in the north, and the conflict between the two Koreas resulted in the Korean War in

1950. During this transitional period, sports did not receive much attention from the people.

After the Korean War, the Ministry of Education in South Korea introduced a new curriculum into schools at all levels. Physical education at the elementary level focused on the notion of play, while that at the secondary level emphasized sports (Kwak, 1990). Korean society as a whole still perceived sports from the militaristic point of view. Sport was viewed primarily as competition, and in competition, winning was of the utmost value. This view of sport sometimes resulted in heated competition between the teams concerned, and teams were often observed to play games as if they were on a battlefield.

In 1961 a military regime came into power in the south which promoted and supported sports. To prepare for the 1964 Tokyo Olympic Games, the military government took measures that became the cornerstone for the future development of sports in South Korea. These included the establishment of National Sport Promotion Laws, National Sports Week, National Sports Day, a National Fund for Promoting Sport, Sports Training Centres, and a Sports Science Institute (Korea Sports Council, 1965, 1972, 1982). There is no doubt that this series of sport initiatives has contributed to the establishment of South Korea as one of the sporting superpowers. The first Olympic gold medal in Korean sport history was won in 1976, and twelve years later in 1988, Korea hosted the Summer Games and ranked fourth in terms of the number of medals won. Since 1988, Korea has remained among the top ten medal-winning participants at the Summer Olympic Games.

Professional sport, however, only began in 1982 with the foundation of professional baseball teams. Now there are professional teams in basketball, football, wrestling, *ssirŭm* (the traditional Korean style of wrestling), boxing, bowling, and golf (Ministry of Sports, 1983, 1986). With increased leisure time and awareness of health and fitness, approximately 35 per cent of Koreans participate regularly in sports and physical activities (Ministry of Culture and Tourism, 1998).

The early development of football in Korea

The development of football in Korea closely mirrors that of modern sport. Football was introduced before the Japanese rule and practised as a school subject. During Japanese rule, football games became another way to express nationalistic sentiments and resistance against Japan. Under modern Korean governments, football became a symbol of the national power of the industrialized Republic of Korea.

Football in the pre-Japanese colonization period

Official records state that the modern game of association football was first formally played in Korea in 1905 when a Frenchman named Martel, then a teacher at a foreign language school, taught the game to the secondary school students (Korea Sports Council, 1990). However, other stories and many unofficial records date the introduction of football much earlier. Presently it is widely accepted that it was in the year 1882, towards the end of the Chosŏn dynasty, that football was first introduced into Korea (Association for Development of Korean Soccer, 1990). The British ship, HMS *Flying Fish* approached the port at Incheon and applied for permission to enter. While waiting for permission, the sailors played football near the pier, being watched by curious Koreans. The ship left without entering the Korean port, leaving a football behind. Korean spectators took the ball and imitated the game. This is the first recorded incident of a football in Korea (Lee *et al.*, 1998). One month later, another British ship was admitted to the port, and also the capital city, Hansŏng, (or Hanyang, now more commonly referred to as Seoul, which means 'capital' in Korean). The sailors played a game of football in the recreation ground of the Military Training Centre, and the game attracted a large number of spectators. When the sailors left, they gave the balls to the spectators, who again played the game in imitation (Association for Development of Korean Soccer, 1990).

Numerous other records testify to the popularity of the game among Koreans. Court translators who travelled to foreign countries enjoyed the game and formed the Korea Football Club in 1896. A football team was formed in Paejae Secondary School in 1902 (Paejae Secondary School, 1965) – the first Mission School in Korea, originally founded by Henry Appenzeller in Seoul in 1885. In 1903, a football team was formed by the Seoul YMCA, and played the game in red and white shirts. Football rapidly gained a following during the period from 1905 to 1910. One account shows that Korea Football Club beat Seoul YMCA football team in all their matches during this period (Kwak *et al.*, 1994). In addition, seminaries established by foreign missionaries and schools held sports days, and students, parents, and all the village people often participated in the events. The most popular sports were track and field and football.

There were no consistent football rules at this time. There were no goal-posts, and stones or pieces of wood would mark the goals. There was no regulation of the height of the goal posts, and in order to be recognized as a goal, the ball had to pass over the goalkeeper's head. There were no lines marking the boundary, and of course, there was no pitch size regulation. Players had traditional hairdos, and wore shoes made of straw. There was no limit to the number of the players, as long as both teams had equal numbers of players. No real technical skills were developed, not even passing or trapping the ball. The most advanced technique in the game at this stage was to kick the ball high (Paejae Secondary School, 1965).

Football during the period of Japanese colonization

As with other sports during this dark period, anecdotes about football revolve around the conflict between the oppressed and the oppressor. A couple of anecdotes will suffice to show the conflicts. Paejae Secondary School formed a football team in 1902, but it was not until 1914 that goalposts were erected in their playing field. The founder of the school, Henry Appenzeller, discussed the matter with national movement leaders Lee Sang-Jae and Yoon Chi-Ho, and painted the goalposts white to remind the students of the 'white-clothed people', which was a nickname Koreans preferred to be called, and which helped promote national pride. The Japanese police understood the meaning of the colour white, and threatened to ban the game entirely, and so it was decided that the goal posts would be re-painted black (Paejae Secondary School, 1965). There were many occasions when Koreans competed with Japanese teams. According to Kim Jong-Ryol, who later became president of the Korea Sports Association, when he was a player, his team had to play against the Japanese, who seemed unbeatable in skills and technique. Just before the game, the Korean coach brought the players together and said, 'You are not just playing football. You are fighting for the independence of the Korean people' (Korea Sports Council, 1965, p. 167). Upon hearing this, the players could not be defeated and won the game against all the odds. There are many similar stories told about Korean sporting victories against the Japanese.

There were also occasions when Korean players were treated unfairly by the ruling Japanese government. One such incident concerned the selection of national team members to represent Japan in the 1936 Berlin Olympic Games. During this period, Korea was not recognized as an independent country and therefore Koreans had to enter the Olympics as a part of the Japanese team. Hansŏng football team (referred to as 'All Seoul' or *Keijô* by the Japanese) won both the All-Japan Football Competition, which was normally the Olympic team selection contest, and another major football tournament. It was expected that the Olympic team would therefore be formed mostly by members of the Hansŏng football team, but in the event only two players from the Hansŏng team were included (Lee *et al.*, 1998). Korean players appealed but with no success. Such incidents in sport aggravated hostile feelings towards the Japanese even further, while sports events also provided opportunities for these feelings to be expressed.

Two further points are worth noting in relation to the development of football in Korea during this period. In 1912, Hyun Yang-Woon brought home from Shanghai a football rulebook published by the English FA and translated it (Association for Development of Korean Soccer, 1990). This rulebook was to have a major impact on shaping the popular football game into a more organized sport. However, the dissemination of the rules governing the game did not seem so successful judging from what happened in the years immediately after. In 1920, Chŏsun Sport Association was established, and the first official football game by Koreans was held the next year. However, the game was dogged with disputes concerning the rules. Such disputes about the football rules persisted until 1933 when the Chŏsun Football Association was formed and started to regulate official matches.

A second important event that occurred during the period was the establishment of the Seoul–Pyongyang football rivalry. The two cities are now capitals of the two Koreas. Even during the Japanese annexation, the two cities had a great number of football fans and citizens who enjoyed the game (Association for Development of Korean Soccer, 1990). The *Chŏsun Daily* newspaper hosted an annual football match between the two cities until the division of Korea. The match helped make the game of football a nationally popular sport for Koreans. This is one reason why Koreans express their wish to revive the match whenever there are inter-Korea talks involving sports relations.

Football after Japanese colonization

Soon after liberation from Japan, the Chŏsun Football Association, that had been forced to dissolve in 1942, was re-formed again and renamed the Korea Football Association or KFA (Korea Sports Council, 1965), as it has remained to the present. The Association held the first All-Korean Football Games in October 1945. In June 1947, it joined FIFA and first appeared in the international arena at the 14th Olympic Games held in London in 1948. In 1954, the Korean football team progressed through the World Cup qualifying tournaments and played in the finals held in Switzerland. The Korean team encountered sophisticated skills and techniques of world-ranking teams for the first time here.

Although most European fans of football over the age of 40 will best recall the North Korean team that travelled to England in 1966, the South Korean football team was also successful in Asia. South Korea won the first two Asian Cup competitions held in 1956 and 1960. Other victories followed in the Asian region, winning the Merdeca Cup, King's Cup, Asian Games, and Asian Youth Football Games (Association for Development of Korean Soccer, 1990). The South Korean team secured its place in the region and was known for its unbeatable fighting spirit and mobility. It came to be admired and dreaded by other Asian teams, who referred to it by the nickname of the 'Asian Tiger'.

In 1971, South Korea staged President Park's Asian Cup Football Competition, which invited world-class teams. The tournament provided opportunities for Korean teams to gain experience of playing matches with the most competitive teams in the world, and also for Korean people to watch the most sophisticated football skills and techniques. The competition was renamed the Korea Cup in 1995 (Lee, 2000), and remains one of the most important annual international football competitions held in Asia.

The year 1983 marked another important date for Korean football. It was the year that saw the start of the 'Super League', a professional football league. It was the first professional football league in Asian countries. It offered Korean fans the joy of spectatorship, offered opportunities for young football players, and stimulated the commercialization of sport in Korea. The league started with five teams and has since expanded to ten. It was renamed the K-League in 1996. Although it kicked off almost a decade before, it is possible to see differences as well as close similarities with the organization of the Japanese J.League. Participating teams were required to select a new name that stressed the regional affiliation of the team rather than the main sponsor. Another duty was the payment of a large lump sum into the so-called 'K-League Football Promotion Fund'. The K-League consists of cup games and league games. In 2001, the Adidas-sponsored Cup tournament started in March, the usual beginning of the annual Cup round. The ten K-League teams are divided into two groups. All teams of the A- and B-group face each other twice on a home and away basis. The winner and the runner-up of each group participate in a final round at the beginning of May, and the final is played out among the winning teams in two games (home and away) at the end of the month. The K-League proper usually starts at the end of the Cup competition, although in 2001 the Confederation Cup led to a delay until mid-June.

For League games, clubs are paired with each other three times, home, away and at a third site. For example, since the restructuring of the K-League in 1996, Seoul has lost all of its previous three teams. Currently, no K-League club is based in the capital, thus the newly constructed World Cup Stadium in Seoul will not be used as home ground in the near future. However, as well as the Tondaemon Stadium in Seoul, it can be used for the 'third' match. Until 2001, the leading four at the end of the season proceeded to a play-off round; this system has now been abandoned. Another innovation was the end of the 'V-goal' (golden goal) in extra time to decide a winner, as games have been limited to ninety minutes, with a win, loss or draw as final result. When the K-League is decided, the Korean Football Association Cup starts. Besides the ten K-League clubs, the elite of amateur football, company and university teams, participate. Games of the KFA Cup are played out in elimination style and usually take place from mid-November to the end of December.

When it started in the early 1980s, the Super League attracted considerable attention. However, as baseball remains effectively the national sport, and basketball began to lure away the young generation from football, spectatorship decreased. By 1997, there was an average attendance of only 6,700 spectators per game. It was only after the 1998 World Cup that interest began to rise again. Average attendances rose to 15,000, and while there were over 2 million spectators to all K-League games in 1998, the aggregate number reached 2.8 million in 1999 (Lee, 2000).

Since 1945, Korean football teams have represented Asia and participated in the Olympic Games six times: in 1948, 1964, 1988, 1992, 1996 and 2000 (Association for Development of Korean Soccer, 1990; Korea Football Association, 2001). Since 1988, there have been four successive appearances in the Games. The South Korean team has also appeared five times in the World Cup finals: in Switzerland in 1954, Mexico in 1986, Italy in 1990, America in 1994, and France in 1998. South Korea has become the most frequently participating team among Asian countries.

The K-League and soccer in Korea

The K-League is at the centre of professional football in Korea. The K-League represents the highest level of football skill and culture in Korean football. All promising Korean football players want to participate in the K-League, and do their best to be selected. There has been a steady growth in the number of spectators. Almost all the mass media cover stories from the K-League: major TV networks, cable television networks, satellite TV, Internet TV, radio, newspapers, and magazines, including the ones specializing in football as well as in general sports. The Korean national TV stations KBS1 and KBS2, and private stations, MBC and SBS, broadcast football games regularly and report the highlights and results in the news. The sports TV channel, SPORTS, and football channel, SBS-soccer, cover the League's activities in detail. Newspapers, magazines, and radio report personal and game records and discuss upcoming games. The K-League is also planning to sponsor a lottery (similar to the newly launched '*Toto*' in Japan) which will distribute prize money according to the punters' ability to predict the final scores of matches.

When the K-League first started in 1983 there were five teams in the league. Soon after, the Hanil Bank team joined and there were thus three professional teams (Daewoo, Yukong, and Pohang Steel/POSCO) and three amateur teams (Kookmin Bank, Hanil Bank, and Hallelujah, founded by evangelical Christians). In 1987, the amateur teams were excluded from the League and Hyundai and LG joined the other three professional teams. In 1989, Ilhwa joined the League and these six teams played until 1993 (Kwak *et al.,* 1994). Four more teams have joined since: Cheonbun (Jeonbuk) in 1994, Cheonnam (Jeonnam) in 1996, Suwon in 1996, and Taejon Citizens in 1997. Now the League has ten teams and 400 registered players. Since 1995, the teams have changed their names to reflect both their regional and sponsor affiliations (K-League, 2001). We shall briefly outline the history of each of them.

Pusan I.cons

Pusan I.cons was founded in 1979 as an amateur team, and went professional in 1983. Pusan (Busan) is the second largest city in South Korea, with a population of 4 million. As a port located at the south end of the peninsula, it is a centre of international trade. Pusan will host some of the World Cup Games and the Asia Cup in autumn 2002, in the newly built Busan Stadium. Daewoo sponsors the local team. As Pusan Daewoo, the team won the 1984 Super League, the 1987 Professional League, the first Asian Football Cup, the Asian Club Championship, and the 1991 Professional League. In 1991, Pusan recorded twenty-one consecutive game victories. In 1997 the team won three competitions in the same season, an achievement never before accomplished in Korean professional football history. Although Pusan is a traditional baseball stronghold, football has become very popular recently. This is the place where the biggest audiences, amounting to up to 20,000 per game, usually are to be expected. One reason for this success is the local star player Ahn Jong-Whan who is revered by his female supporters like a film star or pop idol. Thanks to his talents, he is the first Korean to play in the Italian professional football league. In 2001, Ahn started to play for the Italian Serie A club Perugia where Japan's star player Nakata Hidetoshi also began his career abroad in the 1998–99 season. In July 2001, defender Sim Jae-Won, another member of the national team, was taken under contract by the German team Eintracht Frankfurt.

Taejeon Citizens

Without the World Cup, this club most likely would not have come into existence. Taejeon (Deajeon), a city of 1.35 million inhabitants, is traditionally football's nowhere land. Taejeon Citizens were founded in 1997, after the plans for the Daejeon World Cup Stadium were publicly announced. In the first season, average turnout at the games was still very low, only about 2,000. Only after the local hero Kim Un-Jung scored twice in decisive games in the Asian Youth Championship in 1998 against Japan, did enthusiastic support became the trademark of Taejeon Citizens and the number of spectators tripled in the next season. The team was rewarded for its fair play in 1997 and 1998. Youthful ambition, mobility and teamwork characterize the team. As the latest addition to the K-League, the team is trying hard to advance into the upper ranks. Team sponsors include Kyeryong Construction, Donga Construction, Hanwha Logistics, and Hana Bank, but the financial situation is particularly difficult for this young team without a main sponsor. The team's keeper, Choi Eun-Sung, is one of the national side's substitute keepers.

Bucheon SK (Puch'on)

Formerly founded as Ukong in 1982, Bucheon Sun-Kyoung has the longest history in professional football. Bucheon is located between Seoul and Incheon, and has a population of 0.8 million. Since Seoul and Incheon have no football team, the team has no difficulty securing supporters from the metropolitan cities. In fact, as Bucheon has no appropriate facilities to offer, Bucheon SK's home stadium presently is in Seoul. But there are rumours that Bucheon SK will find a new home ground in the new Incheon Munhak Stadium of nearby Incheon, where the team might move after summer 2002. The sponsor, Sun-Kyoung, is ranked fifth in gross sales volume in Korea. In 1984, the team won the first season of the Super League. The team is famous for aggressive play and achieved second place in the K-League and won the Korea Fire Insurance Cup in 1999.

Seongnam Ilhwa Chunma

Seongnam is a middle-class suburb in the south of Seoul. Seongnam Ilhwa was founded in 1989 in Seoul, moved to Cheonan in 1996 and finally settled in Seongnam in 2000. The team has a remarkable record of achievement during its ten-year history. It won the 1992 Adidas Cup, and won three consecutive K-League titles in 1993, 1994 and 1995. Victories were added in the Asian Club Cup, Afro-Asian Club Cup, and the Asian Super Cup. The Moonies own this team.

Suwon Samsung Blue Wings

Suwon is located in southwest Seoul with a population of 1 million and is the home of a brand-new World Cup stadium. The Suwon Samsung Blue Wings were founded in 1996. Nonetheless, the team won the 1998 K-League (sponsored by Hyundai), the 1999 K-League (referred to as the 'Buy Korea Cup') and the 2000 Ticketlink Super Cup and Adidas Cup. These remarkable achievements were made possible by Samsung's generous financial support, the introduction of a 4–4–2 formation and the largest supporters club, 'Grand Blue'. In 2001 the Blue Wings also won both the Asian Club Championship (beating Jubilo Iwata of the J.League in the final) and the Asian Super Cup. The general manager of the team is the former manager of the national team, Kim Ho; players Cho Sung-Hwan and Choi Sung-Yong are well-known names on the roster of the national team.

Anyang LG Cheetahs

Anyang is a satellite city of Seoul. Anyang Lucky Goldstar Cheetahs were founded in 1983, and as with most other teams, their name refers to the place as well as to the main sponsor, the company Lucky Goldstar, or LG. The team has its own training field and weight training facility. The team has won the K-League three times in 1985, 1990 and 2000, and has ranked in second place three times in 1986, 1989, 1993. It has also won the KFA Cup twice in 1988 and 1998 and ranked second place in the Adidas Cup three times. Forward Choi Yong-Soo, who is currently playing in Japan with JEF United Ichihara and is a regular member of the South Korean national team, came originally from the Anyang LG Cheetahs.

Ulsan Hyundai Horang-I Tigers

Ulsan is an industrial city in the South West of Korea facing the Pacific Rim. The coastal city is home to several Hyundai companies, which are the main sponsors of the Tigers. Thanks to the location of Hyundai Industries, the new World Cup venue Munsu Football Field was timely opened as the first of ten new World Cup stadia in April 2001. Ulsan Hyundai Tigers was founded in 1983 and ranked second place in the same year. In 1986 it won the K-League and has ranked highly since professional football began in Korea. Ulsan Hyundai allegedly paid their goalkeeper, Kim, the highest annual salary ever paid to an athlete in Korea in 1999: 220 million won. The national team player and defender Yoo Sang-Chul is the most famous export of the team. After having played for Yokohama Marinos in 2000, he is currently playing for the J.League club Kashiwa Reysol.

Cheonbuk Hyundai Motors

Cheonbuk Hyundai Motors was founded in 1994 with support from the citizens of Cheonbuk Province. The team was recognized with the Fair Play award in 1996 and with the Year's Best Attack award in 1997. It won the KFA Cup in 2000. The president of Hyundai Motors is the owner of the team.

Cheonnam Dragons

Cheonnam Dragons were founded in 1994 with the support of forty-eight shareholder groups and joined the K-League in 1995. Korea's second football stadium had already been opened in this East Korean city in 1992. In 1997, the largest number of spectators ever in the history of professional football gathered at Kwangyang stadium, the home of the Dragons. Kwangyang is also home to the POSCO Steel Refinery and the engineers eagerly support the team. The KFA Cup Winner of 1997, the Dragons handed Kashima Antlers of the J.League a devastating 4:1 defeat inside the Tokyo National Stadium in the Asian Cup Winners Cup.

Pohang Steelers

Pohang Steelers was founded in 1973 as an amateur team (Pohang Atoms). In 1995, the team became an independent corporation and has led the development of football in Korea since. In 1990, it built the first stadium exclusively for a football team in South Korea. The team achieved 200 victories in total, including three K-League championships. The Steelers have produced over forty Korean national team players. In 1994, 1 million spectators came to see the team's games and 2 million in total attended in 1999. Pohang is located near to Ulsan in the South West and is home to POSCO, the main sponsor. A famous son of the team is Hwang Sun-Hong who left Korea in 1997 for the J.League team Shonan Hiratsuka (now Bellmare) and is currently one of three Koreans playing for the Japanese Kashiwa Reysol; his team-mate Hong Myung-Bo is originally from the Steelers. While his exit left the Pohang Steelers in a formidable crisis, it recently found its new stars in the K-League newcomers Lee Jung-Woon and Lee Dong-Gook, who finished high school in 1998 and played in 2000 for Germany's Werder Bremen.

Korean star players and coaches, supporters and the national team

Arguably the best and, certainly the most famous, football player Korea has ever produced is Cha Bum-Keun. He has made an outstanding contribution to Korean football, and a great impression on Koreans. Cha was born in 1953, and educated at Kyoung-shin High and Korea University, two prestigious schools for football in Korea. In 1972, at the age of 19, he joined the national team and remained there until 1978. From 1979 to 1988, he played in the German Bundesliga, except for a brief leave of absence in 1986 to play in the Mexico World Cup finals for the South Korean team. He was in the top eleven foreign players selected by reporters at the 1986 World Cup finals, and altogether scored 100 goals during the ten-year period (Lee *et al.*, 1998). These brilliant achievements have not yet been matched by any other Korean player. After retiring as a player, he became manager of Ulsan Hyundai Tigers from 1991 to 1994. He was at the helm of the Korean team that went to the 1998 World Cup, but failed to get beyond the qualifying rounds. He is currently running football classes for children.

Today there are promising young Koreans playing in Europe and overseas. For example, 22-year-old national team striker Seol Ki-Hyun played at Royal Antwerp and now at Anderlecht, midfielder Ahn Jung-Whan in Serie A with Perugia, and Lee Dong-Kook in Germany with Werder Bremen. Kang Chul and Choi Sung-Yong played for the Austrian side LASK Linz, Hong Myong-Bo, Whang Sun-Hong and Park Ji-Sung are all playing in the Japanese J. League. Ko Jong-Soo in the K-League, and Lee Chun-Soo with the Korea University team are likely to be included in the national team in the 2002 World Cup finals. Two interesting faces on the current South Korean roster are Ryang Kyu-Sa, the first North Korean player to play in the K-League, who has joined Ulsan Hyundai from Tokyo Verdy in the J.League, and Park Kan-Jo, a third-generation Korean born in Japan who was nominated for South Korea for the first time in a friendly against Yugoslavia in May 2000.

Coach Park Chong-Whan, the long-time head coach for the national youth team, is by far the most respected coach produced by Korea. He was born in 1938, and graduated from Chunchon High and Kyounghee University, also famous for their football teams. He was selected as the right back for the national team at the 1964 Tokyo Olympic Games, but a leg injury forced him to retire. As a PE teacher and football coach for high school teams, he showed excellent leadership and led his teams to victory in many games. One of his most impressive and remembered achievements was that of leading the national youth team to the semi-finals of the fourth World Youth Football Competition held in Mexico in 1983. The Korean youth team went to the finals to represent the Asian region. The records at the time show a 1–1 tie with China, and two wins over the United Arab Emirates (4–0) and Iraq (2–1). In the first round of the finals, Korea was beaten 0–2 by Scotland, but beat Mexico 2–1, and Australia 2–1, to go into the quarter-finals. Korea defeated Uruguay 2–1, but was finally defeated by Brazil 1–2. Korean fans were excited by the games, and were proud of the young hopefuls. Korean team members wore red uniforms in all these games, and the fierce fight by the Korean youngsters earned them the nickname the 'Red Devils' by the media (Association for the Development of Korean Soccer, 1990). The name has been kept as the name for the national team supporters, and to many of the supporters, who were too young to watch the games, the victories remain a legend.

Park moved to the Ilhwa club when it was founded in 1989, and made another record by leading the young team to three consecutive championship victories. He was appointed as head coach of the national team, but his dominating leadership style was not received well by some of the older players in the team. In response to the 2–6 defeat by Iran in the Asian Cup semi-final game in 1996, he resigned. From 1997 to 1998, Cha Bum-Keun took charge of the national team. After an unsuccessful World Cup tournament in 1998, Huh Jeong-Moo took the helm. Recently Guus Hiddink, the former manager of the Dutch team that had defeated Korea 5–0 in the 1998 France World Cup finals, has taken over. Hiddink is the first foreign head coach to lead the full national team in the century-old history of Korean football.

The Red Devils, who paint the stadium with red whenever the Korean national team plays, do not call themselves fans or supporters: they call themselves, 'the player No. 12' (Red Devils, 2001). They deny being just fans. They demand to be recognized as a part of the team. They want to boost the team spirit and morale with systematic cheering. The Red Devils never sit quietly during the games. They are busy moving themselves, just like the players they are cheering for.

The Red Devils is not a well-organized or structured group. It is a voluntary fan club with a group homepage and access to the Internet. Those spectators who come in red and fill in the application form can become a member on the spot. The volunteer managers of the Red Devils can estimate the number of the members only by the number of those who appear at stadia. The Red Devils made a debut in the football arena on 10 August 1997 for the occasion of a goodwill game with the Brazilian team. The members showed up in red and with placards. Other spectators were surprised to see the well-organized cheering, and joined them eventually. They have a repertoire of cheering. When the games are held outside Korea, they follow the team abroad.

When the Korean team played Japan in a qualification match for the 1998 World Cup finals, many enthusiastic Red Devils members crossed the Korean Channel to join 5,000 Japanese-Koreans in cheering for the Korean team. Several hundred Red Devils members who could not join the others in Japan cheered for the team in front of a large multi-vision television screen in a street in Seoul. The popularity of the Red Devils is evidenced in the dramatic increase in the number of applicants. Unofficially, it is estimated that there are a thousand active members, and tens of thousands of less active members. Some of the more active members made President Kim Dae-Jung an honorary member, and presented him with a red uniform featuring the inscription of '12th' (Red Devils, 2001). The Red Devil managers and members are keenly aware of the hooliganism in some countries, and try to exert discretion in using verbal and non-verbal expressions and actions. It is also interesting to note that the group rejects any financial or administrative support from football teams or government offices.

At the time of writing (November 2001) the Korean national football squad for the 2002 World Cup is not yet finalized. In many ways the team has still not recovered its best form since the 1998 World Cup. The Korean Football Association has been testing various players through training and in competitive matches with other national teams in the build-up to the finals. Hiddink was appointed following poor results in the Sydney Olympic Games and the Asian Cup, where South Korea came third, but Japan won the trophy. Hiddink's contract extends to 2002, and the Korean national football team will compete in the 2002 World Cup under his leadership. Recently the Korea Football Association's Technical Committee has named a squad of twenty-four players for the national team training camp (Korea Football Association, 2001). Hiddink is assisted by three assistant coaches for offensive and defensive training – Pim Verbeek, Park Hang-Seo, and Jung Hae-Sung – and also a goalkeeper coach – Kim Hyun-Tae.

Conclusion

The FIFA World Cup finals is arguably the world's biggest sports occasion. The 17th World Cup in 2002 will be the first global sports festival of the twenty-first century. It is promising for the future of soccer culture in Korea, Japan, China and other member countries of the Asian Football Confederation (AFC) that the event is to be held in Asia for the first time. We have shown that sport, and especially soccer, has had a special meaning for Koreans ever since it was introduced at the end of the nineteenth century. During the Japanese occupation it was used as a means of resistance. At other times it was a tool of reunification. At other times still it has served as a symbol of national pride. Because of this, co-hosting the World Cup has greater significance for Korea than just staging another sporting event. In addition to its economic and political significance it may influence both inter-Korea relationships and Korea's international relations.

References

Association for Development of Korean Soccer (1990) *The 100 Years History of Korean Soccer*, Seoul: Rasara Publishing Co.
Hangsŏng newspaper (1910) 'Celebrate the sports day of Daesung School', 17 March, p. 2.

Kim Bu-Sik (1988) *Samguk Sagi*, trans. Lee Min-Soo, Seoul: Eulyu Publishing Co.

K-League (2001) 'Introduction to K-League teams and players', online at <http://www.k-leaguei.com/players/index.jsp>. (Accessed 20 September 2001.)

Korea Football Association (2001) 'List of Korea national football team players', online <http://www1.kfa.or.kr/eng/football/national/players/0,1652,S192,00.html>. (Accessed 24 September 2001.)

Korea Sports Council (1965) 'The history of Korea Sports Council', unpublished report of Korea Sports Council.

Korea Sports Council (1972) 'The blue book of sports,' unpublished report of Korea Sports Council.

Korea Sports Council (1982) 'The white book of sports,' unpublished report of Korea Sports Council.

Korea Sports Council (1990) 'The 70 years history of Korea Sports Council,' unpublished report of Korea Sports Council.

Kwak Hyŏng-Ki (1990) 'The procedure of the development of modern physical education and its historical meaning,' unpublished doctoral dissertation, Graduate School of Seoul National University.

Kwak Hyŏng-Ki *et al.* (1994) *The History of Korean Sports*, Seoul: Knowledge Publishing Co.

Lee Byoung-Do (1973) *The History of Korea*, Seoul: Eulyu Publishing Co.

Lee Hak-Rae (2000) 'The 100 years history of Korean sports,' unpublished report of Korean Association for Health, Physical Education, Recreation and Dance.

Lee Jin-Soo (1987) *A Study on Wharang Thought on Physical Activities in Shilla Era*, Seoul: Bokyoung Publishing Co.

Lee Min-Pyo *et al.* (1998) *Soccer: Knowing Well and Playing Well*, Seoul: Tae-Keun Publishing Co.

Ministry of Culture and Tourism (1998) 'The five-year plan for the national sports promotion,' unpublished report of the Korean Ministry of Culture and Tourism.

Ministry of Sports (1983) 'Sports Korea,' unpublished report of the Korean Ministry of Sports.

Ministry of Sports (1986) 'The long-term plan for national sports promotion,' unpublished report of the Korean Ministry of Sports.

Nahm, Andrew (1996) *Korea: Tradition and Transformation*, New Jersey/Seoul: Hollym International.

Paejae Secondary School (1965) 'The 80 years history of Paejae Secondary School', unpublished report of Paejae Secondary School.

Red Devils (2001) 'Introducing the Red Devils', online at <http://www.reddevil.or.kr/>. (Accessed 24 September 2001.)

6 The development of football in Japan

John Horne with Derek Bleakley

Introduction

At the first football match held in Japan after the Great Kantō earthquake in September 1923 a brief memorial service was held in honour of William Haig. A large silver 'cup was displayed, and behind it, in a shrine of flowers, was a large photograph of Haig, which the officials and the members of the two teams saluted before the match' (Roscoe, 1932–33, p. 67). Haig had been a vice-consul at the British consulate in Yokohama. He had helped to establish the All-Japan Inter-Middle School Association Football Tournament and then encouraged the British Ambassador to request a gift from the English Football Association (FA) of a trophy that could be presented to the equivalent organisation in Japan. It was subsequently reported (*The Times*, 3 January 1919) that Lord Kinnaird and Lord Lonsdale of the FA had responded positively to the request. The Foreign Secretary, Lord Balfour, was of the opinion that the 'encouragement of the sport' through the provision of a trophy would 'contribute to the cordiality of unofficial Anglo-Japanese relations' (*The Times*, 23 January 1919). In fact, the Japanese had no equivalent to the FA. Hence it was Kanō Jigorō, the Japanese representative on the International Olympic Committee (IOC), president of the Japan Amateur Sport Association (JASA), founder of the modern martial art of judo, and principal of the Higher Teacher Training Institute in Tokyo (currently Tsukuba University), who initially took possession of the solid silver trophy on 28 March 1919. Only in September 1921 (when the Football Association of Japan, to give it its first official English translation, or the Japanese FA, was finally established) did the trophy find its intended home. The JFA had sixty-five member clubs when it was inaugurated. Later that year the British Ambassador, Elliot, presented the trophy to the captain of Tokyo Football Team, the first winners of the All-Japan Football Tournament, or Japanese FA Cup. The All-Japan Tournament marked the start of competitive domestic football for adults in Japan. It is one of history's ironies that Haig's death during the 1923 earthquake robbed him of the chance to see his plans for football in Japan develop any further.

The history of the development of all sports is full of such stories. Featuring people, places, dates and ironies these accounts, which naturally derive from real events, nonetheless can be criticised for sustaining individualistic origin myths. Of course, without individuals, their enthusiasms, passions and actions, things would not get done. As we will note later in this chapter, the growth of football in Japan since the 1980s certainly owes a lot to the work of men such as Naganuma Ken, Okano Shun-ichiro, Kawabuchi Saburō and Murata Tadao. But the development of sports, like all historical events, involves wider social influences and processes. In particular, and in keeping with the overall theme of this collection, we will examine the way in which the development of football in Japan is a product of different social, economic and political interests which dominate society at specific moments. This chapter looks at these wider interests and influences as a way of making sense of the actions of the individual people involved. It aims to provide a contextual framework within which to better understand the position of football in Japan over the past 100 years and especially at the beginning of the twenty-first century. A companion chapter deals with international dimensions of Japanese football.

Football in Japan: before the Pacific War

As is obvious from the previous comments, football has not just developed in Japan since the birth of the Japanese Professional Football League (or J.League) in the early 1990s. According to the official history of the Japan Football Association (JFA, 1996) organised association football is recorded to have been first played by Japanese nationals nearly 140 years ago in September 1873. Accompanied by thirty-three subordinates, Lieutenant Commander Archibald L. Douglas of the Imperial British Royal Navy had been sent to Japan to teach the essential elements of naval warfare and strategy. In their free time the group played and taught football to their students at what was to become a naval academy in the Tsukiji district of Tokyo. Another British teacher is also recorded as teaching the game at the School of Engineering in Tokyo in the following year. After the Meiji restoration of 1868 there was little resistance to absorbing western culture, and in the case of football, the sport may have been regarded by some of the Japanese elite as a western variant of the ancient game of *kemari*. *Kemari*, or kickball, had originated in China and been adopted by the Japanese nobility in the sixth and seventh centuries. While involving the use of the foot to kick a ball, *kemari* was not, however, played as a competitive game, but rather as a co-operative effort to keep the ball in the air.

Progress in absorbing the modern game of football was slow. The transition from traditional Japanese garb to western dress was a gradual one and there were other priorities during modernisation. The game was, however, played regularly by members of the foreign communities that had settled in Japan, especially around the ports. Kobe Regatta and Athletic Club (KRAC) and Yokohama Country and Athletic Club (YCAC) are thought to have staged the first of many 'inter-port' football matches in 1888. A Scottish chemist – Alexander Sim – formed KRAC in 1870, in the third year after the opening up of the city as a port to foreigners.

In 1886 the Japanese Ministry of Education created a number of selective 'higher middle schools' to serve as preparatory institutions for entry into the Imperial universities. Many of the head-teachers of these institutions – renamed 'higher schools' in 1894 – inspired by the example of the English public schools (Eton, Harrow, Rugby, etc.) believed that games should be a central part of the educational experience of their students. Football was not central to this extra-curricular sporting diet, while it formed a part of primary school physical education lessons (*taisō*) from the 1870s (see Guttmann and Thompson, 2001, p. 92). It was not until 1896 that football was formally introduced at the Tokyo Higher Teacher Training Institute. From 1900 students at Tokyo Imperial University and a few other institutes of higher education also began to play it. Graduates began to teach football all over Japan in middle and higher schools. In 1911 the Japanese Amateur Sports Association (JASA) was established as an umbrella organisation for all sports in Japan, and the Football Association of Japan (JFA) affiliated to it in 1925.

During the 1920s physical education teachers were advised that *a-shiki shūkyū* (the pre-World War Two literal translation of 'association football'), also known as *sokkā* (English pronunication) or *sakkā* (American pronunciation), was too rough for young children. One manual, *Jidō supōtsu* (Children's Sports) warned that the game should be restricted to those over the age of 15 as it could harm children's health (Ishikawa, 1928, p. 166). In this way the sport remained confined to older middle and high school pupils and students. The schools football championship, established with William Haig's assistance, was originally called the All-Japan Inter-Middle School Soccer Tournament, and then renamed the All-Japan Middle School Tournament between 1925 and 1947. It continues to this day and remains the longest-running football competition in Japan. In the first year, students from three cities – Toyonaka (near Osaka), Nagoya and Tokyo – emerged to contest the trophy. The city of Kobe also became renowned as a dynamic football region during this period – two of its schools winning the tournament sixteen times between 1918 and 1940.

By the mid-1930s, as university teams began to dominate domestic football, political developments were exerting a strong influence on sport in general. In 1935 a new tournament, the All-Japan All-Comers Tournament, was introduced, and a new trophy, the Football Association of Japan Cup, was presented to the winners. The trophy sent from London in 1919 was now destined for the winners of a less important tournament. The new tournament, as the title suggested, could include teams from annexed countries in 'Greater Japan', including Korea. In 1935 Hansŏng (present-day Seoul), but known as 'All-Keijō' by the Japanese, became the first Korean football team to take part in the tournament and proceeded to win it. All-Keijō's victory prompted a heated debate in Japan about the inclusion of Korean players in the Japanese football team for the 1936 Berlin Olympic Games. Japan had qualified without having to play a game and hence became the first Asian team to take part in the Olympic football championships. The Japanese squad entered for the Olympic championship included two Korean players. On 4 August the team, including one of the Koreans, sensationally defeated Sweden 3–2 after trailing 0–2 at half time. The Japanese media hailed it as 'the miracle of Berlin'.

Football in Japan: after the Pacific War

After the war football was re-introduced into the school curriculum during the US occupation, while other traditional Japanese sports and physical activities – perceived as too martial in spirit – remained proscribed. An All-Japan football tournament was organised from 1946 but conditions in the country were such that it was not until 1950 that it was run on a nationwide basis. The attendance of the Emperor at the All-Star game at the Meiji Jingu Stadium in April 1947, the first football match he had attended since the final of the All-Japan Tournament in 1929, was followed by the presentation to the JFA by the Imperial Household Agency of a cup, which from 1951 onwards was presented to the winners of the All-Japan Tournament, or Emperor's Cup.

For nearly the next forty years football in Japan remained essentially amateur. As Japanese companies came to act as the main source of support for organised sport in this period it might better be described as 'corporate-amateur'. After a decade of isolation from the football world, links had to be re-established and the development of the game at the grassroots attended to. Initially in the 1950s the Emperor's Cup was dominated by university teams, but towards the end of the decade football had began to take root in company sports teams. In 1954, Tōkyō Kōgyō and, in both 1956 and 1958, Yawata Steel, became the first two company teams to reach the final of the Emperor's Cup. In 1960 Furukawa Electric became the first company team to actually lift the trophy.

In June 1965 the 'Japan Soccer League' (JSL), featuring company teams, was launched. The original intention was a national championship involving both university and company teams. Because of a conflict between the proposed spring to autumn football season and the summer to winter Japanese academic year, leading university teams declined to take part. The JSL was therefore composed entirely of company teams, regarded by their owners as either a welfare facility or a publicity tool (see Table 6.1). The clubs had neither the status nor the independence to make decisions in their own long-term interests. Nonetheless, in the second half of the 1960s the JSL, in combination with university teams such as Waseda, helped to produce some valuable players for Japan, such as Sugiyama Ryūichi of Mitsubishi and Kamamoto Kunishige of Yanmar.

Table 6.1 The Japan Soccer League (JSL) Champions, 1965–92

Year	Champion	J.League Team Equivalent
1965	Toyo Industrial	Sanfrecce Hiroshima
1966	Toyo Industrial	Sanfrecce Hiroshima
1967	Toyo Industrial	Sanfrecce Hiroshima
1968	Toyo Industrial	Sanfrecce Hiroshima
1969	Mitsubishi Heavy Industries	Urawa Reds
1970	Toyo Industrial	Sanfrecce Hiroshima
1971	Yanmar Diesel	Cerezo Osaka
1972	Hitachi	Kashiwa Reysol
1973	Mitsubishi Heavy Industries	Urawa Reds
1974	Yanmar Diesel	Cerezo Osaka
1975	Yanmar Diesel	Cerezo Osaka
1976	Furukawa Electric	JEF Ichihara
1977	Fujita Industrial	Shonan Bellmare (formerly Bellmare Hiratsuka)
1978	Mitsubishi Heavy Industries	Urawa Reds
1979	Fujita Industrial	Shonan Bellmare
1980	Yanmar Diesel	Cerezo Osaka
1981	Fujita Industrial	Shonan Bellmare
1982	Mitsubishi Heavy Industries	Urawa Reds
1983	Yomiuri Club	Verdy Tokyo (formerly Verdy Kawasaki)
1984	Yomiuri Club	Verdy Tokyo
1985–86	Furukawa Electric	JEF Ichihara
1986–87	Yomiuri Club	Verdy Tokyo
1987–88	Yamaha	Jubilo Iwata
1988–89	Nissan	Yokohama F. Marinos
1989–90	Nissan	Yokohama F. Marinos
1990–91	Yomiuri Club	Verdy Tokyo
1991–92	Yomiuri Club	Verdy Tokyo

Sources: *Japan Football Association Guide Book* (2000); *Rising Sun News*, online
<http://www.wldcup.com/Asia/jfl/history.html>.

Despite early successes – the league drew an average of 7,491 fans per game in 1968, the year Japan won bronze at the Mexico Olympics – the interest of the Japanese media in the JSL and the sport of football in general was lukewarm. By 1973 the league was struggling and drew an average of 2,897 spectators per game. In fact, overall during its twenty-seven seasons, the JSL attracted only 9,739,110 spectators, an average of 3,972 per match (*The Japan Times*, 6 November 2001; JFA, 1996, pp. 236 and 244). It was the mid-1980s before more noteworthy developments in Japanese football occurred. In 1985 the Asian Football Confederation (AFC) reinstated the Asian Club Competition that had started in 1967 but had then been abandoned between 1972 and 1984. Japanese attitudes to this initiative had been cautious, as problems had been encountered reconciling the demands placed on Japanese clubs by the Asian competitions with their domestic commitments and essentially amateur status. In 1986 Furukawa Electric (later to be renamed JEF Ichihara in the J.League) made history by becoming the first Japanese club to win the Asian Club Championship. Also significant for domestic football was 26 October 1985. This is a key date in the history of Japanese football despite the fact that it marked yet another defeat at the hands of Korea in a World Cup qualifying match. This time the first leg was played before a capacity crowd at the National Stadium in Tokyo. Despite having failed to qualify for the World Cup finals to be played in Mexico, spurred on by a sense of popular interest in the sport, a committee of the JFA was established to consider the development, for the first time, of professional football in Japan. The JFA recognised that it had to adopt an increasingly professional approach to the game. From 1986 it had allowed a few selected players to sign 'special licences', or in effect become professional football players. From the 1987 season all clubs in the JSL were given the freedom to establish professional contracts and fifty-seven players signed. An indication that club football in Japan had begun to improve in the second half of the 1980s was when three sides played in the finals of the Asian Club Championship. Two of them emerged as winners: Furukawa (as already noted) in 1986 and Yomiuri (to be renamed Verdy Kawasaki) in 1987 (the third was Nissan, later renamed as Yokohama F. Marinos). It was the decision in 1989 by the full JFA committee, which by this time included Naganuma Ken, Murata Tadao, Okano Shun-ichirō and Kawabuchi Saburō, to establish a Japan Professional Football League, or 'J.League', which laid the basis for a regular, fully professional, club competition. To ensure a more durable foundation for the sport, the J.League was to be one of three football-related projects launched simultaneously. Alongside the establishment of a professional league, the aim was to strengthen the national team and to secure the rights to host the 2002 World Cup finals. The announcement of the intention to launch a professional football league was given a warm welcome in the media, and economic conditions could not have been more favourable. Had the decision been delayed a year or two, when Japan's bubble economy had burst and the beginnings of the 'Heisei Recession' were visible, it is possible that the J.League project would not have gone ahead.

The rise of the Japan Professional Football League (J.League)

Although for most of the outside world the J.League started in May 1993 amidst much publicity (and a capital injection estimated at £20 billion by some observers), the tenth anniversary of the Japan Professional Football League, the J.League's governing body, was actually celebrated at a Tokyo hotel on 1 November 2001. As a trial for the real thing the following year the J.League staged the Nabisco Cup tournament from September to November 1992 for the ten J.League founder members, including the former Mitsubishi Motors, Furukawa Electric and Toyota Jidosha. Reborn as Urawa Red Diamonds, JEF United Ichihara and Nagoya Grampus Eight, respectively, each with an official slogan, mascot, and team song, these three teams, along with seven others, were expected to attract between 15,000 and 30,000 fans twice a week from May 1993 onwards. Tables 6.2 and 6.3 show how the composition of the J.League, since 1999 divided into two Divisions, and the Japan Football League (JFL), formed out of the JSL, evolved from the formal kick-off date in May 1993 to the start of the ninth J.League season in March 2001.

In 1993 the J.League chairman, Kawabuchi revealed that the original plan was to begin the J.League with just six teams, as in his estimation there were only about 100 players in Japan capable of playing at the professional level at the end of the 1980s, when the idea for its development was laid down. This plan also took into account the allowance of three professionals from abroad for each team (as in Japanese Major League baseball). Seven conditions were imposed on clubs applying to join. The first was that the club had to be a registered corporation specialising in football, a stipulation designed to force the management of each club, as well as players and coaches, to be professional. Teams were also requested not to have the names of their owner as the team name. J.League football, unlike the JSL and professional baseball, would not be used simply as an advertising tool. J.League teams were to have a balanced ownership, representing 'home towns' (or cities) and regional prefectures as well as sponsors. Nor at the outset was any team allowed to be based in central Tokyo. Verdy had made their home in Kawasaki, and their application to relocate to Tokyo after success in the first J.League season – stimulated no doubt by the ambitions of the key sponsor, the giant media company Yomiuri, to emulate the success of their professional baseball team (Yomiuri Giants) to become 'Japan's team' – was turned down by J.League officials. The J.League was seen as a major tool of urban redevelopment and relocation away from the capital and hence a second condition was the cultivation of a 'home town' environment, and each club was expected to forge strong links with its local community. The third condition was to secure the regular use of a 15,000-capacity stadium equipped with floodlights. The fourth condition imposed was that each club should operate a reserve team and teams at the U-18, U-15 and U-12 levels. The fifth condition imposed was that each club should include professional contracts with at least eighteen players, and that coaches employed at all levels should hold the appropriate licence. The other two conditions were disciplinary in nature: a US$1 million membership fee was required from each club, as was agreement to comply with the rulings of the J.League and the JFA.

The J.League method of distributing media revenues from broadcasting rights equally to all J.League teams irrespective of performance also challenged the prevailing practice in professional baseball that permitted the Giants to amass a dominant financial position. Despite the conditions governing team location, most of the J.League teams that have prospered since 1993 have been located in the large population centres stretching out from Chiba Prefecture in the east to Hiroshima in the west. In 2001 two J1 (First Division) teams – the renamed Tokyo Verdy and FC Tokyo – shared a stadium in Tobitakyū in western Tokyo. The downplaying of the role of club

Table 6.2 J-League Division teams 1993–2001

Club	Home town and prefecture	Main sponsors	Slogan
[From 1993 – the original 10 J.League teams]			
Verdy§	(1993) Kawasaki, (2001) Tokyo	(1993) Yomiuri, (2001) NTV	com a bola no pe
(F.) Marinos*§	Yokohama, Kanagawa	Nissan	sail on to victory
AS Flugels*	(1993) Yokohama	(1993) ANA, Satō Kōgyō	take to the skies
Antlers§	Kashima, Ibaraki	Sumitomo Kinzoku, Kashima	dashing beauty
JEF United§	Ichihara, Chiba	JR East, Furukawa Denkō	the mighty front
Red Diamonds§	Urawa, Saitama	Mitsubishi	red in Urawa
Sanfrecce§	Hiroshima, Hiroshima	Mazda, Hiroshima	pour the heat on
Gamba§	Osaka, Osaka	Matsushita Electric (Panasonic)	the swift attack
S-Pulse§	Shimizu, Shizuoka	(1993) TV Shizuoka, (2001) JAL	pulsing with excitement
Grampus Eight§	Nagoya, Aichi	Toyota, Tōkai Bank	here we go
[From 1994]			
Bellmare	Hiratsuka, Kanagawa	(1994) Fujita, (2001)	winning waves
Jubilo§	Iwata, Shizuoka	Yamaha	fleet elite
[From 1995]			
Reysol§	Kashiwa, Chiba	Hitachi	heat it up
Cerezo§	Nagai, Osaka	Yanmar Diesel, Capcom, Nippon Ham	los lobos victoriosos
[From 1996]			
Purple Sanga	Kyoto, Kyoto	Kyocera	[no information]
Avispa§	Fukuoka, Fukuoka	Fukuoka, Sanyō Shinpan	[no information]
[From 1997]			
Vissel§	Kōbe, Hyōgo	Itō Ham	time is now
[From 1998]			
Consadole§	Sapporo, Hokkaidō	Toshiba	[no information]

Table 6.2 Cont.

Club	Home town and prefecture	Main sponsors	Slogan
[In 2000] Frontale	Kawasaki, Kanagawa	Fujitsu	in the front
[From 2000] FC Tōkyō§	Tōkyō, Tōkyō	Tokyo Gas	sexy Football-beauutiful our new beginning 2001

SOURCES: *Japan Football Association Guide Book* (2000); *Rising Sun News*, online <http://www.wldcup.com/Asia/jfl/history.html>.

Notes

* Clubs merged in 1998 after the withdrawal of Flugels' main sponsors led to the change of Marinos' name from 1999.
§ Members of J.League (J1) in 2001.

Table 6.3 J.League Division Two (J2) teams in 2001

Club	Home town and prefecture	History
Albirex Niigata	Niigata, Niigata	Regional champions in 1997; joined J2 in 1998
Kyoto Purple Sanga	Kyōto, Kyōto	Kyoto UV Tech before 1994; joined J.League in 1996; relegated in 2000
Kawasaki Frontale	Kawasaki, Kanagawa	Formerly Fujitsu Kawasaki; joined J2 in 1998; J1 in 1999; relegated 2000
Montedio Yamagata	Yamagata, Yamagata	NEC Yamagata before 1996; joined J2 in 1998
Omiya Ardija	Ōmiya, Saitama	NTT Kanto before 1998; joined J2 in 1998
Oita Trinita	Oita, Oita	Regional champions in 1995; joined J2 in 1998
Sagan Tosu	Tōsu, Saga	PJM Futures, then Tosu Futures before1997; joined J2 in 1998
Vegalta Sendai	Sendai, Miyagi	As Brummel Sendai regional champions in 1994; joined J2 in 1998
Ventforet Kofu	Kōfu, Yamanashi	As Kofu Soccer Club joined JFL in 1994; joined J2 in 1998
Mito Hollyhock	Mito, Ibaraki	As Prima Ham Tsuchiura joined JFL in 1997; joined J2 in 2000
Shonan Bellmare	Hiratsuka, Kanagawa	As Bellmare Hiratsuka joined J.League in 1994; relegated to J2 in 1999
Yokohama	Yokohama, Kanagawa	Formed after Yokohama Flugels folded; promoted from JFL in 2000

Sources: *Japan Football Association Guide Book* (2000); *Rising Sun News*, online <http://www.wldcup.com/Asia/jfl/history.html>.

sponsors in favour of the hometown's name is still marked compared with Japanese baseball, although the rule has been tested to the limit from time to time by some of the clubs.

As Yomiuri and Nissan respectively, Verdy Kawasaki and Yokohama Marinos were the cream of the old JSL. The two teams played the opening game of the J.League on 15 May 1993 in front of a capacity crowd of 59,626 spectators at the National Stadium in Tokyo. Hence it was not so surprising to see that they accomplished championship successes in the first three seasons. Verdy Kawasaki won the first and second Suntory championships in 1993 and 1994. The following year – during which two commentators on Japanese football announced after the first stage that 'the standard looks higher this season, and the J.League's playing field is now about as level as it can get' (*World Soccer*, July 1995, p. 43) – Yokohama Marinos won the first stage and, although Verdy won the second stage for the third time, it was the Yokohama-based team that became overall J.League champions in 1995. Subsequently Kashima Antlers – sponsored by both the town's local authority and local employer Sumitomo Metal – and Jubilo Iwata – based on the old Yamaha side – became pre-eminent, winning alternating J.League championships in 1996, 1997, 1998 and 1999. In 2000 it was Kashima's turn again, only this time they accomplished the 'grand slam' by winning the domestic treble of J.League, Nabisco (League) Cup and (JFA) Emperor's Cup.

From the outset it was planned to expand the J.League gradually over ten years and eventually to allow relegation and promotion between the J.League and the semi-professional/amateur JFL. Teams in the JFL that wished to be considered for J.League status not only had to finish in the top two positions of the JFL but also had to pass basic stadium requirements, and other criteria, such as potential level of spectator interest and local community support. One example of this rule in operation was when Honda of Hamamatsu won the JFL championship in 1996 but because of the lack of a suitable stadium did not join the J.League. There was some suggestion that additional pressure by motor company rivals Nissan (Marinos), Toyota (Grampus Eight) and Yamaha (Jubilo) might also have proved conclusive in the decision, although other considerations were the preparedness of Honda to sponsor a football team as well as the Honda team's location close to other existing teams in the same prefecture.

In the first three seasons of the J.League all clubs played each other four times on a home and away basis, in two stages. Hence in 1995 the Suntory-sponsored first stage ran from mid-March to mid-July and the second Nicos-sponsored stage from mid-August to mid-November. Teams received three points for a win of any kind. Unlike British, and most other European leagues, if scores were level after full-time, a period of 30 minutes 'golden goal' extra time was played. If the game was still tied, results were resolved on the basis of a penalty kick shoot-out. Teams losing a penalty shoot-out received one point during the 1995 season. With the gradual expansion of numbers of teams in the J.League and hence the number of competitive games per season increasing, the J.League was reorganised for the 1996 season. The two-stage system was abandoned in favour of a single format with two (home and away) meetings. The break in the summer enabled the national team to compete in the Atlanta Olympics while the Nabisco (League) Cup competition took place.

The total number of competitive league matches was reduced to thirty home and away games; the two-stage format was re-introduced after just one season in 1997 and has remained since. Formally, this means that should the same team win both stages, there would be no need for any additional championship decider matches to be played. In practice, since the beginning of the J.League this has never happened. It does lead to some unusual conclusions to the season. In 1999, for example, Shimizu S-Pulse, managed by former Tottenham Hotspur player Steve Perryman, secured sixty-five points on aggregate (including winning one stage) yet were beaten on penalties in the final championship decider by local rivals Jubilo, who had finished sixth overall with forty-nine points after a very poor second stage performance. In 2000 the best team on points aggregate was Kashiwa Reysol (fifty-eight points) but without a single stage victory the team had to watch as Kashima eventually took the championship for the third time against Marinos, managed by another former Tottenham Hotspur player, Ossie Ardiles.

At the end of 1998 two divisions (J1 and J2) were created out of the then existing J.League and semi-professional teams in the JFL. Those clubs left out of these divisions comprised a 'new JFL' – a *de facto* 'Third Division'. Unlike J1, where the number of teams was fixed at sixteen for the next four seasons (and this has now been extended until 2005), the number of teams in J2 and JFL depend on the number of teams promoted and relegated or withdrawing from the leagues above and below them. In the case of the JFL, these are the regional leagues played on a prefectural basis. JFL sides are required to have associate J.League membership and meet most of the J.League criteria mentioned earlier. Hence teams in the JFL in 2000 that retain a clear corporate identity similar to Japanese baseball teams – such as Honda Motors, Sony Sendai, and JATCO – would have to alter their names if they aspired to compete in J2.

Another change introduced into the J.League from 1999 was the dropping of the penalty shoot-out as a way of deciding tied matches. For the first time since its creation, the J.League permitted drawn games. Again, as a commitment to consistency, the J.League announced that a new points system would apply for at least three seasons. From 1999 therefore three points have been awarded for a win in the ordinary 90 minutes of play, two points awarded for a win in extra time through the scoring of a 'golden' or 'victory' (or 'V-) goal' (i.e. the first goal scored in the 30 minutes extra-time period), and one point awarded to each team for a draw after 120 minutes play.

After an initial boom in the first three years, average crowd sizes in the J.League began to decline. In the 1997 season average attendances dropped close to 10,000. The J.League has started to develop its 'star' teams – Kashima Antlers and Jubilo Iwata – as well as its disappointments and underachievers – Verdy, Marinos, and Grampus Eight. Devoted fans consistently turn out to see some of the less successful ones – Urawa, Consadole, and S-Pulse. Yet none of the teams have yet got such audience-'pulling' power as the Yomiuri Giants baseball team. There are even rather predictable jokes about the worst of them:

> Two J.League fans spend the whole day fishing out in the middle of Lake Otsu. Toshi turns to Nobi and says, 'I hear Kyoto Purple Sanga lost today'. 'How do you know that?' Nobi asks. 'Well, it's a quarter to five, isn't it?'
> (*Sports World Japan*, August 1998, 47, p. 45)

With qualification for the FIFA World Cup (France'98) by the national team and the prospect of co-hosting the 2002 World Cup with South Korea, it was clearly possible that football would be back in fashion if the changes brought in after the 1998 season created an exciting spectacle. Although revenues from spectators and the media broadcasting rights have declined (see Horne and Manzenreiter, this volume), some teams have weathered the economic storm. Others have been faced with economic problems. The most extreme example was Yokohama Flugels which was closed down at the end of the 1998 season (although their last competitive game was the winning of the Emperor's Cup in January 1999) and merged with the other Yokohama team Marinos. If in parts he features crude stereotypes of Japanese football fans, English journalist Jonathan Birchall (2000) paints a sympathetic account of the campaign organised by Flugels supporters against this imposed decision. The rise of the 'new Flugels', Yokohama FC, financed by the large international sports marketing agency founded by Mark McCormack, International Management Group (IMG), Citibank and the German tool company Bosch, is one of the most interesting developments to result from the first closure of a J.League team.

Between 1993 and the start of the 2001 J.League season 29,649,817 spectators have attended 2,106 matches with an average of 14,079 per match. Since its formation in 1999 over 2,100,000 people have watched J2 Division matches, with an average of 5,420 per match (*Nihon Puro Sakkā Riigu*, 2001, pp. 372–373). In the first stage of the 2001 season average attendances for J1 matches reached 16,702. In the second stage the record attendance for a single J.League match was smashed as 60,533 spectators crowded into the new Saitama Stadium 2002 to watch Urawa Reds play Yokohama F. Marinos. Clearly interest in football in Japan has picked up as 2002 approached. The concluding section will consider the key factors that have been influencing this upward movement in football attendances and the general growth of a stronger football culture in Japan. While the success of the national team in the run-up to 2002 and the higher profile given to Japanese football players playing outside of Japan in the Japanese and world sports media have both played a part, we will discuss these aspects of Japanese football in the world outside Japan in more detail on pages 121–129.

Aspects of contemporary Japanese football culture

In 1991 football ranked 22nd in terms of sports participation by the total population, but, significantly, was second in popularity to baseball amongst 15–19 year olds (*Asahi Shinbun*, 1992, pp. 65–66). Football enjoyed greater involvement and more popularity than baseball in high schools at the end of the 1980s and beginning of the 1990s. A survey conducted in December 1992 found 31.4 per cent of respondents wanting to attend a J.League game at a stadium, compared with 33.5 per cent for baseball. Football had most appeal for children and young adults. The seeds of Japanese interest in it had clearly become greater in the 1980s and early 1990s. The corporate sponsorship and staging of international football competitions such as the World Football

Club Championship (Toyota Cup) from 1981, the FIFA World Youth Championships, and the winning of the Asian Cup in 1992 had encouraged them. In addition the J.League had been packaged and sold as a new, trendy, leisure pursuit. It was marketed as *shinhatsubai*, as a 'new, improved product, now on sale', which is a well-known marketing principle to Japanese consumers (Watts, 1998). Central to this was the role of Hakuhōdō, Japan's second biggest advertising company, who portrayed football as international, casual, fast and lively, in contrast to the more slowly paced and traditional game of baseball. As a commercial sport it was deliberately targeted at a younger audience than that for baseball in Japan.

One of the medium-term football aims of the launch of the J.League was to broaden the pool of Japanese football players and thus assist in the creation of a stronger national side. In the 1960s and 1970s there was a handful of good players, but a large supporting cast was lacking. In the 1980s, however, more Japanese boys and girls began to play football than baseball at school and in university. Rather than send players abroad it was hoped that, by attracting leading players from Europe and South America to Japan, Japanese players could learn from their example. In the event, Ramon Diaz, Guido Buchwald, Leonardo, Jorginho, Salvatore Schillaci, Sampaio, Zinho, Alexander Torres, Patrick Mboma, Hugo Maradona, Carlos Caetano Bledorn Verri (Dunga), Hristo Stoichkov and Dragan Stojkovic have all played in Japan since 1993.

One of the most recent ways that football has begun to be more firmly integrated into Japanese popular culture is the recent launch of a football lottery, *Toto*. After trials in Shizuoka prefecture in 2000, the soccer lottery *Toto* was introduced nationwide in March 2001. Following a lengthy debate about the potential social consequences, a *Toto* system was introduced that was based on similar football-related gambling schemes in other countries. The Ministry of Education (Monbu Kagakushō) manages the *Toto* through an affiliated organisation, the National Stadium and School Health Center of Japan. A single bet costs 100 yen and participants can win up to 100 million yen for correctly predicting the outcome – win, draw or lose – of the thirteen J1 and J2 matches played on a weekend. Some 50 per cent of the total revenue is allocated to prize money, and by June 2001 seven people had already won the 100 million yen prize. After prize money and marketing costs (not meant to be greater than 15 per cent of revenue) are deducted, the earnings from *Toto* are divided into three – for sports associations, local public corporations and central government. The local public corporations are also expected to use the money to promote sport in general.

By its twelfth week *Toto* sales had reached 3.87 billion yen and it was clearly a big success. In June 2001, however, it was revealed that the Japanese World Cup Organising Committee (JAWOC) had asked for 3 billion yen from the proceeds of the first year. There was an outcry from other sports organisations including the Japanese Olympic Committee (JOC), especially since the slogan of the new lottery, 'for all sports of Japan', adorns virtually all of its publicity. The government-affiliated organisation responsible for *Toto* estimated that revenue would reach 80 billion yen and profits would be 16.5 billion yen in the first year. Thus 5.5 billion yen would therefore be equally divided among the three recipients. JAWOC wanted to have 3 billion yen of the 5.5 billion yen share allocated to sports organisations, such as JOC, claiming that it had already included the amount in the 60.7 billion yen estimated for the cost of running the 2002 World Cup. How the controversy was to be resolved would not become evident until later in the year. While concerns about the impact of this new gambling culture on young people have been raised, '*Toto* culture' is playing a part in cementing the activities of J.League teams into Japanese popular culture, and thus balancing the internationalism of the 'world game' with local concerns.

Conclusion

Football and other sports in Japan have always been manipulated by different interest groups to accommodate new demands and initiate new ways of thinking. For much of the post-1945 period, sport, except for professional baseball and made-for-television shows like professional wrestling, was organised and facilitated on an amateur basis or by companies. Football, at this time, thus became a part of popular culture through corporate sponsorship. Since the early 1990s, however, football in Japan has been actively marketed as something to be consumed differently from other sports, especially baseball. Baseball was conceived of as inward-looking, traditional and local whereas football has been portrayed as outward looking, (post-)modern, and global. Essentially because financial success is crucial for any new sport that tries to break into an established popular culture, football in Japan has deliberately utilised different marketing strategies and targeted different clients (or a different spectator base) than the main professional sport of baseball.

In addition to these economic marketing strategies football has been assisted in Japan by one more ideological influence. Japan's biggest contribution to world football culture so far is probably *Tsubasa Ōzora*, better known as 'Captain Tsubasa' (or 'Oliver Atom' in France). Originally filling thirty-six volumes of *manga* (comic books), stories featuring this character were a best seller throughout the 1980s, not only in Japan. Translated into Arabic, Italian, Spanish, Thai, Malaysian, Korean, Chinese, French and many other languages, the cartoon and the subsequently produced animation series seized the imagination of entire generations of young football players all over the world. A second series began in 1993 where the hero eventually left Japan for the Nou Camp in order to play for Barcelona. Baseball is not the only sport that can claim a field of dreams.

An emphasis on place of residence, increasingly replacing an emphasis on the place of work, or the company, which predominated after 1945, has also been a feature of the new professional football league. Finally, an emphasis on consumption, especially through the marketing of 'new improved products', in contrast to an emphasis on production, which had existed for most of the post-1945 period, has been a key feature of the football culture developed in Japan since the launch of the J.League. Football in Japan is itself at the centre of a contradictory pull between the enthusiastic amateurs keen to generate football as a popular cultural 'practice' and those with an interest in the exploitation of the commercial opportunities that football as 'spectacle' provides.

In Japan the specialised football stadium and football spectating experience are both relatively novel social environments. Hence instructions were issued at the outset of the J.League as to how to behave: 'Be the twelfth player in the stadium'. Yet the experience was also a familiar one with such features as competition showdowns, via 'penalty shoot-outs' and championship play-offs. As with all sports, football offers Janus-faced possibilities to different social groups in Japan. As one Japanese informant told a British journalist: 'In Japan, when you start talking about football, before you know it, you're talking about society, the education system and the political economy' (Birchall, 2000, p. 111).

References

Asahi Shinbun (1992) *Japan Almanac, 1993*, Tokyo: Asahi Shinbun Publishing.
Birchall, Jonathan (2000) *Ultra Nippon: How Japan Reinvented Football*, London: Headline Book Publishing.
Guttmann, Allen and Thompson, Lee (2001) *Japanese Sports: A History*, Honolulu: University of Hawaii Press.
Ishikawa Torakichi (1928) *Jidō supōtsu* [Children's Sports], Tokyo: Kōbunsha/Bungei Shunjū Sha.
JFA /Japan Football Association (1996) *Nihon Sakkā Kyōkai 75 nen shi. Arigatō, soshite mirai e* [The 75-year history of the Japan Football Association], Tokyo: Bēsubōru Magajin Sha.
Nihon Puro Sakkā Riigu (2001) *J.League Yearbook 2001*, Tokyo: Toransuāto.
Rising Sun News <http://www.wldcup.com/Asia/jfl/history.html>. (Accessed.)
Roscoe, N.K. (1932–33) 'The development of sport in Japan', *Japan Society of London, Transactions and Proceedings*, 30: 53–71.
Sports World Japan, August 1998, 47, p. 45.
Watts, Jonathan (1998) 'Soccer *shinhatsubai*. What are the Japanese consumers making of the J.League?', in D.P. Martinez (ed.) *The Worlds of Japanese Popular Culture: Gender, Shifting Boundaries and Global Cultures*, Cambridge: Cambridge University Press, pp. 181–201.

Further reading

For more detailed references to the sources informing this chapter see the following.
Horne, John (1996) '"Sakka" in Japan', *Media, Culture and Society*, 18, 4: 527–547.
Horne, John (1999) 'Soccer in Japan: is *wa* all you need?', *Culture, Sport, Society*, 2, 3: 212–229.

Horne, John (2001) 'Professional soccer in Japan', in Joy Hendry and Massimo Raveri (eds) *Japan at Play*, London: Routledge, pp. 204–218.

Nogawa Haruo and Maeda Hiroko (1999) 'The Japanese dream: soccer culture towards the new millennium', in Gary Armstrong and Richard Giulianotti (eds) *Football Cultures and Identities*, London: Macmillan, pp. 223–233.

7 Korean football at the crossroads
A view from inside

Leonid A. Petrov

Introduction: Korean football between Asia and Europe

Football is said to be a game played not by feet but by brains. Thinking speed and mental fortitude govern the game. These qualities, as well as physical endurance, must be nurtured and trained in football players from childhood. It is this ability to concentrate and make quick and educated decisions that ultimately distinguishes winners from losers. It is also said that the East will never understand the West. Emotional incongruity between the Orient and the Occident has been the source of cultural misunderstandings and religious conflicts. In this respect, the phenomenon of football which is universally loved and understood creates an extraordinary cultural bridge. Quick reactions and cohesive teamwork, if complemented by outstanding physical fitness, deserve respect and admiration in any country.

Korean historians tend to find the roots of the game deep in their national history. The first official chronicles *Samguk Sagi* [Records of the Three Kingdoms] that contain references related to a ball-kicking game called *ch'ukku* was compiled nine hundred years ago. However, football in its modern form came to the isolated Korean kingdom relatively late. Korean Football Association (KFA) historians name 1882, when the British battleship *Flying Fish* entered the port of Chemulp'o (today's Incheon) and its sailors taught the locals how to play (KFA, 2001). Since then, the game has always been associated with the West and its traditions.

Antipathy towards Japan, the coloniser, impelled Koreans to admire Europe and America even more. Nevertheless, throughout the first half of the twentieth century European culture and expertise were destined to be copied from the Japanese patterns of modernisation. The first football-related administrative bodies in Korea were in imitation of its Japanese counterparts. In 1928 the first Chosŏn Referees Association (Chairman: Sin Ki-Jun) and then in 1933 the Chosŏn Football Association (Chairman: Pak Sŭng-Bin) were set up in Korea.

Korean football was not recognised by the world community until after Korea regained its independence in 1945. The newly established Korean national team qualified for the Olympic Games in London in 1948. In 1954,

South Korea qualified for the World Cup in Switzerland and twice, in 1956 and in 1960, won the Asian Cup. However, during the 1960s and 1970s professional football in Korea continued to retain many specifically Asian features. Being traditionally based on a hierarchical structure of power and clan ties, Korean society was not ready to produce an adequate number of professional players adept in playing the creative and brisk game the West was suggesting. Koreans themselves knew that the problem existed, but to eliminate outdated practices a great deal of patience and courage was required.

In Korea, corporal punishment in education and particularly in physical training was widely practised. The Confucian morality to which Korea has ardently adhered for the last half a millennium does not restrain a senior from beating a junior. On the contrary, the virtues of filial piety and fraternal respect are unimaginable without periodic thrashing. Even nowadays, school and college students may be flogged by their teachers and beaten by senior students. Thus, the coach who plays a role of a benevolent 'father' has all moral rights to bash his prodigal 'children', presumably for their own benefit. Anecdotes about the furious coach who during the half-time break hits a slack player with his own boot are so common as to induce nothing but a rueful smile.

Interestingly, even after the collapse of the Communist Bloc, many Koreans still had the impression that its outstanding achievements in sport, ballet, arts and sciences were exclusively due to severe beatings and fear. Maybe it was the case for North Korea, but definitely not for Eastern Europe. Considering their society highly democratic, football authorities in South Korea often hesitate to impose even minimal elements of discipline on their elite players. An unsatisfactory game result is a more likely reason to attract the anger of the Korean sponsor than a drinking incident among the players.

Despite the tremendous interest which the South Korean population demonstrates in football, the game has never been quantifiably as popular as, for example, baseball. The poor quality of playing fields and the shortage of stadia seriously impeded the development of professional football in the country: the Korean Super League was established only in 1983. Severe winters and the short growing period for grass restrain ordinary schools and colleges from having anything more sophisticated than a bare earth sports field. The low level of professionalism among school football coaches often reduced the content of their training to a mere endurance exercise. In provincial towns, the coach would simply hold a loudspeaker and drive his motorcar behind the group of exhausted youngsters galloping along the hard asphalt road.

Needless to say, favouritism and bribery were omnipresent in Korea's sports circles. To secure a place in the playing squad, parents of a team member were expected to treat the coach to a tailored suit, an expensive gift or an envelope full of cash. To monitor and eliminate such malpractices, special Technical Committees were established in the structure of all provincial football associations in Korea. However, in disputes with the local groups, the inadequacy of the legal framework frequently left the Seoul-based KFA powerless. Like anywhere in the world, football in Korea has always been torn between club and country. Pursuing their immediate interests, professional clubs or universities could easily refuse to dispatch their player to join the national team for scheduled trainings or games.

On the international football scene, South Korea has for a long time demonstrated better results than Japan. The Korean determination to win is well known and is reflected in their no-nonsense style of aggressive play. However, due to the reasons mentioned above, for decades Korean football retained the qualities of 'Asian football'. As the competition for the top place in Asia intensified and Korea began to worry about its superiority, emulation of European football traditions became indispensable. Searching for solutions, Korea turned, as so often, to emulate the experience of Japan. In 1960, Dettmar Cramer, a German who also coached Franz Beckenbauer and many more footballers all over the world, was invited to come to Japan to help the Japanese establish a strong amateur football programme which later led to the formation of the Japan Soccer League (JSL). Cramer's influence had a lasting impact upon Japanese football and clearly enabled Japan to take the bronze medal at the 1968 Olympic Games in Mexico City.

In the late 1980s, to make sure that Korea would not be overtaken by Japan, the KFA also invited Cramer to serve as a technical coach and to help develop the Korean League. However, due to thorny relationships with professional clubs and their coaches the ageing foreign expert failed to attain anything significant. Public interest in his activity and financial support for it were also limited. As a result all Cramer's efforts to boost the quality of football education at high school and university levels proved to be futile. Nowadays, very little trace can be detected of his work in Korea.

In July 2000 at the China Football Conference held in Beijing, when asked to give some advice to Chinese soccer organisers, Dettmar Cramer said: 'You need patience. You can build a mansion overnight, but you can't develop a footballer overnight.' The following year, Cramer talked more about the process of preparation of young players in different regions:

> Developing young players is the same the world over. The priority should be improving technical skills. Many countries in the last decade went the wrong way. The priority by Federations and big clubs was selection based on size, physical fitness and strength and training was then based on enhancing these qualities. I think this was wrong. Whether Youth or Professional, soccer is a technical game. Of course physical and mental fitness and tactics are important but the core of the game is skill and technical training should be the foundation of youth development.'
>
> (Galustian, 2001)

In preparing their professional players, therefore, Koreans went the way which Cramer had described as 'wrong'. Nevertheless, Korean national teams continued accumulating skill and experience through participation in international competitions. They qualified for World Cups in Mexico 1986, Italy 1990, USA 1994 and France 1998. The 1994 World Cup became the most successful event ever for the Korean squad. In a pulsating game, where they came back from a 3–0 interval deficit to lose just 3–2, they really could have accounted for Germany, the former world champion. The secret was simple: on the bench beside the Korean national coach, Kim Ho, was a Russian technical adviser. Employed by the KFA for the last six months of preparations before the Cup's finals, 48-year-old Anatoli Bychovets managed to elevate the technical and physical level of the team to a new height. For this, Bychovets quickly gained the unfeigned affection of Korean footballers and the outspoken abhorrence of their coaches.

In contrast, despite the efforts of its Dutch-born head coach, Johans Oft, the Japanese national team failed to qualify for the 1994 World Cup finals. Understanding numerous positive aspects of the foreign football influence, the Japan Football Association (JFA) promptly replaced the ineffective Dutchman with a Brazilian football star, Paolo Roberto Falcao. The expectations were that Falcao would be able to lead the national squad until the 1998 World Cup in France (Cho, 1994). It should be mentioned that the fad for foreign coaches and instructors had already taken hold in the Asian football world. The Polish coach Peknicek took over the helm of UAE football from the Ukrainian-born Valeri Lobanovsky, who left only to assume the same position in Kuwait. Saudi Arabia employed Ivo Bortman, and Evaristo Masedo was training Qatar (Ch'oe, 1994).

Thus, the KFA began looking for an appropriate person from overseas to train the national squad in Korea. After the 1994 World Cup, though, there was little doubt that if any foreigner were to assume this post, it would be Bychovets, the former USSR head coach and winner of the 1988 Seoul Olympic football competition gold medal. After a series of negotiations with the Russia Sport Union, the KFA officially invited Bychovets to train and lead the Korean Olympic and national teams until the 1996 Olympiad in Atlanta.

Russian coach and Korean players

Problems associated with the decision to appoint a foreigner to the sensitive position of the national head coach began mounting immediately. Inside the Korean football community, various groups and forces created opposition to the choice of Chung Mong-Joon, KFA President who in May 1994 was elected vice-president of FIFA. Angry protests, emanating predominantly from the heads of professional football clubs, were based on traditional mistrust of foreigners and anticipation of inevitable communication problems and cultural predicaments. Pak Chong-Hwan (Ilhwa), Hŏ Chŏng-Mu (Posco), Ch'a Pŏm-Gun (Hyundai) and other professional clubs' head coaches had their own expectations concerning the contract worth half a million dollars. In other words, the atmosphere surrounding Bychovets' appointment was not particularly welcoming, exactly as it was when Cramer came five years earlier.

Anatoli Bychovets, who was also a former KGB colonel (in the 1980s he coached the Dynamo Moscow club which unofficially belonged to the Ministry of Internal Affairs), was prepared for a struggle. He promptly initiated a number of moves to deter potential enemies and surround himself with loyal and professional people. For example, Bychovets sacked his previous Korean interpreter whom he had long suspected of informing his rivals on the team atmosphere and his coaching methods. In order to form a devoted and professional coaching side of the future team, Bychovets also intended to invite a Russian trainer for goalkeepers and a physician but the KFA briskly vetoed these requests as superfluous.

The role of interpreter in professional sport is tantamount to the role of military interpreter in war. In the sweet moment of victory, nobody really appreciates him, but when things go wrong, the interpreter is the first to be blamed. Along with specific vocabulary and professional slang, a sports interpreter is usually expected to understand the hidden implications which always lie in discussions between the coach and players. Working as a Russian–Korean interpreter, one must keep in mind that, despite the commonality of a tumultuous past and certain cultural similarities which unite these two Siberian peoples, the task of establishing the working communication between Koreans and Russians is particularly difficult. Both Koreans and Russians have difficulties in understanding each other's logic and, when irritated, demonstrate exceptional bigotry.

Bychovets spent two months interviewing and testing interpreters in Seoul and Moscow. For political purposes, the KFA at first demanded that the interpreter must be an ethnic Korean. But as a result of the Stalinist national policy the younger generation of Koreans in Russia and Central Asia (to where they were resettled in 1937 by the almighty leader of the world proletariat) do not speak the language of their ancestors. People of the older generation were not suitable for such a peripatetic position either. Finding a suitable Russian-speaking person in South Korea was even harder: since 1945, fervently anti-communist South Korea had been living in hermetic isolation from anything Russian. Finally, when the Korean media began mocking his meticulous search, Bychovets decided that the only factor to be counted in selecting an efficient combat interpreter was the knowledge of languages and teamwork skills. Apart from interpreting daily meetings, theory classes, interviews and brawls, the future interpreter was expected to perform the duties of personal secretary, video camera operator, ballboy and odd job man. Finally, the author of this article – a recent graduate of the Department of Oriental Studies, St. Petersburg State University – was chosen to do the job. In late August 1994, hardly having any understanding of football and its rules, I was summoned to join the team for its inaugural training.

As the national team in Korea did not have a base of its own, training sessions were normally conducted in Kangnŭng (eastern coast) or Masan (southern coast) where the optimal combination of quality football fields, accommodation and food could be found. At that time, Korea was assiduously preparing for the 1994 Asian Games in Hiroshima. In the long-standing competition between Korea and Japan, football had acquired a particularly high profile. Both the KFA and the JFA spared nothing to outperform each other. With the new foreign coaches in control, expectations of winning gold medals were ubiquitous. However, for Bychovets, whose main task was preparation for the 1996 Olympics, the upcoming event was simply a landmark in the process of building a powerful national squad.

Due to restrictions imposed on the age of players participating in Olympic qualifying games and finals, Bychovets planned to create a mobile U-23 team composed of recent high school graduates and university students and augmented with several over-23 celebrities. The very first step in fulfilling this plan was to identify those Korean football stars who would become role models for the younger players. Preparation for the Asian Games included friendly matches against the Ukraine national side, Saudi Arabia Olympic, and the Brazilian Vasco Da Gama professional club teams. The first results were so impressive that Korea became almost certain about its victory in Hiroshima.

In the meantime, in the atmosphere of great optimism the Japanese national team was also preparing for the Asian Games. Composed of Miura and twenty other best national players selected by their Brazilian head coach Falcao, the Japanese squad did not even bother to check in to the dormitory-style overcrowded Sports Village on the outskirts of Hiroshima. Despite staying in a five-star hotel, having exquisite food and training on the best pitches, the Japanese spectacularly lost the quarter-final match to their Korean archrivals. After that undoubtedly most thrilling match of the Asian Games, the JFA sacked Falcao and lost any further interest in the tournament.

Intoxicated by their tremendous success and quick cash bonuses, however, the Korean team began performing exceptionally badly, losing one game after another. It was a disgrace when the goalkeeper Ch'a Sang-Gwang missed the ball randomly kicked by a desperate Uzbekistan player from the centre-field area. Since then, for Korean football fans the very word 'Uzbekistan' has acquired a grim significance akin to what 'Waterloo' meant to Napoleon. Nevertheless, this bitter defeat brought to the Korean Olympic team, and Korean football in general, one positive change: the KFA finally acceded to Bychovets's request to invite from overseas a full-time coach for goalkeepers. Soon after, the Ukrainian-born 48-year-old Semen Altman arrived in Seoul to assume this position.

Almost immediately harsh criticism of the 'foreign coach who failed to mobilise the cream of national footballers' began circulating in the Korean media. A trivial conflict between Bychovets and Noh Chŏng-Yun, a Korean football star playing in Japan, fuelled the scandal. Playing for Sanfrecce Hiroshima professional club, Noh enjoyed the love and veneration of the Japanese public but not of the new Russian head coach. Due to a minor but persisting injury, Noh was not included in the main list of players. Animosity between the two culminated when Noh accused Bychovets of 'communist methods' in managing people and refused to show up for the evening stroll. Apparently, it was the KFA Technical Committee's Chairman, Pak Kyŏng-Hwa, who provoked this incident as well as many other mishaps which continued to haunt the team. In fact, it was Pak's brother who sold Noh to Sanfrecce and, therefore, who was in danger of forfeiting his profit should Noh's reputation be doubted.

The fracas was stopped but, in order to maintain the balance of interests, the proportion of Koreans in the team's coaching staff was immediately enlarged. Along with the second coach Kim Sŏng-Nam, a younger brother of the KFA General Manager, the Halleluiah amateur team's coach Yi Yong-Mu was hurriedly employed. Yi's frequent absences and unsolicited introduction of pastoral care hours for players found little resonance in the heart of the former KGB colonel. In fact, Bychovets was not against God but he was against the existence of two priests in one chapel. After the first open brawl occurred in Saudi Arabia between Bychovets and the Chairman of the Technical Committee, Yi Yong-Mu was dismissed. But the signs of dissent brewing behind Bychovets's back persisted.

Korean Cup Ramen

After the sweeping success in the first round of qualifying matches against Hong Kong and Indonesia, in June 1995 the team left for France to partici-pate in the traditional competition of Olympic squads in Toulon. But instead of developing the Korean players' ability to overcome European and South American football, Bychovets found himself struggling with a crisis which nearly resulted in his resignation. While preparing the team to play against the U-23 teams from France, Mexico and Scotland, Bychovets discovered that his second coach, Kim Sŏng-Nam, had organised a rebellion against the foreign coaching staff.

Initially, Kim subverted the team's atmosphere by complaining that there was no need to come all the way to Toulon while in Seoul at that very moment there was the Korea Cup competition, a perfect opportunity to earn extra cash bonuses. To buy the support of players, Kim even exploited the common Korean longing for traditional spicy food, awarding several cartons of *Cup Ramen* (instant noodle soup packed in plastic cups) for his supporters inside the team. When they began devouring this monosodium glutamate concoc-tion for breakfast, lunch and dinner, the boys soon developed diarrhoea and other gastric disorders. Not surprisingly in Toulon the team lost three matches in succession.

Suspecting that there was a broader conspiracy brewing, Bychovets accused

Kim Sŏng-Nam of mutiny and demanded his immediate replacement. Indeed, the rigorous discipline, hard training schedules and constant performance control which marked the daily life of the team created a potential for discontent. It is also possible that Kim's plan was simply to ascend to the top position in Korean football himself, but due to Bychovets's rapid and firm counter-attack the whole plan failed. To remedy the precarious situation, without delay the KFA fired Kim and employed two other Korean coaches nominated by the unyielding Russian. After that the team's performance began improving, but the mediocre result in July 1995 at the Merdeka Cup in Malaysia was clear evidence that the repercussions of the Toulon crisis still persisted.

Resilience and tremendous will for victory helped Koreans in winning the first round of the Olympic qualifying matches. Of particular importance were the games against Indonesia. Trained on the playing fields of Italian club Sampdoria, where several of the players were included in the Primavera (youth squad), the Indonesian Olympic team was perfectly prepared by its German head coach. To deter the attacking force of Indonesian strikers (Kurniawan and Indriyanto) Bychovets set off his 1–4–4–1 formation and won both matches in Jakarta and Seoul. It must also be mentioned that the Indonesians were alleged to have used a range of 'dirty tricks' varying from attempts at match-fixing to off-the-ball fouls. During the two games, several Korean players were hospitalised with injuries. For example, in the first minutes of the match in Jakarta, Korean defender Pak Ch'ung-Gyun received a shocking face injury from Kurniawan.

Preparing the team physically and theoretically, Bychovets especially emphasised the importance of matches against the non-Asian teams. For this purpose, the KFA arranged more trips for the team to Europe, North Africa, Australia and America. During the first year of preparation (November 1994–November 1995), the Korean Olympic Team completed a total of 392 training sessions and played 51 matches. The information table, which Bychovets presented to KFA as his annual report, shows that those games ended in 29 victories, 13 draws and 9 defeats (see Table 7.1). Every single match played by the team was video-recorded and then scrupulously analysed at special theory classes. A total of 116 hours of such classes was delivered throughout that period. Bychovets put so much effort into these theory classes that he was easily upset if he saw anyone dozing off. To make some of those hours more interesting, Bychovets obtained a video cassette featuring the brightest episodes from earlier Olympic and World Cup tournaments. Some of this footage showed Bychovets himself scoring goals at the 1968 Olympic Games in Mexico City.

Those video classes were supplemented by so-called 'interview meetings' where Bychovets individually discussed match play issues with every member of the team. The players, hailing from different provinces of South Korea, spoke different regional dialects. But the major difficulty in establishing a stable flow of communication between them and the Russian coaches was not

Table 7.1 South Korea national football team playing and training schedule, 1994–1995

	Nov	Dec	Jan	Feb	Mar	Apr	May	Jun	Jul	Aug	Sep	Oct	Nov	Total
Training days	11	26	27	23	24	11	28	12	24	22	5	24	26	263
Training sessions	23	48	46	21	30	19	38	15	39	30	9	36	38	392
Theory classes	4	6	16	12	10	–	12	6	4	10	–	8	28	116
Vacation days	–	5	4	4	7	19	3	18	7	9	25	7	4	112
University tournaments	–	–	–	–	16–31 Mar	–	10–25 May	–	–	–	6–19 Sep	13–24 Oct	–	4
Matches vs national teams		Saudi Arabia (1:0)(3:0) (1:0)	Japan (1:1) Colombia (0:1)	Yugoslavia (1:0) Hong Kong (3:2) Japan (2:2)(6:7)					Malaysia (1:2) Iraq (2:2)			Trinidad & Tobago (0:0) (2:0)		W6 D4 L2
Matches vs W8	Russia		Denmark	China (0:0)	Switzerland			Ghana	France				Mexico	Norway
Olympic teams	(3:0) (1:1)		(0:0)(1:2) Australia (1:1) Japan (1:0)	(2:1) Tunisia (5:0)			(1:0)(3:0)	(0:1) Mexico (0:1) Scotland (0:1)				(2:1)(0:0)	Sweden (0:3) Russia (0:1)(2:1)	D6 L6
Matches vs professional clubs			Hong Kong Hong Kong (4:1)(2:0)	Hong Kong (2:1)(6:0)	Italy (3:0)(4:0) (1:0)		Botafogo (0:0)(0:2)			Costa Rica (7:1)(1:1) (1:1)			Belgium (2:1)(3:0) Goteborg (2:1)	W11 D3 L1
Olympic qualifying matches							Hong Kong (5:0) Indonesia (2:1)			Hong Kong (7:0) Indonesia (1:0)				W4 D0 L0
Won (W):	W1	W3	W4	W3	W5	–	W4	W–	W–	W3	–	W2	W4	W29
Drew (D):	D1	D0	D3	D3	D0	–	D1	D–	D1	D2	–	D2	D1	D13
Lost (L):	L0	L0	L1	L1	L0	–	L1	L3	L1	L0	–	L0	L2	L9

in the language or cultural differences but in the enormous distance which had traditionally existed between a teacher and a student in Korea. The linking role of interpreter was to help overcome this gap. Nevertheless, after two years of work, when asked by the journalists about the major difficulty for a foreign coach working in Korea, Bychovets lamented that it was the lack of understanding.

The Confucian tradition of fraternal respect often contradicted the basic principles of football. The very idea of a team is understood in Korea as a strictly hierarchical body with a captain at the top and the youngest member at the bottom. Each player knows exactly his role and position in the team and prefers to abstain from taking any extra responsibility. For example, when dribbling the ball in the rival's penalty area a virtuous Korean player would never use a golden opportunity to score the goal himself but invariably start looking for an 'elder brother' who could do it. In Korean society, individualism was traditionally considered a sin. Similarly, in football teams, the desire to be 'like everyone' often surpassed the desire to be 'the best', giving way to a pack mentality.

Moreover, a tiny conflict of interests between player and coach in Korea could immediately grow into fully fledged dissent. If a footballer did not see his name among the 'best eleven', the ideals of teamwork and patriotism would instantly become meaningless to him. Overwhelmed by a narrow-minded envy such players were no longer supporters of the team but rather its fifth column. Bychovets spent two years struggling against this destructive tendency in Korean football and finally seemed to achieve his goal. Despite countless difficulties, his Olympic Team was bound to succeed, albeit in Asia only.

The best Asian team

The final qualifying tournament in Kuala Lumpur was considered the decisive battle on the way to the Atlanta Olympics. Four teams in Group 'B' (Korea, Saudi Arabia, China and Kazakhstan) met for an exhausting struggle in March–April 1996 where Korean fighting spirit underwent a surprising decline followed by an equally miraculous resurrection.

Preparations for this crucial tournament began several months beforehand, in the middle of winter. Bychovets took the team to California to gain more experience in playing against Olympic squads of North and South America. The results were quite modest but the team continued hard training in the utmost southern point of South Korea, the island of Cheju. Thus, by the time the team arrived in Malaysia, the physical and emotional condition of the players was rather worn down. After a draw with Saudi Arabia and a shaky victory over Kazakhstan, the team's spirit was on the verge of collapse. Before the game against China, the KFA President Chung Mong-Joon met with Bychovets and tried to encourage him to win and qualify for the Olympics. Chung was talking about Atlanta, France and the great prospects for Korea to host the 2002 World Cup, but in his words Bychovets discerned a sorrow for the waning chance to win. Clearly, the President came to bid farewell to the diligent foreign coach.

With the arrival in Kuala Lumpur of the Technical Committee's Chairman the team was beset by mysterious problems. On the day when the match against China was scheduled, Ch'oe Yŏng-Su – the principal centre forward – collapsed during morning exercise. Ch'oe declared that he could not walk and asked for a wheelchair. The team doctor spent hours trying to restore the rising star of Korean football to health. KFA officials prescribed an intensive session of Chinese acupuncture. Just hours before the game against China any Chinese doctor visiting the team would be treated with a large dose of suspicion. To mislead the enemy, Ch'oe was even given a pseudonym. Although the best specialist in Kuala Lumpur was invited, all his efforts were in vain: despite some obvious improvement, Ch'oe Yŏng-Su felt 'not a hundred per cent'.

Thanks to the strategic and tactical genius of Bychovets, as well as to the sudden rainstorm which postponed the match for more than an hour, the team managed to restore its credentials. For the Russian coach, who had in his hands the updated list of the Chinese playing squad, this hour was just enough to reconfigure the routine 1–4–4–1 formation into the surprising 3–5–2. Yi Ki-Hyŏng and Yi Woo-Yŏng superbly performed the roles of two centre forwards. As the team's triumph was apparent, striker Ch'oe Yŏng-Su began feeling 'much better' and even asked Bychovets to let him play. Korea spectacularly beat China (3–0) and then Iraq (2–1), securing its place in the Olympic finals. The celebration reached its zenith when the team won the politically important final game against Japan (2–1) and snatched the primary place in Asian football. President Kim Young-Sam, who was watching the game from Seoul, immediately called to Malaysia to congratulate the team members. This call was broadcast by major South Korean TV and radio stations in real time and was probably designed to raise presidential popularity, slightly tarnished by a corruption investigation. President Kim praised the team members for heroism and invited them for lunch at his Ch'ŏngwadae Palace.

This nimbus of glory which began surrounding the Olympic team allowed the KFA to rest on their laurels. A number of international matches which Bychovets requested in the process of preparation for the trip to America were cancelled. It was springtime and when the first sprouts of grass began growing, the team was denied access to any decent football pitches in the country except the poorly maintained grounds of the Military Academy in T'aenŭng. Accommodation conditions were also downgraded. Instead of the usual five-star hotel, the team was shanghaied into the ragged sports village in Nowon-ku, on the outskirts of Seoul. In June 1996, Bychovets called for an urgent training tour to Europe. Games against Scotland, Northern Ireland, Belgium, Denmark, Norway and Russia undoubtedly strengthened and enriched the team. But after their return to Korea, the summer rainy season (*changma*) began. During the last weeks before the departure for Atlanta, team training looked more like a water-polo exercise.

To ensure that the team members were theoretically well informed, the KFA augmented its official delegation with the General Director of the Korea Sport Science Institute. Dr Sin Dong-Sŏng illuminated the players on the mechanism of dehydration and preached against masturbation (Koreans are notoriously conservative in sexual matters). But the favourite topic of this scholar–bureaucrat was the harmful role of air conditioners. Even in Washington, DC and Birmingham, Alabama, where the team arrived in the middle of July, Dr Sin lectured about the dangers of artificial temperature adjustment for sportsmen. He made sure that the bus, which the Korean team used for travelling from the hotel to the training and game venues, had its air conditioner turned off. As the mean temperature in Birmingham was +32°C, after an hour-long ride in a hot and stuffy coach players felt exhausted even before the game began. This scientific obscurantism continued to be practised despite the vocal protests of Bychovets.

It must also be mentioned that the Korean team arrived in America without their second goalkeeper, Yi Un-Jae, who had spent two years preparing for this trip but was diagnosed with TB just several days prior to departure. The young but remarkably talented midfielder Ko Chŏng-Su was also hospitalised. In other words, things did not look good. In such adverse circumstances, Bychovets' new 3–6–1 system was often criticised as a very defensive one. Both defenders and midfielders man-marked their opponents and completely forgot about attack. The libero also played very deep. It was no surprise that in the three games the Koreans scored only twice. Originally, the team's tactic was based on the quick counter-attack, but often the ball was held too long or the deep passes that were supposed to reach an attacking player were not accurate enough. Even if they did get into a promising position their efforts were often too hasty or lacking in precision (FIFA, 1996). At the earlier stage of the Olympic tournament, Korea did defeat Ghana (1–0) but failed to overcome Mexico (0–0). The waning physical condition and numerous injuries, which were received during the game against Mexico, undermined the fighting spirit of the team.

The final blow was delivered by Italy. By the third match of the competition, the Italians had already lost two games to Mexico and Ghana and thus had no chance of proceeding to the next round. Korean footballers knew that and did not expect to face any sustained defence. Nevertheless, led by the popular coach Cesare Maldini, the Italians managed to mobilise for the last bout and in a hard struggle defeated Korea (2–1). Analysing the Korean team performance, the FIFA Technical Report on the 1996 Olympic Football Tournament reads as follows:

> Their positive qualities were physical fitness, speed and discipline. But creativity and the ability to surprise opponents were lacking. The self-confidence needed to succeed against established football nations like

Italy or Mexico seems still to be lacking. In addition, despite the longer period of preparation and the matches against European and South American teams, they were not experienced enough against this kind of opposition.

In preparing his team to play not against European muscles but against European brains, Bychovets appeared to be insightful. But his two-year-long attempt to remove the Asian label from Korean football had failed. The only news which could console devastated football fans in Korea on that day was that the Japanese team had also dropped out of the Olympic tournament.

Whither the World Cup?

The defeat of the Olympic team in America did not overshadow the convivial atmosphere which was brought to Korea by FIFA's decision regarding the joint staging of the 2002 World Cup. Korea's expectations to host the World Cup had been escalating and reached a peak in early 1996. Interest in football quickly transformed into a national obsession. Diego Maradona visited Korea to give football master classes for schoolchildren; housewives were wearing T-shirts and caps welcoming the 2002 World Cup to Korea; non-government organisations were bombarding FIFA with letters warning that if the decision were not made in favour of Korea the whole nation would plunge into deep distress. Animosity dating to Japan's occupation of the Korean peninsula dominated the bitter bidding campaign.

However, this movement was hardly supported by any practical actions. As previously, the improvement of football fields and the construction of new stadia remained a wish list of the Korean football community. The only pitch which could conform with the highest international standards, the Chamsil stadium in Seoul, kept its doors closed to national team training. The KFA had to require its national squads to tour around the country hunting for vacant grounds. In contrast, by 1996 Japan had already spent billions of yen improving existing football facilities, renovating the old and constructing new stadia across the country. Japan's first dedicated football training facility, the J.Village, was opened in Fukushima in July 1997. Designed for intensive training of the Japanese national team, and for use by J.League, JFL and L-League clubs, that facility also welcomed football teams run by business companies, universities, high, intermediate and elementary schools.

The final decision concerning the venue for the next World Cup was made at the end of João Havelange's presidentship, when FIFA politics proved decisive. In a move underscoring the acrimony toward Havelange, world football's ruling body was prepared to award South Korea the 2002 World Cup. The fifteen potential votes for South Korea were not so much out of support for the bid, but mainly to deal Havelange a humiliating public defeat (Associated Press, 1996). If Havelange had not relented, the executive committee would have voted 15–6 in favour of South Korea. But Lennart Johansson, UEFA president and rival of Havelange, won support from European, Asian and African members of FIFA's executive committee and lobbied strongly for both Korea and Japan as co-hosts.

Japan, which had been opposed to having co-hosts, agreed to go along with the plan when it became clear that South Korea would otherwise win the vote. Havelange, who previously had ruled out co-hosting and spoken in favour of Japan's bid, backed down on the day before the scheduled 1 June vote. Thus, both South Korea and Japan were hurriedly selected to share the tournament. On 31 May 1996, when Havelange announced that FIFA had agreed to change its statutes and allow for dual hosting, both Korea and Japan felt in some way disappointed. For example, in his live TV interview the KFA General Manager talked about his great delight mixed with regret that the whole event must be shared with the Japanese. The reaction of the JFA General Manager was more straightforward – he simply resigned.

The consequences of that disillusionment are still palpable. Disagreement concerning the opening and closing ceremonies, the order in which the co-hosting countries should be officially named, as well as the ongoing scandal about the Japanese high school history textbooks, have already damaged the image of the 2002 World Cup. The economic downturn, together with the renewed flirtation with strong nationalism in Korea and Japan, is not the best background for this global festival either. Mutual disparagement and distrust between the two archrivals often prevail over the spirit of cooperation, prompting sceptical remarks akin to the one made by a Japanese journalist saying that 'South Korea seems washed in high hopes that the 2002 World Cup will be as successful as the 1988 Olympics' (*The Korea Times*, 19 October 2000).

Both Korea and Japan continue to prepare their national teams for the great football competition. However, the main hurdle for the co-hosts' success on the pitch will be whether the two nations can reach the last 16 in the 32-team tournament. Korean football, once a powerhouse in Asia, disappointed local fans with its poor performance in the 1998 World Cup and 1999 Asian Cup, and even failed to qualify for the 2000 Sydney Olympics. The reason for the quick decline of the national team after Bychovets was probably its swift return to the habitual methods of selecting and training footballers. A quickly changing sequence of local head coaches between 1996 and 2000 brought to Korean football nothing but disappointment. All were removed from the position due to poor performance, while one even had his training licence suspended.

Finally, after the JFA chose a French coach Philippe Troussier, the KFA's reluctance to hire another foreigner also dissipated. Since early 2001, the Korean national team has been led by the former Real Madrid head coach, Dutchman Guus Hiddink. It seems that Hiddink is not having an easy time, and that he suffers from the same kind of adjustment problems Cramer and Bychovets faced when they first came to Korea. Hiddink's main task is to deconstruct and reconstruct the way the Korean national team plays (Varcoe, 2001). Interestingly, two-thirds of Hiddink's current team players are former members of Bychovets' Olympic squad.

In other words, the history of Korean football is repeating itself in cycles: every five years the Koreans hire a European coach and enable him to mould their best players into a formidable team of international standard. But after the contract is over and the guest coach has gone home, things return to their normal, Asian routine. Due to this long-lasting vacillation between the global and the home-grown, Korean football, as well as football in Japan, has not yet achieved the result it deserves. They are both still lingering at the crossroads, uncertain whether to follow the generously paid recommendations of their foreign tutors or continue groping for their own-style football. In this sense, will the 2002 World Cup help Korea be resolute and make the decision?

References

Associated Press (1996) 'FIFA friction spurred 2002 World Cup deal', 14 June 1996, online: <http://archive.sportserver.com/newsroom/ap/oth/1996/oth/soc/feat/archive/061496/soc19496.html>. (Accessed 10 September 2001.)

Cho Byŏng-Mo (1994) 'Il taep'yo taep'ok mulgari' [Japan national team is ploughing through], *Sŭp'ochi Sŏul*, 17 September, p. 6.

Ch'oe Kyu-Il (1994) 'Taeri chŏnjaeng' [The war of proxies], *Ilgan Sŏp'och'i*, 23 September 1994, p. 9.

FIFA (1996) *Technical Report, 1996 Olympic Football Tournament*, online: <http://www.fifa2.com/olympics/atlanta96/techreport/index.atlanta96.html>. (Accessed 10 September 2001.)

Galustian, Alfred (2001) 'Dettmar Cramer, Interview with Alfred Galustian', *Coerver Coaching*, online: <http://www.coerver-coaching.com/interview_01.shtml>. (Accessed 10 September 2001.)

KFA (2001) *History of Football in Korea*, online: <http://www1.kfa.or.kr/kor/football/history/summary/0,1654,A20237,00.html>. (Accessed 10 September 2001.)

The Korea Times (2000) 'Editorial "Calls addressed to Seoul ASEM"', 19 October, online: <http://www.hankooki.com/kt_op/200010/t20001019170256481161>. (Accessed 10 September 2001).

Varcoe, Fred (2001) 'S. Korea must buck up before World Cup', *The Japan Times,* 21 June, online: <http://www.japantimes.co.jp/cgi-bin/getsp.pl5?sp20010621fv>. (Accessed 10 September 2001).

8 Japan in the world of football

John Horne with Derek Bleakley

Introduction: Japan in the football world before 1945

The Fédération Internationale de Football Association (FIFA) was formed in 1904 and five Summer Olympic Games had been held before the first Far Eastern Games were held in Manila, in the Philippines in 1913. The Far Eastern Championship Games were a series of international athletic meetings conducted roughly along the same lines as the Summer Olympics under the auspices of the Young Men's Christian Association (YMCA). Yet it was 1917 before Japan entered an international football tournament for the first time, when the third Far Eastern Games were staged in Tokyo. On 9 May China beat a team of students from the Tokyo Higher Teacher Training Institute representing Japan. The following day a team consisting of ten of the same players did even worse – losing 15–2 to the Philippines. The pace of progress in developing knowledge of the sport in Japan had been so slow that it was observed that it was only during the tournament that some Japanese players realised for the first time that the ball could be headed as well as kicked! Nonetheless, playing the football tournament on home soil had the effect of drawing the existence of the game to the attention of a much wider audience.

As noted in a previous chapter, in the 1920s opportunities for non-students to play the game remained very scarce. The emphasis was placed initially on promoting the game in higher and middle schools. From 1922 league competitions between college teams were also introduced. The nucleus of the national team in the 1920s was students from Waseda University in Tokyo. They won their first international match, 2–1 against the Philippines, at the Far Eastern Games played in Shanghai in 1927. Fixtures between Japanese and Korean club teams began in 1926, but because Japan had annexed Korea in 1910, these games were not looked on as true internationals. In 1928 a Japanese delegation travelled to Europe to attend the Olympic Games in Amsterdam. Whilst in Europe they were invited to visit the headquarters of FIFA. Japan's application to join world football's governing body was provisionally accepted in July 1928 and full membership was formally approved in May 1929. Like many other national football organisations therefore, the JFA joined FIFA before the English FA.

Domestically the All-Japan Tournament became a focal point of the football calendar and from 1928 university teams began to take part in fixtures with Korean teams. The benefits of university students training together for extended periods of time were felt in 1930 when Tokyo once again staged the Far Eastern Games. For the first time in an international Japan fielded a selection of the best players available, rather than one established team representing Japan. A 7–2 win over the Philippines and an exciting 3–3 draw with China were enough to give Japan a share of the title. As we have noted in an earlier chapter in 1935, when 'All-Keijō' (Seoul) became the first Korean team to take part and win the All-Japan Tournament, the victory prompted a heated debate in Japan about the inclusion of Korean players in the Japanese football team for the 1936 Berlin Olympic Games.

After 1936 political developments and eventually the outbreak of war hindered the development of football in Japan. Japan withdrew an application to participate in the 1938 World Cup finals, and this left the way open for the Dutch East Indies to claim its place as the first Asian country to take part in them. A 4-0 win for an 'All-Kantō' students team, effectively a Japan XI, against a touring amateur English team, Islington Corinthians, in April 1938, suggested that some progress was being made on the football field. However, plans to host the 1940 Olympic Games in Tokyo were cancelled, sporting links with many countries were disrupted and in 1940 the trophy sent by the English FA disappeared. It is widely believed to have been requisitioned by the military authorities. Although JFA annals record a tournament in Manchuria in 1939, the East Asian Games in Japan in 1940 and finally three matches played in Manchuria in August 1942, the opportunity for Japan to develop as a significant football playing force in the pre-war period was thus lost.

Japan in the football world: 1950s–1990s

Both the JFA and the Deutscher Fussball Bund (DFB) were reinstated to FIFA in 1950. Japan returned to international football the following year when the team achieved third place at the Asian Games in March 1951. But the real test for Japanese football came later that year when Helsingborg became the first professional foreign football club to tour Japan. The Swedish team played six games, won them all, scored thirty-six goals and conceded none. Japan had learned that it had a long way to go in football terms. Partly because of this, and other experiences against foreign opponents right up to the 1980s, which demonstrated the huge gap in playing standards, the JFA preferred to invite club sides, rather than national teams, as opposition. Because of Japan's geographical position, a long way from the mainstream of football, foreign teams invited to Japan also tended to play a series of games once they arrived. Travel in the other direction took longer to develop. Japan joined the newly formed Asian Football Confederation (AFC) in 1954. In the same year Japan entered the FIFA World Cup qualifying competition for the first time. Only one other Asian country was in the qualifying group and the

Republic of Korea were the opponents. Public opinion, as well as South Korea's President Rhee, would not permit a visit by a Japanese team to Korea and so both matches were played in Tokyo. The first official competitive football match between Japan and Korea took place on 7 March 1954. Despite taking an early lead, thanks to a goal by Naganuma Ken, Japan was defeated 5–1. In the second match, played a week later, the teams drew 2–2. This was enough to send South Korea to the 1954 World Cup finals. Naganuma went on to manage the national side in the 1960s and become president of the JFA in the 1990s.

Football remained an amateur sport in Japan, and in Japanese eyes, the Olympic Games remained more important than the World Cup. Despite this, the 1950s saw few international successes for Japanese football. The national team qualified for the 1956 Melbourne Olympics but were eliminated in the preliminary rounds by Australia. In 1956 the AFC launched the Asian Cup, open to both professional and amateur teams, but until as recently as 1992 Japan took a lukewarm approach to it, either declining to take part or sending a 'B' team. In 1958 Japan even declined to enter the qualification round for the World Cup finals. In the same year the Asian Games were held in Tokyo and the National Stadium had been built especially. In the football tournament, however, defeats by the Philippines and Hong Kong meant that Japan were knocked out in the early stages. When South Korea eliminated Japan from the qualifiers for the football tournament to be held at the 1960 Rome Olympics as well it was an especially hard blow since Tokyo had already been selected as host for the following Olympics to be held in 1964. The next year Korea once more dispatched Japan from the qualifiers for the 1962 World Cup. The first 1962 World Cup qualifier, played in Seoul in November 1961, marked the first ever visit to the Republic of Korea by any sports team from Japan. Although there was no success on the pitch for Japan, diplomatically it could be argued that football played a small role in fostering links between the two countries where few other channels existed at this time. Apart from Korea, Burma was the first country to be invited to play a friendly match, but it was not until 1961 that the first European country, Yugoslavia, was invited to play a full international in Japan.

The 1960s were a very important decade for the growth of football in Japan. The national team made their first ever tour of Europe in 1960 and although only one of the ten games was won, valuable experience was gained and contacts were established. The following year a German coach, Dettmar Cramer, was appointed as manager of the national team. In 1964, at the Tokyo Olympics, the Japanese team reached the quarter-finals of the football competition having beaten Argentina 3–2. The success against Argentina – on a par with the victory over Sweden twenty-eight years earlier – made a lasting impression on the scorer of Japan's second goal, Kawabuchi Saburō: he went on to become chairman of the J.League. Success at the Olympics also prompted Cramer to make further recommendations to the JFA on coaching, grounds, pitches, the need for international experience and a national football league.

As noted in the previous chapter, in the second half of the 1960s the Japan Soccer League (JSL), in combination with university teams such as Waseda, helped to produce some valuable players for Japan, such as Sugiyama Ryūichi of Mitsubishi and Kamamoto Kunishige of Yanmar. They helped fuel interest in the sport further through their success in Mexico in 1968 when the Japanese Olympic team gained a third place and the bronze medal. Prior to the Olympic Games valuable experience had been acquired by playing teams of varying quality. British teams ranging from Middlesex Wanderers, Stirling Albion to Arsenal all played a part in the build-up. In Mexico Japan beat Nigeria and France and drew with Brazil and Spain before being defeated by Hungary in the semi-finals of the competition. A convincing 2–0 victory over the hosts, Mexico, secured the bronze medal and the Team Fair Play Award.

In the 1970s and 1980s, while a few solitary individuals played in professional leagues in Europe and elsewhere, the promise of the 1968 Olympic games achievement was not maintained. Illness prevented Kamamoto from playing in the qualifying round matches for the 1970 World Cup. Failure to qualify for the Mexico World Cup in 1970 and successive World Cup and Olympic football tournaments, combined with the absence of an effective youth development programme, meant that for the next two decades Japanese fans had little to cheer about at the international level. To use a cliché, it was as if, in building up the bronze medal winning team, all the Japanese eggs had been put into one basket. Although interest in football was sustained for the dedicated fans in Japan through the JSL, the hosting of international events, such as the FIFA Asian Youth Championships in 1965 and 1971 and FIFA World Youth Championships in 1979, and the establishment of the Japan Cup in 1978 (an annual international tournament which in 1985 was renamed the Kirin Cup after the new sponsors), there was a failure to capitalise on the developments of the 1960s.

It was the mid-1980s before more noteworthy developments in Japanese football occurred. In 1985 the Asian Football Confederation (AFC) reinstated the Asian Club Competition that had started in 1967 but then been abandoned between 1972 and 1984. Japanese attitudes to this initiative had been cautious, as problems had been encountered reconciling the demands placed on Japanese clubs by the Asian competitions with their domestic commitments. In 1986 Furukawa Electric (later to be renamed JEF Ichihara in the J.League) made history by becoming the first Japanese club to win the Asian Club Championship. As noted already in an earlier chapter, 26 October 1985 became a key date in the history of Japanese football despite the fact that it marked yet another defeat at the hands of Korea in a World Cup qualifying match. The capacity crowd at the National Stadium in Tokyo that watched the first leg inspired some members of the JFA to establish a committee to consider the development, for the first time, of professional football in Japan.

Japanese football: internationalism at home and abroad

The type of football played by the teams in the J.League has usually depended on their managers and players and therefore one aspect of the 'internationalism' of Japanese professional football has been the fact that different J.League teams have playing styles reflecting the world game. Hence Kyoto were hailed as a 'Brazilian' team in their first season (although this did not prevent them from establishing the record for losing the most consecutive J.League matches), Fukuoka and Marinos have been seen as 'Argentinean', and JEF United Ichihara and Sanfrecce Hiroshima played a 'European'-style game in the early seasons. It has been on the playing field that the true internationalism of football in Japan has been most visible. Although regulations prohibited more than three foreign players per side from being on the pitch at any one time at the outset of the J.League in 1993 (and this was revised in 1998 to three foreign players in total per team squad), there have always been foreign players, as well as managers, in the J.League. Brazil has been the main source of imported players. Since 1993 more than 130 Brazilian players have appeared for J.League teams – more than half the total number of foreign players. Despite the scaling down of foreign players, eighteen out of the forty-two foreign players at the start of the 2001 season were from Brazil.

While the launch of the J.League saw the number of footballing greats playing in Japan grow initially, the downturn in live attendances, the economic difficulties of some of the clubs and changes to J.League regulations about numbers of foreign players per team, have all contributed to a decline in the number of really famous names from European and South American club sides playing in the J.League. That the flow of talent has been slow in going the other way can be explained partly by the lack of it, but also because the relative benefits of staying in Japan have usually outweighed the cost of going abroad to play. In 1996 Miura Kazuyoshi (Kazu), a leading forward in Japan's national side at the time, returned to Verdy in the J.League after a year's loan to Genoa in Serie A in Italy. As a young player he had spent five years in Brazil (with Santos) and regularly trained in Brazil to maintain a permanent residence permit there. His performance in Italy was not very impressive but he was hailed as a leading star because of his form at the start of the J.League. He also played a season at Dynamo Zagreb in Croatia. Following Kazu's example, a few Japanese players began their careers with second division South American teams. The next Japanese star footballer to leave the J.League for Europe was Nakata Hidetoshi, a young mid-field player formerly with Bellmare Hiratsuka who made the biggest impact on the British media in the Japan national team at the 1998 World Cup finals. Nakata initially joined Perugia in Italy's Serie A after the 1998 World Cup and made an instant impression by scoring twice on his debut in September. According to newspaper reports, 500,000 Perugia shirts bearing his name and his No. 7 were being shipped to Japan for fans following his progress (*The Guardian*, 16 September 1998, p. 31). Nakata was also voted Asian Football Confederation player of the year in 1998 and became the subject of a documentary focusing entirely on himself when NHK had cameras tracking his every move during a J.League game before the World Cup. Hailed as the 'Japanese David Beckham' by some sections of the English press in 2001, Nakata has not in fact played very effectively for the past two seasons with Serie A sides.

In 2000, and with the visibility that relative success for the national team has given, overseas clubs started to recognise the talent of more Japanese players. Jō Shōji (Real Valladolid) and Nishizawa Akinori (Espanyol) went to the Spanish league initially, although without much success on the field of play. In 2001 Nishizawa joined Bolton Wanderers while other players joined Feyenoord in the Netherlands (Ono Shinji), Boca Juniors in Argentina (Takahara Naohiro), Cerro Porteno in Paraguay (Hiroyama Nozomi) and Arsenal in the English Premiership (Inamoto Junichi). Nakata meanwhile has moved to Roma and then most recently Parma within Italy's Serie A. A major problem for Japanese players remains that the relative financial return for playing abroad is small compared with staying in Japan. Nishizawa, for example, had to take a pay cut as part of his transfer to Espanyol even from one of the less successful J.League teams, Cerezo Osaka.

Apart from their improving ability and increasing visibility on the world stage through the expansion of football as a television content filler, one more explanation for the rash of transfers of Japanese players abroad since 2000 has been the steady involvement of foreign managers at J.League teams. At the start of the 2001 season half of the J1 club managers were foreign. From England both former Tottenham Hotspur players Steve Perryman and Ossie Ardiles have found opportunities to manage J.League teams (S-Pulse, Marinos, Reysol). Arsene Wenger, currently manager of Arsenal in the English Premiership, was another successful import to Japan from France. Wenger managed Nagoya in 1995 and 1996, being named J.League manager of the year in 1996 and was retained as a technical adviser to the JFA. His own subsequent success with Arsenal, and the triumph of the French team at the 1998 World Cup finals, have enhanced his reputation even further in Japan where he is often invited back as a media pundit. It was on his recommendation that fellow Frenchman Philippe Troussier, previously the manager of Nigeria, and South Africa's national team at the 1998 World Cup finals, was appointed as manager of the Japanese national team in August 1998 (*World Soccer*, October, 1998, p. 46). In each of these ways football in Japan has been tied symbolically to the world outside Japan.

Tragedies and miracles: supporting the Japanese national team

At the end of the twentieth century two brutal facts recorded in the football history books are: that neither of the two countries chosen to co-host the 2002 World Cup has ever won a single game in a World Cup final; and that Nakayama Masashi's goal against Jamaica was the only goal ever scored by Japan in a World Cup final. As we have noted already, the Japanese national soccer team had often been beaten by their near neighbours South Korea in World Cup qualifying matches before 1993, the year of the J.League launch. For Koreans, soccer had long enjoyed a special position as a sport at which they could regularly defeat the Japanese, and thus sustain some national prestige. A Korean newspaper report from December 1928 indicates the intensity of feeling generated by the sport among Koreans during the occupation of Korea by Japan:

On the day before departure an enthusiastic crowd of students, seniors and students from other universities came to say goodbye to the soccer team of Seoul University, wishing them all the best for the victory. The gathered students asked the players to win the cup . . . and to triumph, even when injured. Ah, what is behind that? It is not only soccer fever but also the objective of beating the Japanese perfectly. Our blood is running so fast and getting hot . . . We attach great importance to this journey.

(quoted in Jung, 1996, p. 167)

In the early 1990s, one Japanese journalist, Ijiri Kazuo (1994, p. 77) suggested that many Japanese felt that this was acceptable: 'We beat them at baseball; they beat us at soccer.' It is little wonder then that when in the 1993 World Cup Asian Zone qualifying tournament South Korea lost to Japan some called it 'the worst humiliation since the 1910 annexation' (ibid., p. 77). It has been suggested that it was as a direct result of this defeat that the South Korean Football Association put forward its bid to host the 2002 World Cup finals in competition with that of Japan. At the same time the reaction of the Japanese audience to the victory also confirmed a new level of intensity of involvement in the game. According to one commentator, 'the fans regularly sang *kimigayo*, the (then) de facto, (now de jure) national anthem before each game of the tournament' (ibid., p. 77). A few days after Japan's defeat of Korea, on Thursday 28 October 1993, the final matches of the Asian Football Confederation qualifying tournament for the 1994 World Cup were played in Doha, Qatar. With 30 seconds remaining Japan were leading Iraq by two goals to one and seemed to have secured a place at the 1994 finals. Then, from a corner kick, the captain of the Iraqi team headed an equalising goal, which sent Saudi Arabia and South Korea, despite their earlier defeat at Japan's hands, through to the US finals instead. For the Japanese team, and over 1,000 of their supporters who had accompanied them to the Gulf, there was a sense of disbelief. For those millions of Japanese watching what has become known as 'the tragedy of Doha' at home – in what amounted to the fifth largest television sport audience ever in Japan – the feeling of anti-climax was profound.

What these responses also suggested was that by the early 1990s football had become a symbolic battleground for a 'new Japan', in which some of the old arguments about the singing of the national anthem – especially for its connection with militaristic nationalism – were being challenged. It was, in fact, only in August 1999 that the Japanese government, still facing fierce opposition, passed legislation that formally designated *kimigayo* as the national anthem and the *hinomaru* (a red disk on a white background) as the national flag of Japan. It is as if support for the national football team, and other displays of sporting nationalism, offer a way of overcoming a complex that many Japanese people have felt over nationalism and expressing national identity since 1945 (on sporting nationalism, see Bairner, 2001). Kawabuchi, Chairman of the J.League, told English reporter Jonathan Birchall (2000, p. 212) that he felt it was a 'good kind of national awareness'. Another Japanese journalist commented after the key World Cup qualifying play-off against Iran in Malaysia in 1997 that it 'was probably the first time that so many Japanese flags had been taken to that region since the Japanese military invasion in 1942' (ibid.). He continued, 'The young probably didn't associate the flag and the anthem with the dark implications of the past. For them it's just another way of cheerleading' (ibid.).

After narrowly failing to qualify for the 1994 World Cup finals the Japanese national team began a process of rebuilding. In 1995 the team won the Asian Football Confederation Marlboro Dynasty Cup in Hong Kong, played against China and South Korea. In the summer Japan's national team official sponsor, Kirin, supported the Kirin Cup, an invited competition between Japan and one South American and one European national team. In 1995, it was the turn of Ecuador and Scotland. Later that summer Japan travelled to England for the equivalent sponsored event, the Umbro Cup, involving Sweden and Brazil as well as the host country. So successful was the latter tournament for Japan that *World Soccer* columnists were moved to write, 'if proof was needed that the J.League is not all hype, it has been given. Just two years since it began, Japan's young sons are rising in every age group of the game' (August 1995, p. 42).

Commentating for BBC television on the England–Japan match played at Wembley Trevor Brooking and Barry Davies offered a more mixed response. At half-time, with Japan trailing 1–0 to a lacklustre England side, Barry Davies offered the view that 'The Japanese are showing with the round ball what they have already with the oval ball, that they are learning the game.' Early in the second half a missed scoring opportunity prompted Brooking to comment that 'They seem to get a bit excited when they see the goal posts within range. That was almost schoolboy stuff.' A few minutes later, however, he had to eat his dismissive words. 'Straight out of the Premiership', he exclaimed after Ihara equalised with a deft near-post header. The final result, a narrow 2–1 defeat was a highly creditable performance. The rise of 'Japan's young sons' has fluctuated since then, but in the summer of 2001 when the national team twice beat England's other sporting *bête noire*, Australia, and seven Japanese football players are featuring in the football world's major leagues, it is difficult to argue any longer that the words 'Japan' and 'football' are such an odd couple.

Conclusion

Our view is that football and other sports in Japan have always been manipulated by different interest groups to accommodate new demands and initiate new ways of thinking. For much of the post-1945 period, sport, except for professional baseball and made-for-television shows like professional wrestling, was organised and facilitated by companies. Sports, including football, at this time thus became a part of popular culture through corporate sponsorship – part of *kigyōshugi* (company-centredness). As this system has started to break up, with the impact of greater economic realism amidst the 'Heisei Recession', football in Japan has been actively marketed as something to be consumed differently from other sports, especially baseball.

As we showed in an earlier chapter, since the beginning of the 1990s, when the Japanese 'developmental state' has faced challenges on several apparently contradictory fronts, football has played a significant role in balancing several of them. In various ways football has been used to incorporate an emphasis on internationalisation – *kokusaika* – and at the same time an emphasis on the hometown – *furusato*. At a time when concerns about national identity have been expressed quite forcefully through *nihonjinron* (or 'debates about Japanese culture'), international football matches especially have provided opportunities for the expression of a safer form of Japanese national identification and the establishing of clear differences from Japan's 'others' (including Koreans) in the Asia-Pacific region, through the singing of the national anthem, and the waving of the *hinomaru*. Consideration of football provides glimpses of new ideals of masculinity, relationships to paid work, towards place of residence and expressions of national identity in contemporary Japan.

References

Bairner, Alan (2001) *Sport, Nationalism and Globalisation*, New York: State University of New York Press.

Birchall, Jonathan (2000) *Ultra Nippon: How Japan Reinvented Football*, London: Headline Book Publishing.

Ijiri Kazuo (1994) 'Soccer fever', *Japan Echo*, 20, 4: 77.

Jung, Koo-Chul (1996) *Erziehung und Sport in Korea im Kreuzpunkt Freinder Kulturen und Machte* [Education and sport in Korea in the intersection of foreign cultures and powers] Köln: Sport & Buch.

World Soccer, various issues, London.

Further reading

For more detailed references to the sources informing this chapter see the following.

Horne, John (1996) '"Sakka" in Japan', *Media, Culture and Society*, 18, 4: 527–547.

Horne, John (1999) 'Soccer in Japan: is *wa* all you need?', *Culture, Sport, Society*, 2, 3: 212–229.

Horne, John (2001) 'Professional soccer in Japan', in Joy Hendry and Massimo Raveri (eds) *Japan at Play*, London: Routledge, pp. 204–218.

Japan Football Association (1996) *Nihon Sakkā Kyōkai 75 nen shi. Arigatō, soshite mirai e* [The 75-year history of the Japan Football Association], Tokyo: Bēsubōru Magajin Sha.

Part III

State, civil society and popular resistance in football

9 Japanese soccer fans

Following the local and the national team

Shimizu Satoshi

Introduction

It is clear that after the birth of the professional soccer league in Japan (the J.League) in 1993, soccer has raised various issues not only 'on the pitch', but also related to other aspects including the management of professional soccer clubs and the establishment of relationships with franchises. Holding the 2002 World Cup and making preparations for it mean being subject to FIFA regulations and an 'invasion' of soccer fans from around the world. Japan and Korea will soon be engulfed by the huge wave of a sporting mega-event equal to, if not larger than, that of the Olympic Games. One of the considerations after the event will be the extent to which the diverse soccer cultures participating in the World Cup will help create new forms of play and support or change those forms that have developed in Japan and Korea in the past decade. One of the most important aspects of wider soccer culture worth studying is the character of soccer supporter cultures. In this chapter, I discuss some of the most significant features of soccer supporter cultures and subcultures in Japan. It is based on interviews, small sample surveys, observations and participant observation. It focuses on the behaviour of the supporters of just one J.League team, the Urawa Red Diamonds (hereafter Urawa Reds), who enthusiastically cheer on the club in organized groups that approximately consist of 15,000 participants, the largest in the J.League.

The chapter will first of all provide some background to the team. Next I will make some brief comments on how I went about analysing soccer supporter cultures in Japan, in contrast to Western European traditions, especially in England. As one of my main concerns was to let the fans speak for themselves about the significance of soccer in their lives I utilize interviews and observations of Urawa Reds fans at home and abroad following the national team to help us tell the story. The chapter concludes with some further reflections on the contrasts with other studies of soccer supporter cultures.

Japan's 'Man. United'

Urawa is a northern suburb in the Tokyo Metropolitan Area, in Saitama prefecture, approximately forty minutes by train from Tokyo central railway station, with a population of 480,000 people. On 1 May 2001 Saitama City itself was established through the amalgamation of Urawa, Ōmiya and Yono – the combined population of this new city is over 1 million. Urawa Red Diamonds began as Mitsubishi Heavy Industries Football Club in the company-team Japan Soccer League (JSL) established in 1965. Mitsubishi were not unsuccessful during this period – winning the championship four times in 1969, 1973, 1978, and 1982 – but as with other JSL teams they could not develop as a truly independent soccer club without changes in the wider infrastructure. Even when the J.League kicked off in 1993, and despite one of the J.League conditions of acceptance being that company names did not predominate, the chief company sponsor, Mitsubishi, did not completely relinquish its name from the team. For most of the 1990s Urawa were known as Mitsubishi Urawa Reds, and it is only since 2000 that the team have adopted the name Urawa Red Diamonds on their shirt badge. The name 'Red Diamonds' still refers to the company's logo of the three stacked diamonds that combines the three oak leaves of the Tosa crest and an allusion to the three ships, borrowed from the Tosa in 1870, that laid the cornerstone of the Mitsubishi Shipping Industry.

At the start of the J.League Urawa promised to be the 'Manchester United' of Japan. Wearing the same shirt colours, consequently utilizing the nickname 'The Reds', attracting considerable passionate support, and importing European, especially German, coaches and players such as Guido Buchwald and Uwe Rahn, Urawa were meant to go places. While other J.League teams have often struggled to even half-fill their stadia, Urawa has had little trouble in filling Komaba Stadium. When attending a home game at Komaba, one always realizes that a soccer stadium is a place where various cultures interact. Shouts and chants from the 'Urawa Boys', which is the name of the core group of Urawa Reds supporters, echo throughout the stadium. The cheer 'Warrior', based on a song which accompanied the television performances of the 1992 professional wrestling tag team champions Terry Gody and Steve Williams (and originally performed by the rock group Kiss) is very popular. Like England supporters during the World Cup in France in 1998, Reds fans also sing the up-tempo theme song from the film *The Great Escape*, composed by Elmer Bernstein:

> Here we go! We are the Reds! La, la, la. La, la, la, la. La, la!
> Here we go! We want a goal! La, la, la. La, la, la, la. Reds!
> *(Repeated again and again)*

Other cheers are performed in French:

Allez, allez, allez au Urawa! Allez, allez, allez au Urawa!
Allez, allez, allez, qui! Allez, allez, allez, qui!
Allez, allez, allez au Urawa!

The area behind the goal ('end') is a space of wild enthusiasm and excitement. Fans become fascinated, pursue pleasure and throw themselves into cheering. Using all parts of their body, supporters jump up and down, clap hands and never cease to shout in reply to the voices of their leaders. In the midst of this fervent carnival, nobody is aware of the creolization process of diverse cultures which are represented by the songs and chants made from different languages, the rituals of supporting habits and soccer culture's own origins. Then, with loud music blaring, the players enter the pitch. Precisely at that moment, a large vertical red, white and black banner with a red heart-mark in the centre, in which the figure '12' is emblazoned (representing the supporters), is hung from the second balcony of the stands, and supporters turn their eyes to the players while watching the curtain. Be 'the twelfth player in the stadium' requested the J.League when it kicked off in 1993. Urawa fans appear to need no more encouragement:

Urawa Reds! Cha, cha, cha-cha-cha! *(Clapping hands)*
Urawa Reds! Cha, cha, cha-cha-cha! *(Clapping hands)*

Then, several men standing close to the leader of Urawa Boys begin to set off smoke candles. Guards try to stop them, but another group of supporters prevent them from approaching the men. Cameramen near the pitch, always searching for dramatic photos, rush over in an attempt to take pictures of the scene. While watching the scene, supporters in the bleachers continue cheering and turn their attention to the kick-off.

Yet Urawa has not performed as well on the pitch as their ambitions or their support would suggest. In fact, they were the first of the J.League founder teams to be relegated at the end of 1999 when promotion and relegation were formally introduced between J1 and J2 Leagues. They only stayed in J2 for one season, however, and attendances in J2 reached their highest average ever thanks to the devotees of the Urawa Reds.

Violence and representation by Urawa Reds supporters

Relegation at the end of 1999 drove Urawa Reds supporters towards ever more reckless acts, as their discontent had become a source of their energy. In fact, Urawa Reds supporters have been represented as 'hooligans', or unruly fans, since the start of the J.League in 1993. In 1994 the Reds last game of the season took place at Toyama Stadium. Yokohama Marinos defeated the Reds 6–3. The next day, one newspaper article was published with the heading 'Urawa let in six goals. Supporters go wild!' and the subheading 'The manager should quit. Riot in grounds' (*Nikkan Sports*, 20 November 1994).

Having lost four consecutive games, the players bowed to their fans in apology. Soon after, the supporters started to express their anger towards the manager, 51-year-old Yokoyama Kenzō. 'Resign, Kenzō!' they shouted repeatedly. Then they lit smoke candles and threw empty cans and trash. The stadium was thrown into an uproar. Nearly thirty supporters broke out onto the pitch and, despite the efforts of the team officials and security guards, they made their way to outside the locker rooms, shouting, 'Hand in your resignation, Kenzō!' and 'Come out and apologize!' Fortunately the riot quietened down within ten minutes after Urawa defenders Taguchi Yoshinori, 29, and Ikeda Futoshi, 24, went out to speak to the fans to try and calm them down (*Nikkan Sports*, 20 November 1994).

Disruptive acts by Urawa Reds supporters have continued to gain public attention. Headlines such as 'Coins thrown at Fukuda' (an Urawa Reds forward), and 'Radical supporters lose it!' featured in newspapers in 1997. When the team lost four consecutive games it was reported that 'nearly 500 supporters threw raw eggs and coins at Fukuda Masahiro as he was getting on a bus to leave the stadium' (*Nikkan Sports*, 8 May 1997). Also, when Reds supporters responded to apparent provocation by Nagoya supporters and raided the supporters' seats behind the Nagoya goal, it led to the headline, '30 people riot in Nagoya' (*Nikkan Sports*, 11 May 1997). On 29 July 2000, while the Urawa Reds were playing in Hokkaidō against Consadole Sapporo, Reds supporters lit smoke candles and threw plastic bottles at spectators in the Consadole section. After the game, they chased a cameraman who was filming them onto the pitch.

Clearly media coverage, especially newspaper reports, has helped to shape an image of Reds supporters. Furthermore, many books about the Urawa Reds (Crazy Calls and Todoroki, 1994; Ōsumi, 1998; Yamaoka, 1998; Yoshizawa, 1998; Toyota, 2000; Yamanaka, 2000; Seio, 2001) have reconfirmed these events and sustained the image of Reds supporters as unruly. Some of the books emphasized the distinctive masculinity and image of 'delinquency' concerned in soccer supporters' culture. These books may have become one of the main factors in attracting supporters to the Urawa Reds in recent years (Shimizu, 2000).

Making sense of soccer supporting, and the *Match Day Program*

Despite apparent similarities, the actions of the Urawa Reds supporters need to be understood in a different way from the hooliganism often observed in Britain from the 1960s onwards (Williams *et al.*, 1984; Dunning *et al.*, 1988; Murphy *et al.*, 1990). In my view, it is necessary to approach the behaviour of Japanese soccer supporters from a perspective other than that which concentrates purely on the violence alone. As concrete case studies, based on ethnographic research into the lived experiences of soccer supporters clearly demonstrate (Marsh, 1978; Marsh *et al.*, 1978; Ogasawara, 1998; Giulianotti,

1999, Robson, 2000), soccer supporter culture behaviour should be considered in the light of research on youth cultures and subcultures and the relationship with norms of masculinity (Cohen, 1973; Clarke *et al.*, 1976; Taylor, 1982). This is particularly true in the Japanese case.

Historically, Japanese subcultures often were created in line with perceived images taken from Europe and America. A similar process shaped the emergence of soccer supporters' culture in the 1990s when ardent fans started to fuse rock music and fashion with soccer and professional wrestling. Urawa Reds fans sometimes communicate their ways of cheering and opinions to the club through *Match Day Program (MDP)*, a fanzine. *MDP* is edited by Saitama Newspaper's *MDP* editorial office and is sold for 300 yen every time the Urawa Reds have a game at Komaba Stadium. According to a small investigation carried out in April 1998, 80.6 per cent of fans attending games purchase *MDP*. This figure was obtained by polling people lining up at the gates for a match. As the total number of people polled was only 216 it cannot be considered as truly representative (see Shimizu and Iida, 1999, for further discussion).

In *MDP*, Urawa Reds players, tactics, and the team's point of view are introduced. In addition, staff members from the *MDP* editorial office suggest how cheering should best be done. Featured articles refer to the memories and impressions that newspapers and books have created. *MDP* also includes opinions on the supporters' actions, while supporters themselves can exchange views about the team. Hence *MDP* is likely to be the most convenient and reliable source of information for Reds supporters who frequent Komaba Stadium. *MDP* also helps supporters think about and act on the opinions of others (Saitama Shimbun, 1998). In fact, after the season dramatically ended in 1994, the Reds team had an *MDP Special Edition* published to explain the club management and policy of the then manager, Yokoyama Kenzō. This edition also included supporters' contributions. Indeed, *MDP* may have been established precisely as an attempt to stop any violence from happening. In practice, however, this is hardly possible. For some supporters, it is very hard to keep calm when their favourite team keeps losing or when the team is playing a game that may decide their place in the league rankings. With rising frustration levels, they often act on it, ignoring all rules and regulations.

On the Withered Lawn

Since April 1998, I have been closely following a supporters group called *Kareta shiba no ue de* ('On the Withered Lawn'), which consists of fifty members (including fifteen women) born between 1959 and 1978 and is led by a 33-year-old man. 'On the Withered Lawn' formed following the break-up of the 'Crazy Calls', another fanatical group that cheered on the Urawa Reds before the Urawa Boys.

The leader of the Crazy Calls was called Yoshizawa Kōichi. This key man of the Urawa Reds supporters developed his ideas by drawing on knowledge of spectacular subcultures, like rock and punk cultures in Britain. In 1994, in *The Red Book: The Fighting Twelfth Players of The Reds,* Yoshizawa explained:

> I began to target young people, especially teenagers, as they tend to be more sensitive, but I only focused on boys . . . Why did I focus on teenage boys? Whatever you start to like or become enthusiastic about when you are a teenager, you tend to carry on liking it even when you get older . . . Something that a man will like in the future is usually introduced when he is young . . . I researched what would really appeal to teenage boys, and then I realized that there was a common theme, 'delinquency'.
>
> In the Fifties, there was Elvis Presley and James Dean, and in the Sixties, the Beatles and The Rolling Stones represented the 'Counter Culture'. The Punk movement took over in the '70s with The Sex Pistols and The Clash. The theme 'delinquency' always came up when I thought about what young people were enthusiastic about over the century. Of course, from an adult's point of view, the very word 'delinquent' does not sound very good, but I think young people use the word to describe something cool. Crazy Calls focused on those people who wanted to be cool, and they stimulated people into realizing that soccer is an exciting and great sport.
>
> (Crazy Calls and Todoroki, 1994, pp. 120–122)

He also commented that 'We decided that we should attract attention to ourselves as supporters, and therefore we should be introduced to the media as Crazy Calls' (ibid., p. 129).

Yoshizawa and his fellow Crazy Calls members concentrated on chants using lyrics and rhythms that derived from rock, and strove hard to develop exciting performance schemes with high visual appeal. Yoshizawa explained that the actual chants were 'based on rock music, because rock has always been popular in Urawa. We also referred to hit tunes, and changed the lyrics so that they would rhyme' (ibid., p. 39). The resulting form was a kind of macho behaviour, partly borrowed from rock subcultures, and occasionally demonstrating a violent form of masculinity. The image of 'delinquent men' became a kind of 'marketing strategy' to sustain media interest. At the same time, Crazy Calls' style grew popular among many other supporters.

A male university student (born in 1978) who also became a member of 'On the Withered Lawn' after belonging to Crazy Calls told me:

> The reason why the supporters attract people is that they try to purposefully project a macho image. It does not mean that everyone should be macho, but there are some people who still want to try to do that . . . I have been a supporter ever since the first year of the J.League, so five years now. I think I am more macho without realizing it. This must be the

difference between someone who aims to be a supporter and someone who has long wanted to be one. I am not saying that women are not good enough, but the people you can rely on in case of an emergency are either young people or men in their 20s and 30s. In such cases, physical strength is needed and this is connected to fighting power, although I do not want to think that way too much . . . As society is becoming less macho, there is more desire to be macho. But we know there would be problems if we took things even further such as excluding women from society.

(Interview, 4 May 1998)

Wives and girlfriends of the 'On the Withered Lawn', about five members, usually sit behind the men who always take up their position standing in two lines at the terrace behind the goal. Watching the men while chatting among themselves, the women never mingle with the men, neither at the stadium nor in 'Sakagura Riki' ('Sake Cellar Riki'), the main drinking establishment of Urawa Reds supporters. Urawa Reds supporters regularly go to Riki's following a match to chill out from the excitement and (especially during 1999 when most of the field-work for this chapter was undertaken) soothe each other's disappointment after losing a game. Riki's is also used by supporters as a place to refresh themselves in preparation for their return to daily life the next day, as the pre-match ritual for the most dedicated fans includes waiting in line all night long, drinking alcohol, and standing and cheering throughout the match. For those who cannot see the match live, it is a place to get together with the supporters who did see it after getting off work. Some of the keenest supporters have moved to live near to Komaba Stadium and Riki's so that they can meet with other supporter friends, drink and discuss the Reds and other soccer-related subjects and return home late on foot or by bicycle.

Allez Japon! Japanese soccer supporters abroad

During the 1998 World Cup in France, for the first time elements of the Japanese soccer supporters' culture in action abroad became visible to a global audience. A substantial number of Japanese fans flew to France, a flight of some twelve hours, only to discover that many of them did not have tickets for any of the matches. One product of the ticket scandal, when some thousands of Japanese were left without a valid ticket in France, led to an image of Japanese fans as eager to pay exorbitant sums to watch their team. Some sections of the local French media criticized the Japanese for profligate spending. After such a long distance journey, however, it is understandable that many wanted to get in to see the games they thought they had already paid to see! Television and newspapers reported Japanese fans walking around soccer stadia holding pieces of paper with the words 'Need Ticket' on it written in English or French, and haggling with ticket scalpers (see *Asahi*

Shimbun, 14 and 20 June 1998; also *Nikkei Weekly*, 8 October 2001). Hence, when Japan's national team played its first match, against Argentina in Toulouse, Japanese supporters occupied 70 per cent of the regular seats in a stadium with a seating capacity of 36,500. An additional 10,000 or so Japanese supporters gathered at a park near the stadium to watch a 'virtual' World Cup match projected on to a large screen (*Asahi Shimbun*, 15 June 1998). 'Allez Japon', and other cheers for individual players, were heard all around the place for over one hour before the kick-off (*Asahi Shimbun*, evening edition, 15 June 1998). One player commented afterwards, 'I felt as if I were standing in the National Stadium in Tokyo'. When there were no matches scheduled, Japanese supporters rushed to shop at famous brand stores or do some sightseeing. A luxury shop in Lyon, where the match with Jamaica was held, introduced a special shift for Japanese shoppers, increasing the number of Japanese sales staff and changing the assortment of goods to match the taste of Japanese people. It was apparently successful, since it was reported that sales tripled (*Asahi Shimbun*, evening edition, 26 June 1998).

What significance did the 1998 World Cup have for the Japanese supporters? Irrespective of the Japanese team's victory or defeat, they went sightseeing and shopping. While some male supporters professed themselves to be 'delinquent' and tried to portray their 'Japaneseness' by wearing, for example, a karate outfit, most of them behaved as rather mainstream Japanese by acting in the same way as the average Japanese travel group. As Japanese supporters were most likely to be encountered in this particular style, it can be concluded that their behaviour sustained a distinctive characteristic of the Japanese people abroad: the tendency to settle for 'passive self-satisfaction', arguably also represented by the performance of the few Japanese professional athletes who have ventured to advance overseas.

Ultra Nippon: travelling with the national team

Every time one of Japan's national football teams includes Urawa Reds players, a group of Urawa Reds supporters sets out on tour to watch the team play, even if the match is played far away. As English journalist Jonathan Birchall noted in his study of 'Ultra Nippon', the hardcore Japanese national team supporters' group:

> Dedicated European fans might make a few trips to Rome or London or Stockholm, but Japanese national team fans are in a frequent-flying category all of their own . . . one company was offering supporters a trip to see the away game against Kazakhstan in Almaty on what was advertised as a three days no nights basis. The lucky fans were to leave Japan on a Friday, travel overnight to the game on Saturday, and leave immediately so that they could get back to Japan on Sunday in time for work on Monday.

> (2000, pp. 209–210)

I was able to witness the involvement of a group of Urawa Reds supporters at another qualifying match for the Sydney Olympic Games, held in Hong Kong in June 1999. A member of the group purchased two Japanese flags (*hinomaru*) before the match. When a guard refused to allow him to pass the gate with the flags affixed to their poles, he removed the flags from the poles and wrapped them around his body. At each national team match, he told me, he wore a black Adidas soccer cap and his fellow Urawa Reds supporters wore blue T-shirts that matched the national team colours. On the T-shirts was the logo in honour of their favourite drinking place, 'Sakagura Riki', as well as a large *hinomaru* mark on the front and the Japanese characters 'Urawa' and '*riki*' (literally, 'force') on the back. A pair of baggy trousers completed the away team supporters' outfit.

Upon entering the stadium in Hong Kong, the group stood in line, held up a large banner with the *hinomaru* mark in the centre and the written words, 'Let's go in high spirits! Let's shout to one another! Let's act as samurai and the sons of Nippon!' Next, following their leader, an individual dressed in a karate uniform with a *hinomaru* mark embroidered on the breast and *hakama* (i.e., Japanese-style trousers), hand-sewn by his wife, shouted another order: 'Spread the large banner!', and the horizontal banner was unfurled. At that moment, many cameramen rushed over and focused their cameras on the spectacular scene. The wives and girlfriends also smiled for the cameras, although in Hong Kong, too, the women followed their habitual convention of watching the match while sitting apart from the male supporter group. In fact, after the game some of the female fans went to the lobby of the Japan national team's hotel and enjoyed the thrill of having their pictures taken with players and getting autographs – of course, most of the players they were interested in were members of the Urawa Reds.

Just before the start of the match, Urawa Reds supporters with Ultra supporters began singing the theme song from the NHK (Nihon Hōsō Kyōkai, or Japanese National Broadcasting Corporation) TV drama *Monokaki Dōshin Inemuri Monzō*, entitled '*Genki dashite yukō*' [Let's go in high spirits]. This television drama serial highlights the traditional narratives in Japan that governed relations between male and female, husband and wife, father and daughter, and mother and daughter during the Edo era (1603–1868). A few key lyrics quoted from the drama were written on the large horizontal banner the supporters held. These displays were clearly conducted with the expectation that the mass media, especially TV cameras and newspapers, would cover them and bring the group's activities to the attention of the wider Japanese public.

The Urawa Reds supporters' visit to Hong Kong was a four-day package tour, during which the members could watch two qualifying matches. As spare time was ample, the group usually displayed tourist behaviour similar to the activities of the Japanese supporters in France. In other words, this supporters' tour was in many ways similar to other sightseeing tours that Japanese people usually take when holidaying abroad (Chon *et al.*, 2000).

When not at the matches, the group boarded a bus and took in the main sightseeing attractions in Hong Kong with the help of a local guide; meals had been prearranged in special restaurants. Almost all of the members of this tour also participated in similar group package tours to watch the qualifying matches and finals of the 1998 World Cup.

Moment of resistance?

As previously stated, the leaders of the Urawa Reds supporters set their sights on 'presenting interesting and stimulating visual images' (Crazy Calls and Todoriki, 1994, p. 122) based on their understanding of various subcultures in America and Britain and mainly focused on one factor, 'delinquency'. Even the clothes and styles of fashion worn by the Urawa Boys are influenced by this way of thinking. The recent styles of performance of Urawa Boys are based on those of supporters in Serie A, Italy. Today, Urawa Reds most fanatical supporters spend every moment entranced in the 'carnival'. Not caring about the real meanings, they call out mixed up chants, songs and performances derived from English and Italian soccer fans, simply indulging in the pleasure that cheering the team on gives them (Giulianotti, 1999).

However, when it comes to cheering on the national team, the group focuses on cheers that are based on their 'Japaneseness', or their sense of Japaneseness, for example, by displaying the lyrics of the theme song from the popular Japanese television drama on their horizontal banner. For them, tying the *hinomaru* flag around their body is part of a performance. Kawabuchi Saburō, Chairman of the J.League, has suggested that for some Japanese soccer supporters, soccer has become connected to their sense of national identity:

> But that's something different from the militarism and patriotism that we had during the war years. I think it is a good kind of national awareness. These days, watching soccer may be the only time when people think about their nationality.
>
> (quoted in Birchall, 2000, p. 212)

In domestic competitions it can seem, superficially at least, that by their actions even Urawa's most fanatical supporters are discontented with the Urawa Reds team and club. I would argue, however, that perhaps the basis of their irritation is really their latent feelings about the conditions in the companies they work for and the Japanese work environment in general. In everyday life, cultural conventions prevent them from expressing their feelings in a straightforward way, which are neither 'Japanese' behaviour nor 'proper male conduct'. As they all have been socialized to believe that their behaviour should be seen as strictly 'Japanese', they follow this idea, even when cheering on the Urawa Reds. Particularly at the game, when TV cameras and the nationwide audience watch every move of the group, they are eager not to infringe public expectations. In addition, the media are most salient in transporting and constructing role models of proper male Japanese conduct.

The work-centredness of contemporary Japanese society remains a major influence on the Japanese at play. It can be argued that for the Urawa Reds supporters discontent stemming from work and the norms of masculine behaviour in Japan are the inspiration behind their leisure time behaviour. Their actions take place in a social environment where the dominant factor is 'a conservative consciousness that tries to maintain a consensual social system based on harmonious judgment' (Watanabe, 2000, p. 261). This can also be demonstrated by the fact that rather than simply cheering on play on the pitch, some supporters believe that they are better deployed in cooperating with the administration of their club to create a better club. That is to say, supporters are attracted to the notion of soccer, and the J.League in particular, as a grand social experiment in which their choices and actions will lead to the creation of an ideal club. As one supporter, an employee of a major general contractor, commented to me: 'I'm more interested in creating a better environment than watching soccer games, like working on the operational aspects such as improving the pitch grass for the Urawa Reds players'. (Interview, 12–14 June 1999).

Alternative choices

People do not just go to Komaba Stadium to be reminded of the impressions and memories of Reds matches or actions taken by supporters. Most of what might be called the 'silent minority' go there with their own thoughts and feelings towards the team. One male worker, born in 1950 near to Urawa and still living there, has been a passionate supporter since 1994. He loves photographs and carries around albums with close-up photos of players. He also has an album exclusively featuring two of Urawa's most famous players – Okano Masayuki and Ono Shinji (who played for Feyenoord Rotterdam in 2001). Some of the photos even have players' autographs. He told me how his commitment to the team developed:

> Whenever some players or their wives or even their children see my wife or me, they always talk to us. There is warmth between us since we recognize and call out to each other. It makes me happy to realize that I am a supporter. Some players ask me about my son and daughter, saying 'Is your daughter here today?' I don't really understand soccer though. My wife is more into it. She was watching games when players who represented Japan were playing. I wasn't. Maybe it's difficult to understand it unless you're really into it. In my case, I'm just a supporter. But because of the photos I've taken, many people talk to me and then we become friends. I think whoever is a supporter finds it addictive, like, 'I want to see it again'.
>
> (Interview, 4 May 1998)

From his comments, it is evident that he enjoys supporting soccer for the opportunity it provides him to expand his social network of friendships. The feeling of being connected with players is also a key aspect of being a supporter.

Another of the members of 'On the Withered Lawn', a man born in Urawa City in 1964, who is a graduate of a private university in Tokyo and works as an employee of a major general contractor, told me:

> I feel I should not just work all the time. I'm calm when I'm working because I'm not involved in production. My job is to sort out companies that are not doing well as the result of the collapse of the bubble economy, so I am in the position to discuss and not to be dismissed. I used to work onsite before, as the company often constructed tunnels. I tried to get my wife interested in soccer in the beginning, but she couldn't get into it. *(He laughs)*. She just told me to do whatever I liked. I won't have anything if soccer is taken away from me. It doesn't mean that soccer is the main thing besides work, but I can afford to do what I want to do.
>
> As for how I feel, soccer obviously wins over work. No matter how hard you try at work, everything depends on capability. Work isn't forever. I could even get fired as the result of restructuring, so I don't feel happy belonging to the company. Ideally, it would be nice to be acknowledged as an individual so that I could proudly say I am being useful for the company and get a reasonable salary. Our legal residence is Urawa City, and I want to bring up my children in Urawa, stay in the region, watch soccer and live with pride in my hometown, even though we are not in Urawa at present. Urawa is said to be a model for the J.League . . . But there are many things that others can't imitate. As I said before, it used to be a kingdom of soccer (especially the All Japan High School Championship). I think those people in their 30s are the ones supporting the team at present, together with some young people.
>
> (Interview, 12–14 June 1999)

Conclusion

Through a series of illustrations of the behaviour, at home and abroad, of members of one of the more flamboyant supporters groups in the J.League, this chapter has offered a glimpse into how various popular cultures, such as fashion and music, have been incorporated into Japanese soccer supporter cultures. Members' involvement as supporters is constructed out of a variety of elements of their daily life. Will it be possible through the J.League project to establish a regional sports club system and continue to operate it by virtue of the 'power of the people'? Will the supporters break away from the 'populist', as articulated by dominant political influences, and become truly independent as a 'popular' group, forming a consensus of opinion and thereby putting 'popular democracy' into practice? Taking into consideration the present political situation in Japan in terms of political history and new conservatism, it is not a particularly favourable climate. Nonetheless, at least in the J.League, the '100 Year Project' has begun!

References

Asahi Shimbun, various issues.

Birchall, Jonathan (2000) *Ultra Nippon: How Japan Reinvented Football*, London: Headline Publishing Company.

Chon, Kaye *et al.* (eds) (2000) *Japanese Tourists: Socio-economic, Marketing and Psychological Analysis*, New York: Haworth Press.

Clarke, John *et al.* (1976) 'Subcultures, cultures and class', in Stuart Hall and Tony Jefferson (eds) *Resistance through Rituals: Youth Subcultures in Post-war Britain*, London: Routledge, pp. 9–74.

Cohen, Stanley (1973) *Folk Devils and Moral Panics: The Creation of the Mods and Rockers*, St Albans: Paladin.

Crazy Calls and Todoroki Yukio (eds) (1994) *The Red Book: Tatakau Rezzu 12-banme no senshutachi* [The Red Book: The fighting twelfth players of The Reds], Tokyo: Daiei Shuppan.

Dunning, Eric, Murphy, Patrick and Williams, John (eds) (1988) *The Roots of Football Hooliganism: An Historical and Sociological Study*, London: Routledge and Kegan Paul.

Giulianotti, Richard (1999) *Football: A Sociology of the Global Game*, Oxford: Polity Press.

Marsh, Peter (1978) *Aggro: The Illusion of Violence*, London: Dent.

Marsh, Peter, Rosser, Elizabeth and Harré, Rom (1978) *The Rules of Disorder*, London: Routledge and Kegan Paul.

Murphy, Patrick, Williams, John and Dunning, Eric (eds) (1990) *Football on Trial: Spectator Violence and Development in the Football World*, London: Routledge.

Ogasawara Hiroki (1998) 'Bunka seiji ni okeru ātikyurēshon' [Articulation in cultural politics], *Gendai Shisō* [Revue de la pensée d'aujourd'hui], 26/4, pp. 250–293.

Ōsumi Yoshiyuki (1998) *Urawa Rezzu no kōfuku* [The happiness of Urawa Reds], Tokyo: Asupekuto.

Robson, Garry (2000) *'No one likes us, we don't care': The Myth and the Reality of Millwall Fandom*, Oxford: Berg.

Saitama Shimbun, *MDP* Editorial Office (1998) *Reddo Daiyamonzu ofisharu matchi dē puroguramu* [Red Diamonds official match day program], Vols 119, 120.

Seio Jun (2001) *Urawa Rezzu ga yamerarenai* [Can't stop being Urawa Reds], Saitama: Land Garage.

Shimizu Satoshi (2000) 'Sapōtā-sono hyōshō to kioku, soshite ima tsukurarete iku mono toshite' [Representations and memories of the supporters], *Gendai Supōtsu Hyōron*, 3: 75–90.

Shimizu Satoshi and Iida Yoshiaki (1999) 'Puro sakkā chiimu to shimin to no kankei ni kansuru kenkyū' [Study of the relationship between professional soccer team and the people], *Purofesshonaru Supōtsu Kenkyū Yosei Hōkokusho*, 2: 31–49.

Taylor, Ian (1982) 'On the sports violence question: soccer hooliganism revisited', in Jennifer Hargreaves (ed.), *Sport, Culture and Ideology*, London: Routledge and Kegan Paul, pp. 152–196.

Toyota Mitsuho (2000) *Seikan: Urawa Rezzu J2 senki* [Comeback: tales from the Urawa Reds in the second division], Tokyo: Magajin Hausu.

Watanabe Jun (2000) *Aidentiti no ongaku: media, wakamono, popyurā bunka* [Music as identity: media, youth, popular culture], Kyoto: Sekai Shisō Sha.

Williams, John, Dunning, Eric and Murphy, Patrick (eds) (1984) *Hooligans Abroad: The Behaviour and Control of English Fans in Continental Europe*, London: Routledge and Kegan Paul.

Yamanaka Ichirō (2000) *Urawa Rezzu wa makenai: We Are the Reds!* [Urawa Reds never lose: we are the Reds!], Tokyo: The Massada.

Yamaoka Junichirō (1998) *Rezzu to Urawa: junai sakkā monogatari* [The Reds and Urawa: a story of pure soccer love], Saitama: Reddo Daiyamonzu Kōenkai.

Yoshizawa Kōichi (ed.) (1998) *Bokutachi no wārudo kappu. Sapōtā ga mita! Furansu e no atsuki kiseki* [Our World Cup as seen by supporters. Exciting traces on the way to France], Tokyo: Kōbunsha.

10 Another kick-off

The 2002 World Cup and soccer voluntary groups as a new social movement

Yamashita Takayuki and Saka Natsuko

> Today's social movements contain marginal countercultures and small sects whose goal is the development of the expressive solidarity of the group, but there is also a deeper commitment to the recognition that personal needs are the path to changing the world and to seeking meaningful alternatives.
>
> (Melucci, 1989, p. 49)

Introduction

The FIFA 2002 World Cup is of major importance for the standing of the host nations, Japan and Korea, in world football, as well as for their bilateral political relationships and domestic economies. At the same time, the social significance of this global sport event is high on the agenda in both countries. We will focus on the social phenomenon of Japan's hosting the World Cup in the light of its global, local and *glocalised* dimensions. As we see it the World Cup can be approached on three social levels: first, on the level of globalisation; second, on the level of regional politics, especially under the influence of the particular nature of the Japanese–Korean past; and third, on the level of Japanese society and culture, in relation to its domestic responses to the changes occurring on a global level. In effect, these three levels intersect and are closely interwoven, and we believe that these relationships are manifested in a new kind of social movement. All over Japan, and particularly in the regions around designated 2002 venues, sport enthusiasts, football lovers and concerned local citizens have established voluntary groups related to the 2002 World Cup. It is our view that these voluntary groups constitute a new social movement that represents local, regional and global influences stemming from the World Cup.

Two of these voluntary groups are discussed in detail later in this chapter. With reference to the work of Alberto Melucci (1989) and Ernesto Laclau and Chantal Mouffe (1985) we will first argue why voluntary groups associated with soccer deserve to be called a social movement. The next section of the chapter discusses the specific social conjuncture that has brought about the existence of these voluntary groups in Japan. Finally, in outlining some case studies, we will demonstrate their key defining features, the way they are formed, and their various human, material and ideal resources. However, in the same way as the 2002 World Cup is a social phenomenon in process, this is research in progress. Our conclusions are provisional; as the World Cup develops so too does the formation of the groups that relate to the event. However, we hope to provide evidence that the volunteer movement in Japan has significance for wider society as much as for the world of sport.

Voluntary activities as a new social movement

When Japan's professional soccer league, the J.League, was established in 1993, numerous voluntary groups were formed or appeared in connection with it. While regular fan clubs always had been evident, the new soccer supporter groups displayed features that exceeded the traditional realms of cheering and participating in sports-related activities. The opening of public forums or holding of symposiums, where professionals as well as laymen were invited to discuss local and national soccer issues, and to express or declare their own opinions, marked them out as novel in the Japanese context. Sometimes, they also cooperated with environmental groups or other social support networks. Another novelty was the way the individuals became involved. Traditionally, the formation of social groups relied on existing networks of social relationships, such as blood ties, territorial bonds or school affiliation. In the case of the groups we have studied, however, participation seems to be based more on a common intellectual outlook, which is constantly being reconstructed through a variety of negotiated interactions. Internet homepages offer a good insight into this particular outlook, which is also represented by the modes of action of members in relation to various events.

These characteristics of football supporter behaviour in Japan are manifested in the groups' organisational form. Members constantly negotiate and influence each other via the Internet to assess resources and surroundings as well as to construct plans or clarify objectives. These processes are not necessarily instrumental in accomplishing the common goals of the groups, but such reflective interaction is a vital aspect of them. As Melucci (1989) indicates, these collective activities indeed contain a self-referential character. While no one will argue against the distinctiveness of these features, it could be claimed that these collective activities merely arise from their members' needs, for example, to create emotional relationships in a convivial environment. However, at the same time we argue that they can also be seen as symptoms of a new type of social movement.

Superficially, these voluntary activities have little to do with politics. They are 'at one and the same time prior to and beyond politics. They are pre-political because they are rooted in everyday life experiences; and meta-political because political forces can never represent them completely' (Melucci, 1989, p. 72). However, they also contain political potentialities, because, as he argues, the basis of social conflict in contemporary society has shifted towards 'the production of meaning'. New forms of subordination have occurred through people's 'incorporation into a multitude of other social relations: culture, free time, illness, education, sex and even death' (Laclau and Mouffe, 1985, p. 161). In common with these authors, we argue that, instead of visible institutional political activities, the core of contemporary politics in Japan is potentially situated in, and based on, an area of invisible meaning, especially the production of alternative meanings and the negotiation of meanings in the network of life-worlds. All areas in a life-world 'can be expressed as resistance against the new forms of subordination, and this from within the very heart of the new society' (ibid.). As Melucci (1989) argues, in this situation, 'the challenge manifests itself by the reversing of the cultural codes'. Therefore, the emergence of a new style of expression, a new way of acting, and the possible generation of new meanings, which voluntary soccer activities clearly represent, are highly political in the environment of contemporary Japanese society. Soccer support groups are thus comparable to voluntary associations concerned with gender issues or the protection of the environment, which are understood as more overtly political. Laclau and Mouffe emphasise the new social movements for 'the novel role they play in articulating that rapid diffusion of social conflictuality to more and more numerous relationships which is characteristic today of advanced industrial society' (1985, pp. 159–160). In addition, they share the common interest of putting forth problems of privately or locally limited concern in the eyes of the public. Due to their role in the construction of the 'public sphere', voluntary groups can overcome essential differences with other social movements, and their members can become empowered to relate to each other on an equal footing. The public sphere is most evident at the local level, from where groups expand their communication network to the national.

The J.League, for example, was inaugurated as a franchise system based on the 'hometown' concept. Therefore supporter groups of particular club teams were exclusively formed on the local level, following the enfranchisement system. While this is a very specific explanation of the emergence of soccer supporter groups, socio-economist Saitō Hideharu (1998) offers an important, more general reason. He states, and we agree, that conditions in all areas of contemporary life exhibit competing, and sometimes contradictory, tendencies. Global mass media images and markets comprise a common standardising code for consumers all over the world. At the same time, however, multiple autonomous decision-making actors arise in each society who will tend to form a new social order based on needs derived from their own life-worlds. Saitō suggests that the relative decline of social control by the state and the globalisation of markets induce the rise of various kinds of social movements in the field of civil society. As states, which have controlled and legitimised dominant meanings, gradually lose some of their authority, global, political and economic agents become more central to actual decision-making instead and the relative autonomy of life-worlds in some areas increases.

Voluntary soccer groups seem to be situated on just such tendencies or social fault lines. They have the potential to construct a new public sphere as it arises out of local life-worlds, in which the experiences and feelings of ordinary people enter into negotiation with the logic of globalising capitalism, and in this case the global political economy of sport. To repeat, the emphasis we place on these voluntary groups does not focus simply on their effects, or the results they do or do not achieve, but rather on the processes by which they operate, and the kinds of new cultural practices, forms of relationships, and alternative perceptions, they create in contemporary Japan.

The traditional Japanese social system of sports and soccer voluntary groups

The emergence of the soccer voluntary groups must be seen in the light of the changes Japanese society and sport in Japan have undergone over the past two decades. Traditionally, sport and physical exercises were primarily seen as part of the education system; even non-school sport heavily relied on this perception. Starting in the 1980s, we can observe a major transformation of the institution of sport. The 'reversal of the situation', as a similar process in France was dubbed by Jacques Defrance and Christian Pociello (1993), was triggered by the shift towards a new market liberalism in political and economic decision-making and public policy.

Two further factors in particular encouraged change: an apparent shift in people's social consciousness, and the development of a new set of sports policies for the mass of the Japanese people. The need felt for greater involvement in volunteer activities has been widely registered in Japan recently. A public opinion survey published by the Japanese Cabinet Office illustrated this change in people's consciousness of life (Prime Minister's Office, 1999). According to the results of the survey, by the late 1990s Japanese people put much greater importance for their future on 'spiritual richness' rather than on 'material affluence'. Affluence had retained a higher position in Japanese people's consciousness for most of the years after World War II. This shift in consciousness started a little before the 1980s, that is ten years after Japanese society had achieved some degree of affluence following the rapid economic growth of the late 1950s and 1960s. Even after the 1990s, when the Japanese economy was hit by a decade of negative growth, this tendency continued to be recorded in similar surveys. Melucci explains this phenomenon more generally as a by-product of post-material society:

> [When] the primary needs of the population are to a large extent satisfied, freedom from needs is being replaced by freedom of needs. Awareness grows that needs are subject to choices and are not mere necessities imposed by want. The cultural dimension of needs supersedes their material determination and opens up new unexplored territory.
>
> (1989, p. 177)

In addition to the shift in social consciousness towards 'spiritual richness', which tends to provide some support for Melucci's argument, a set of policy changes contributed to the transformation of sport in Japan. In the 1970s, the government set out a 'policy for community sport' in order to promote sport in residential areas. This orientation towards 'Sports for All' was supposed to be based on local communities. As such, it necessitated the enhancement of the then insufficient social capital for sports based in local communities. Under this policy, numerous sports clubs came into existence such as the popularly called 'mamas' volleyball', 'mamas' tennis', and 'grassroots baseball' clubs at the community level. However this also brought about, at the same time, the appearance of a new markct.

In the 1980s the former Ministry of International Trade and Industry (MITI) developed a new 'policy for the sports industry'. In order to cope with the new orientation of the economic system towards a service-oriented economy, the expansion of domestic consumption, and to make up for the hollowing out of the domestic industry caused by the transfer of the national production base overseas, MITI devised a scheme to incorporate the sports sector into the domestic market's future mainstream industrial sector. This policy reflected the transformation of the Japanese economic strategy *vis-à-vis* the twenty-first century. Following this policy shift, all kinds of companies rushed into the new market. While no more than 200 commercial sport clubs were in operation before the mid-1980s, the same number of new establishments opened their doors annually thereafter (Yamashita and Taneda, 1997). These companies adapted to the needs of their members, who effectively were customers, and most of them were women. The new core clients led to the creation of a new image of sports. The mass media communicated the soft, graceful, and fashionable, nature of sport, which differed considerably from the traditional image of sports as a form of masculine achievement.

The changing social consciousness and the creation of the new images of sports by the sport industry formed an antagonistic alliance against the traditional sport system. It consisted of the same dualism between privately organised leisure and the supply of the sports industry, as was described by Defrance and Pociello in their study of French sport. The new orientation clearly continued in people's expectations of, and sympathy with, the J.League and in their increasing need for voluntary activism. Consequently, the emergence of soccer volunteer groups, related to both the J.League teams and the 2002 World Cup, can be seen as expressions of these changes in social conditions and awareness.

The emergence of soccer voluntary groups

From its beginning, the J.League has played the role of a cultural change agent because its main idea challenged the traditional Japanese sports system and aimed to replace it with a new system and a new image. The J.League committee members declared their ideas in their statement of goals (or mission statement) entitled the 'J.League Mission' published in 1993. 'The Mission' had its origins in thinking critically about the traditional Japanese system. In the past, sport in Japan was positioned as a part of physical education or fitness activity in schools, or else as a corporate employee welfare and fitness activity. Athletes were fostered under these separate systems, but there was no environment for continuing sport on a lifelong basis. Sport had not become a full part of people's everyday life. The J.League, upon its foundation, made it its mission to establish such an environment in which anyone could enjoy sports appropriate to their age, physical condition, ability and personal goals. The J.League believed that this broader base would also foster many more outstanding athletes (J.League homepage).

The alternative model the J.League referred to was based on the European system, where sports clubs are open to anyone in the community who wishes to participate. The main idea pervading 'The Mission' was the hometown concept. The 'J.League Mission' stated that each club 'must cooperate in sports activities conducted in the area and grow as a club that takes part in activities in the community and promotes sports in the region'.

The message that the 'J.League promotes the establishment of community-based sports clubs under the slogan "The J.League Sports Community for All"' ('The Mission') resonated well with 'the reversal of the situation' Japan had experienced in the field of sports since the 1980s. The inauguration of the new professional football league meant not only the mere appearance of a new commercial sport. It also acted on people at a cultural level. Some journalists and sport critics even described professional football as a new social, rather than merely sporting, phenomenon.

According to its mission statement, various criteria had to be met for the establishment of each team (for full details, see Horne and Bleakley, p. 95 this volume). One of the most important conditions was that of 'hometownship'. Each club had to designate 'a particular locality' as its 'hometown'. Later, after the J.League had implemented a two-division system in 1999, J2 teams were also expected to accept the participation of volunteers in team management. This was not just a requirement of the 'J.League Mission' but as our interviews with some J2 division team managers suggest, it was indispensable in financial terms as well. Hence, volunteers were taken seriously as a local support resource for the teams. Simply put, voluntary activities themselves became one of the constituent factors of the J.League's accomplishment of the objectives laid out in its mission statement as well as the management of teams and holding of games. This central positioning of volunteers served to increase their motivation, and they continued to come, on their own initiative, to investigate any conditions surrounding the J.League that obstructed its development in line with 'The Mission'. 'The Mission', in this way, was both a source of motivation and an asset for the groups. Furthermore, it denoted a common reference point, or point of recognition. It signalled what members or voluntary support groups were expected to do, and as a commonly shared reference frame it enabled them to communicate and cooperate.

The success of 'The Mission' has been mirrored in recent new sports policies and social policies that promote volunteerism. Exhibiting very similar tendencies, these policies have enhanced the value of voluntary participation further. As a consequence, they have retrospectively legitimised the concept of the 'J.League Mission' which is now a mainstream ideal for the reconstruction of the entire field of Japanese sports.

For the sake of completeness, one additional influence on football voluntarism deserves mentioning: the vigour of the voluntary activities seen (and displayed) during the French World Cup in 1998 which therefore acquired the label, 'The Volunteers' World Cup'. This made a strong impression on Japanese supporters who visited France at that time. According to survey research by the Japan Organizing Committee for the FIFA World Cup Korea/Japan (JAWOC), following the 1998 World Cup Japanese people's interest in the 2002 World Cup showed a marked increase. Some respondents answered that they wanted to go to events related to soccer and wished to be involved with voluntary management activities. One supporter explicitly wrote in his private web page, 'Looking at the activities of the French volunteers, I also wanted to be a volunteer in return in a venue city for the 2002 World Cup.'

The present state of soccer voluntary groups

The rest of the chapter deals with our case studies. The voluntary groups or activities, which we have already researched, can be divided into roughly two types depending on the mode of their local affiliation. The Japan Supporters Association (see homepage) and 'Salon 2002' (see homepage) represent non-local types, while 'Alliance 2002' and 'Trinista' are locally based groups.

'Salon 2002' evolved out of one particular research group of the Japan Football Association Science and Research Committee. This research group was established in 1997 as a loose information exchange that appealed not only to researchers, but also to a broad range of individuals with a common 'ambition'. In their own words:

> Salon 2002 is a loose network of people sharing the same 'mind'. Anyone can become a 'member' as long as he or she consents to the 'mind' of Salon 2002. However, a member not only plans to 'take' from Salon 2002, but also always considers what a member can actually 'give' to society, and it is 'give and take' that is the premise of our existence.
>
> (Salon 2002 homepage)

Meetings, which are defined as a 'place of information exchange', or 'a place of encounter with other people', are held once a month. One member circulates the topic of a particular meeting. Research results and reports, but also problems and projects are freely presented. The monthly meeting is also a place for 'Self-PR of a subject donor'. Some of the recent themes presented at monthly meetings have been as follows:

A senior high school teacher/chairman of DUO League: *Does youth soccer change? The history of the DUO League, a view of the Tokyo youth league, and the 'clubizement' of a school athletic club* (N.B. the 'DUO League' attempts to blend school football with local club football.)
A representative of Tokyo TV: *How TV contributes to the exploitation of soccer fans*
Clubhouse Co-operation: *Usage of the homepage of Salon 2002*
FUTSAL (Mini-Soccer) Project: *Do we need a FUTSAL league? Sport in the 21st century, and the present state of the organization of the game*
A photographer: *Dynamo: Football under socialist government*
A university lecturer: *What makes a sports event successful?*
The Ministry of Education (now The Ministry of Education, Culture, Sports, Science and Technology) Sports Advancement Lottery Section: *On the soccer lottery (part 3)*

Members of Salon 2002 seem to agree with the J.League's conception of sport. On the basis of the J.League Mission, they have found an open space where meanings of and about soccer are interpreted and exchanged in an atmosphere of mutual negotiation. In this sphere, all members are on an equal footing. Such a highly reflective and constitutional group poses an important alternative to the traditional way of group order in Japanese society. However, who is in the position to participate in the discussions within this public sphere? We found out that in this case most of the members are well-educated university graduates who belong to the higher social strata (see Table 10.1). As their agenda embraces a broader range of soccer issues, this higher educational background might be seen as an essential requirement for the extension of their intellectual framework. How people who do not command a comparable level of formal academic education deal with these debates is of crucial significance for assessing the importance of this group. While its main function of transmitting alternative opinions from the centre out to various locally based groups cannot be underestimated, also of major importance is the role Salon 2002 plays in the establishment of a continuous negotiation process about meanings. We argue that these may ultimately allow many different kinds of people to construct and extend their own cognitive frameworks. We will return to this issue in the conclusion. For the time being, we can see the seeds of an alternative civil society in Japan in the work of Salon 2002.

Table 10.1 Occupational background of 'Salon 2002' members, 2000

Occupation	Number	Percentage
Football business (including J.League)	21	16.5
University professor	19	15.0
Small and medium-size company	16	12.6
Mass media	13	10.2
Large manufacturer	11	8.6
Government employee	8	6.3
Graduate student	6	4.7
Teacher	5	3.9
Sports business	5	3.9
Scientist in company institution	4	3.2
Self-employed businessman	4	3.2
Student	3	2.4
Medical and other health services	2	1.5
Housewife	2	1.5
Unknown	8	6.3
Total	127	100.0

Starting soccer from barren land: the case of the 2002 World Cup venue cities, Niigata and Oita

As case studies of locally based volunteer groups we selected organisations in Niigata and Oita City. We decided on these cities because both of them were hosting games in the 2002 World Cup finals. In addition, until recently, soccer has not been very popular in either city, and the traditional system of delivering and relating to sports clubs has remained strong.

Niigata prefecture is situated in the centre of Japan and Niigata City is the prefectural capital. The city is home to half a million people. The main industry is agriculture, especially rice production. Niigata City is about two hours from Tokyo by *shinkansen* ('bullet train'), and in cultural terms it is strongly influenced by the capital city. In order to increase awareness of the World Cup, the local government and business circles joined forces and established a professional soccer team, Albirex, in 1997, by merging some local amateur teams. Simultaneously with the establishment of Albirex, that, at the time of writing (October 2001) was playing in the J.League 2nd Division, local soccer fans organised the volunteer group 'Spirit of Niigata'. This group initiated the foundation of 'Alliance 2002' which unified five other supporters' groups. The name describes the alliance between groups. In their own words, 'Alliance 2002 is a movement that has been organized to raise enthusiasm for the World Cup among people in Niigata through grassroots activities. We will discuss and hold lectures on the topic of soccer as culture' (see Alliance 2002 homepage).

Alliance 2002 comprises five main divisions and a 'headquarters' section, which chiefly manages the activities of Alliance 2002. Leadership of the 'headquarters' is not fixed with a permanent base but decided by roundtable discussion. 'Spirit of Niigata' is, as we have mentioned, a volunteer group to support Albirex, and members usually help out with management and administration issues when Albirex has a home game, or with other club events. Activities extend also to co-operation with very different volunteer groups, for example, by holding football games for the physically and mentally challenged. 'Ultra Niigata' is a different kind of supporters' group. Their primary concern is giving support to the national team and another local soccer team, Niigata Shūyūkai ('Niigata Soccer Friend Club') that plays in the Amateur Football League. 'Mokuhachi' ('Thursday 8 o'clock') is a 'mini-soccer' club that meets every Thursday at 8 p.m. for a game of '*futsal*'. Membership is not fixed. Participants pay 500 yen each for the use of the pitch. This income forms half of Alliance's annual revenue (which is, therefore, on an annual basis, approximately 1,000,000 yen).

'Salon 2002 in Niigata' was established using 'Salon 2002' in Tokyo as the model. In a similar way to the metropolitan model, 'Salon 2002 in Niigata' offers lectures and events on soccer and the World Cup in particular to the broader public. Frequently, both 'Salon 2002' groups co-operate in holding symposiums or inviting joint lecturers. On these occasions, they also invite other voluntary groups, soccer players and managers to attend. Once a month, they hold an open seminar, which is sponsored by Alliance 2002. Anyone paying the admission fee of 1,000 yen per event can participate. The following list covers some recent monthly lecture titles and panelists:

> The head of 2002 World Cup Niigata Preparatory Committee: *What do we do as venue city citizens and how do we do it?*
> A former North-Korean national team player, currently playing with a soccer team of North Koreans residing in Japan: *North Koreans and soccer in Japanese society*
> Members of Palrabox, a soccer team for the physically and mentally challenged: *The challenges of the challenged people's soccer team 'Palrabox'*
> Members of Salon 2002: *Grass-roots movements at the crossroads*
> A co-ordinator of sandlot soccer: *Give out bills in the stadium! Sandlot soccer as the frontier of the soccer community*
> Niigata Nippō (Newspaper), FM-Shibata (Radio), and TV-Niigata: *The present and future of Niigata soccer in the media*

Nearly 80 per cent of 'Alliance 2002' members are residents who were born and grew up in Niigata and surrounding districts, but most of the 'headquarters' members consist of businessmen transferred from other areas. Most seem to be middle management level and all are university graduates, some holding doctorates. Representative of this type is one of our interviewees, Mr K., who works for a national finance company as a section head. A 'leader' in 'headquarters', Mr K. said of himself and 'Alliance 2002':

I don't want to be a mere 'behind the goal' fan, but a supporter who plays and enjoys soccer as sporting culture. We actively participate in it. And I wish such concepts and practices to establish roots in Niigata after the World Cup, even if my company moves me to another prefecture.

He also pointed out that as most members of Alliance 2002 had experience of voluntary work in managing soccer conventions, they have a reasonable amount of know-how. Yet the Niigata 2002 Venue Organisation seems unwilling to accept these movements and groups. There continues to be disagreement about the role of volunteers. The organisers seem to want volunteers just to enliven and help in subsidiary work for the World Cup. They do not want these voluntary groups getting involved in management itself. This disagreement is indicative of a conflict deriving from differing perspectives about volunteers' roles, and it also seems to reflect the wider contrast between the way traditional Japanese sports systems have operated and alternative ideas, that have emerged in the past decade.

Simultaneously we foresee another potential conflict arising from the group structure itself. Most of 'headquarters' declare sympathy with the basic concept of 'The J.League Sports Community for All'. However, not all the members hold this concept in common. Gaps are widening between two factions, which are related to two types of supplementary network. One group, based on a local residents' network, appears to regard human bonding, local pride and support for the local team as the sole basis for participation as a venue city in the World Cup. Members are particularly proud of this once in a lifetime chance for Niigata City to appear on the world's (media) stage, which is usually occupied by Japan's mega-cities, Tokyo and Osaka. Being so directly involved in such an event provides most of their motivation. In contrast, 'headquarters' members, who mostly originate from other areas of Japan, seem to pursue a conception of soccer volunteering which has a wider meaning. In terms of uniting traits, both supplementary networks differ from other groups, so that both are 'outsiders' from a traditional viewpoint on Japanese voluntary associations.

At the same time, Alliance 2002 confronts the threat of internal division that Mr K. at 'headquarters' has recognised. In order to maintain a common base, and to promote common concepts, they stage monthly meetings or symposiums. In addition, web pages are used in order to express and explain their ideas. Communication and the exchange of opinions function as a kind of education for all members, including 'headquarters'. However, as in most voluntary groups, members' needs vary and due to their heterogeneity, they are difficult to satisfy. A viable solution to this problem is continuous negotiation among the parties. Such a process of negotiation is very important for the social integration of the group on an instrumental level, and on a wider level to construct multiple power relationships in a nascent, more democratic, civil society. To construct such a space, which allows for the negotiation of opinions on the basis of mutual trust, is the only way to enable multiplicity and co-operation simultaneously. In this sense Alliance 2002 has important cultural and, at the same time, political implications. In the case of Niigata, the conceptual problem is likely to become more apparent after the 2002 World Cup, when local interest and voluntary motivation possibly will decrease.

Oita City, our second case study, is the Japanese World Cup venue closest to Korea. Located in mid-Kyūshū, Oita will be the only prefecture on the southern main island of Japan to host matches during the 2002 World Cup. Despite being capital of Oita prefecture, and having a population of 600,000 (including nearby Beppu), Oita is more rural and provincial than Niigata because of the long distance, both geographically and culturally, from other big cities. Similar to Niigata, football has never had a huge following in this part of Japan. In order to become considered as a venue city of the World Cup finals, a professional soccer team had to be established. Unlike Niigata Albirex, Oita Trinita was built from virtually nothing in 1994. It was only in 1999 that Trinita was successfully turned from a local amateur club into a professional J.League team, which is currently playing in the J.League 2nd Division. According to club sources, 'Oita Trinita' stands for the trinity of sponsors from the business world, local administration, and prefectural citizens.

According to the information leaflet Oita City prepared about the World Cup, 'Oita Trinita have total prefectural support, since not only the prefecture of Oita but also enterprises, companies, and all the inhabitants support it.' Therefore it seems that the 'local' emphasis weighs heavily in Oita City. One staff member of the World Cup promotion division of the local government said in an interview with us that Oita put importance on the linkage between the local and the global: 'We didn't place emphasis on Japanese nationality, because the highlighting of nationality would fade our local colour. We seek to emphasise the global as well as the local.'

Similar to the official promotion line, the consciousness of voluntary soccer supporter groups in Oita has been deeply influenced by this particular aspect of 'local belongingness'. Differing from Niigata, there are only a few independent voluntary groups in Oita. They are aware of each other, but hardly communicate. Cheering on Oita Trinita is at the core of the groups' activities, although some members seem to help with management. However, while soccer volunteers in Oita seem to know about the 'J.League Mission', we could not detect similar significant group activities as in the case of Alliance 2002.

The name of Oita Trinita's official supporters' group, 'Trinista', has its origin in 'Shirashinken (local dialect for 'do your best') Oita Trinita'. The group is outstanding among Oita's voluntary groups, because it is widely accepted to be the representative organ of voluntary supporter groups in the area. Although Trinista is primarily dedicated to cheering on the home team, the group conducts additional activities, such as holding study meetings (called Oita Futcom) and managing a web site. One branch of it, which is named the Minami-Toriyama Research Institution, is in charge of putting forward opinion statements. On this web site, all contributions from supporters, as well as from management, are displayed. Compared with their enthusiasm for cheering, general discussions about soccer seem to be less energetic. The central person in Trinista is Mr M., who is also the key actor in the voluntary supporters' movements in Oita. He works at a technical college, where he coaches the soccer club. Having been on the executive staff of Oita Football Association and an advisor to Trinista, Mr M. is also affiliated to other sports-centred groups as well as being close to other soccer supporter groups and individuals.

Mr M.'s supplementary member network is typical of Oita because it hardly differs from a traditional Japanese one that relies on a local human network. In the case of Mr M., the networks often overlap. Traditional networks and the football supporter volunteers do not necessarily share the same viewpoints. But as both are based on the feature of locality, no conflict endangers the traditional order. Furthermore, members of the volunteer groups seem to place great importance on constructing human bonds and fostering local relationships. These needs for local belonging connect with cheering on the local team and establishing the conditions for participating in hosting World Cup matches in their city. We found that most of the voluntary groups are equipped with supplementary networks that are based on locality. Of course, such kinds of motivation were also observed in Niigata. However, the big difference is that in Niigata, the leaders of 'headquarters' did not come from the local network but had become involved because of their sympathy with the J.League ideals.

We believe this difference in supplementary networks is responsible for the difference in range and level of their activities. Similarly, the social background of members is of great importance in influencing what kind of members join. As Melucci has argued, the leading actors in the new social movements are often members of the 'new middle class', or 'human capital class'. Such people 'work in the advanced information based technological sectors, human service professions and the public sector and have achieved a high educational status and enjoy relative economic security' or are 'marginally affluent' such as students or middle-class housewives (Melucci, 1989, pp. 52–53). The main reason why they tend to lead such voluntary groups would appear to be because of their command over sufficient intellectual resources that enable them to locate specific issues within a wider social context.

In addition to their wider cognitive frame of reference, they are in an advantageous position because they also have access to resources or tools, such as computers, and know how to use them. All 'headquarters' members seem to match this type which explains why, for them, a broader frame of action becomes possible to conceive. On the other hand, these volunteers consistently are confronted with the specific problem of having to co-ordinate all the members' diverse needs. In the case of Oita, the problem seems to be the reverse, as most of the volunteer activities tend to be limited to cheering on their own hometown club. Nonetheless, we expect the Oita voluntary group to continue well after the 2002 World Cup. This forecast is based on the simple fact that the activism there is more firmly rooted in the local, than in Niigata.

Conclusion

In this chapter, we have argued that soccer voluntary groups in Japan bear the seeds of change and the potential signs of a new social movement. But numerous impediments, which are mainly related to gaps in members' perceptions of their own potential, have still to be overcome. These gaps cover a wide range of issues, including the meaning of volunteer activities, the ability to assess circumstances and resources, and the capacity to deal with new media and its implications. We predict a further widening of these gaps after the 2002 World Cup when the core feature of reference, the World Cup finals, are over and latent problems and difficulties are likely to materialise. This does not necessarily mean that conflict will inevitably occur, but it is based on the assumption that most groups will restrict their activities to entertainment and cheering on the local team.

We believe these two types of volunteer groups and their respective problems extend to other areas as well. At the core of these problems is the question of how to satisfy varying needs while having to produce integration at the same time. Therefore, a new form and style of activism to create alternative meanings that fulfil variant expectations and desires are needed. Of fundamental importance is the installation of a permanent negotiation process that involves all members, and thus the construction of a reflective and constitutive public sphere where these discussions can take place. This strategy is not only required in order to integrate the diversity of needs and motivations that members bring together. The process itself is significant, probably even much more important than the effects or results of volunteering activities, because it represents new meanings and offers an alternative method of group organisation. As Melucci (1989, p. 60) also stated: 'The form of the movement is itself a message, a symbolic challenge to the dominant (cultural) codes.' This style of voluntary group organisation, with its emphasis on negotiation of meaning, acknowledgement of other opinions and mutual empathy, may have a synergetic influence on any voluntary group, even if it targets completely different issues from soccer or even sport. Therefore, we argue that the football supporter volunteer groups, which were created out of conviviality, represent a new type of social movement, and even if they seem to be pre- and meta-political in nature, they nonetheless potentially have great political significance in Japan.

References

Alliance 2002 (homepage): <http://www02.u-page.so-net.ne.jp/qa2/tag/HOMEPAGE.html.> (Accessed).

Defrance, Jacques and Pociello, Christian (1993) 'Structure and evolution of the field of sports in France (1960–1990)', *International Review for Sociology of Sport*, 28, 1: 1–21.

Japan Organizing Committee for the 2002 FIFA World Cup Korea/ Japan (JAWOC homepage): <http://www.jawoc.or.jp/index_e.htm.> (Accessed).

Japan Professional Football League (J.League homepage): <http://www.j-league.or.jp> (Accessed).

Japan Supporters Association (homepage): <http://www.jsa-npo.or.jp/.> (Accessed).

Laclau, Ernesto and Mouffe, Chantal (1985) *Hegemony and Socialist Strategy: Towards Radical Democratic Politics*, London: Verso.

Melucci, Alberto (1989) *Nomads of the Present: Social Movements and Individual Needs in Contemporary Society*, London: Hutchinson Radius.

Oita Trinita Supporters Club Trinista (homepage): <http://www.coara.or.jp/~dkslp/trinista/.> (Accessed).

Prime Minister's Office, Public Relation's Office, Minister's Secretariat (1999) *'Quality of life' Opinion Poll*, Tokyo.

Saitō Hideharu (1998) *Kokka o koeru shimin shakai* [Civil society beyond the state], Tokyo: Gendai Kikakushitsu.

Salon2002 (homepage): <http://www.salon2002.net/.> (Accessed).

Yamashita Takayuki and Taneda Yutaka (1997), 'Strategy of sports and fitness business', *The Ritsumeikan Business Review*, 35.

11 The political economy of the World Cup in South Korea

Ahn Min-Seok

Introduction

Throughout the 1980s the 1988 Summer Olympic Games held in Seoul, South Korea, exerted a deep and lasting impact on state and society. The Games played a complementary and supportive role to the major political and economic events taking place there. Internationally, the Games were able to enhance Korean national prestige because they gave the country an attractive appearance through television footage of a scrubbed-clean capital city full of bustling people. Domestically, the Games stimulated many social and cultural changes for South Korea. The country became more culturally open to the West than ever before: nowadays finding a Western-style fast food restaurant in South Korea is no challenging task. Another important change is represented by the massification of sports: the ideology of the Olympics has successfully permeated into Korean society, resulting in the increase in various new sporting and leisure activities.

Just as it is not possible to fully explain South Korean society of the 1980s without referring to the 1988 Olympic Games, in a similar vein, the 2002 World Cup currently has become a major keyword. At the turning point of a new century, the World Cup has replaced the Olympics in South Korea. Thus, it is the right time to analyse the political economy of the World Cup from a critical perspective. This chapter assumes that there are political, economic, and socio-cultural implications and consequences resulting from the World Cup. The study has two main aims: first, it investigates, describes, and discusses the way the interests and values of the Korean state are being permeated through the build-up to the World Cup; and, second, it identifies, assesses, and interprets the implications of co-hosting the World Cup for Korean civil society.

This study applies immanent critique as its main methodological approach. Immanent critique is a method that seeks to evaluate and judge the existing social conditions and arrangements of a social formation by that formation's own internal values and self-espoused ideological claims, rather than by a set of ethical values imposed from the outside. Its aim, then, is to empirically probe whether a given social formation can justify the claims it makes about itself and to identify existing internal tensions with the potential for change (Sage, 1996). The study also employs Cultural Studies as a descriptive/sensitising framework for grounding and informing the descriptions and interpretations of the preparations for the 2002 World Cup. In order to locate our understanding of pre-2002 Korean society more effectively, a brief theoretical discussion about the methodological approach follows. Next we briefly outline developments in Korean society since the Japanese annexation ended in 1945. Then the chapter outlines the relationship between sport and the state in Korea. Finally, the chapter considers the relationship of Korean civil society to the 2002 World Cup.

Theoretical discussion

In considering the significance of the political economy of the 2002 World Cup in South Korea, this study is concerned with understanding the way in which sports, as cultural formations, may be connected to social domination and subordination. Therefore, the study proposes to explore the relationship between sport, as a cultural formation, and power. Since Bob Hollands' suggestive paper published in 1984, one of the leading perspectives with which to look at this relationship has been Cultural Studies. This approach is marked by a more positive approach to the products of mass culture than conventional critical theory and, also by the search to understand the meaning and place assigned to popular culture in the experience of particular groups in society especially the young, the working class, ethnic minorities and other marginalised social groups. Cultural Studies seeks also to explain how mass culture plays a part in integrating and subordinating potentially deviant or oppositional elements in society by utilising the concept of hegemony, derived from Gramsci's writings (1971).

Cultural Studies has advanced the study of sport through the conceptualisation of sport as a cultural form by demystifying commonsensical approaches to sport as natural, apolitical, and a set of social practices conceived of as set apart from society (Hollands, 1984). It has illuminated the inadequacies of mechanistic approaches that viewed sport as a totally incorporated aspect of the superstructure necessarily determined by the material infrastructure. From a Cultural Studies perspective, sport is examined as a historical product with its antecedents – the dominant sporting values and practices – shaped by, but not wholly determined by, dominant social groups.

The pluralist view of sport, culture, and the state, in which sport is not recognised to be part of the state apparatus, is contested by Cultural Studies of sport. In Canada, for example, members of Canada's national sports associations encouraged the expansion of the state's role in sport during the 1960s and 1970s (Gruneau, 1982, pp. 1–38). From this perspective, state and government are never merely neutral facilitators of sport. They not only speak for dominant class interests and regulate sport and leisure culture more broadly, but they also persuade the masses to embrace a consensus that supports the status quo. Ideology promotes the general public to consider society and its norms and values to be natural, good, and just, concealing the inherent system of domination.

From this perspective therefore, the 2002 World Cup may be seen to help consolidate the Korean social order, offering gratifications that act as safety valves to reconcile citizens with a social order otherwise hard to accept. The World Cup may also carry the imprint of values consistent with existing economic and political practices thereby further legitimising the social order. While this study is concerned with the role that the 2002 World Cup, in its present form, plays in reproducing the social structure in South Korea, it also illustrates the potential that hegemony theory has for linking the production of cultural forms, such as mass media, music, and sport, to broader political, economic, and social issues (Sage, 1998, p. 26).

State and society in Korea

In South Korea, just as in every other country, the state comprises a socially constructed set of practices that address human needs for a stable social order and a secure general welfare. At the same time, in capitalist states like South Korea, the state plays an indispensable role in ensuring the reproduction of capitalist social relations, and the powers of the state are used to sustain the general institutional framework of capitalist enterprise. In carrying out these functions, the state is intricately involved with supporting class differences and protecting the overall continuity of dominant class interests against those of other classes.

South Korea is one of the most industrialised countries in Asia. But behind the recent democratisation and incredible economic growth in South Korea are decades of political repression and authoritarianism. World War II brought an end to thirty-six years of Japanese rule in Korea, but it also brought a partitioning of the country into two independent states. In spite of efforts to reunite North and South Korea between 1945 and 1948, no progress was made. Finally, in May 1948 elections were held in South Korea under the supervision of the United Nations; the National Assembly met shortly after the election and elected Syngman Rhee as Chairman. A constitution for the Republic of Korea was adopted in July 1948. It provided for the election by the legislature of a president and vice-president for four-year terms, and Syngman Rhee was elected as the first president. Simultaneously, similar events were taking place in North Korea, and in September the Democratic People's Republic was established, with Kim Il-Sung selected as the Premier of North Korea.

Syngman Rhee was re-elected president in 1952 and 1956, but in both campaigns the internal political scene was marked by intrigue and shifting coalitions; key opposition leaders were assassinated and threats were made on the lives of others. In spite of being re-elected twice, Rhee never enjoyed widespread popularity. His power came primarily from US support and his control over state bureaucracies, especially the police and the military.

Rhee's government ended with the 'student' revolt of 1960 and was replaced by Park Chung-Hee's military coup in 1961. Park consolidated and intensified the repressive state apparatus and pursued a policy of aggressive economic growth. In the case of the latter, he 'encouraged capital accumulation and concentration by siphoning surplus agricultural products and farmers into urban centers, suppressing the labor movement to depress wages, and seeking infusions of U.S. and Japanese capital' (Lie, 1991, p. 40).

Park was assassinated in 1979, and order was restored by Chun Doo-Hwan's military coup in the spring of 1980. The most significant event in Chun's ascendancy to power was the Kwangju massacre during which, according to some observers, the military killed some 2,000 people and injured hundreds more (Clark, 1988). Chun's regime continued Park's main agenda: a repressive state apparatus and aggressive economic growth. As Lie (1991, p. 46) notes, 'the massacre at Kwangju was only the most visible display of state power. Chun also jailed numerous dissidents, sending 37,000 journalists and teachers to military "reeducation" camps. Labor laws were revised to hamper union organization and to squelch militancy.' Large corporate conglomerates (*chaebol*) became more powerful under Chun, as the state and capitalist interests came under increasing pressure from discontented workers, the disenchanted middle class, and dissidents.

In 1987, due to mounting criticism of his government, Chun stepped down as President and was replaced by his right-hand man, Roh Tae-Woo, in the first direct presidential election in sixteen years. Although Roh renounced the legacy of political repression, authoritarianism, and unrestrained economic growth, he was unpopular due to his close ties to the past – he was a former general in the military and was a close associate of Chun. Moreover, despite promises of democratisation, political authoritarianism and repression continued. As Schirmer (1991, p. 26) recounted, 'Amnesty International reports that human rights violations in South Korea increased markedly in the last six months of 1989 with 800 political and trade union activists arrested in major cities in a crackdown on political opposition.' Lie (1991, p. 52) noted that the road to democratisation for South Korea was 'fraught with difficulties, the legacy of three decades of authoritarianism: the gargantuan repressive apparatus, the extreme economic concentration, and the ideology of cultural authoritarianism and vulgar materialism'.

From the beginning of Syngman Rhee's presidency to the present day, active state intervention in the economic system has been a key feature of the growth of the South Korean economy. State discipline over business and labour has been a driving force in the so-called economic miracle of South Korea. The strong central government maintained by all the presidents has supported the development of, and allocated considerable capital resources to, a relatively few family-owned private business conglomerates *(chaebol)*, most of which are owned and controlled by entrepreneurs and their families.

These families are linked, through marriage and other alliances, to each other and to government leadership, creating an inner circle of business and government elites that virtually run the country.

State ownership and control of all major commercial banks, a system of trade controls and industrial licensing, and a system of restrictive foreign investment codes have also helped to shape private investment and production decisions. While these policies have produced some remarkable achievements in economic development, they have resulted in serious internal costs. Farmers, industrial workers, the environment, and democracy have all been sacrificed in the pursuit of export-oriented economic growth (Amsden, 1989; Bello and Rosenfeld, 1990). Kim Young-Sam, elected President in 1993–97, and Kim Dae-Jung, the current President, have tried to democratise politically and economically. While many changes have been achieved, some basic problems and issues remained.

The World Cup and the state

Since the establishment of the modern state, governments have been utilising sports to promote national integration and nationalism. The achievements of their athletes at international competitions serve as symbols of national unity and excellence and provide temporary emotional surges of national passion. Due to the mass media's ability to broadcast worldwide, along with the great influence of sports on people, government involvement has come to expand even more (Gruneau, 1982; Macintosh and Whitson, 1990). South Korea is no exception to the rule, despite its own particular trajectory. The government utilised the propaganda and prestige benefits of hosting the 1988 Olympics for purposes of gaining international recognition, which in turn seemed to produce the more concrete benefits of national development and economic growth. After the Kwangju massacre, to legitimise Chun Doo-Hwan's regime (1981–87), that was without the people's consent, it was essential for General Chun to attach himself to an institution seen by the people as popular or good. The regime, domestically and internationally, was in great need for a kind of icon that would endow it with international recognition. Therefore the Seoul Olympics was regarded as a means to conceal the government's undemocratic and authoritarian behaviour, and to suppress the people's uprising (Ahn, 1990, p. 35). The government tried to realise economic profits, promote social integration and foster a sense of national pride from the sports mega-event, rather than develop people's fitness and improve their quality of life through it.

During the mid-1990s, the democratic government led by Kim Young-Sam (1993–97) maintained the basic policy that utilised sports as an instrument for the promotion of national identity. It is remarkable that both the military regime and the democratic government shared the same sport policy (Ahn, 2000). Kim's government not only continually managed the National Training Center for national teams and athletes, but also led the successful campaign to host the 2002 World Cup.

It is evident that Kim's government went to great pains to host the 2002 World Cup. The President declared his support for it at the end of 1994 and the parliament also resolved to hold the event (*JoongAng Ilbo*, 1995). The application for hosting the event was warranted by the Prime Minister and ministers' signatures as well as the President's letter to FIFA's President. Also, the government supported the fund for the hosting, and President Kim Young-Sam encouraged the professional soccer team owners like Suwon Samsung, Anyang LG and Cheonbuk Hyundai (owners of *chaebol*) to co-operate in the hosting (*Korea Times*, 1996). The government was fully behind the attempt to host the World Cup.

The current government led by Kim Dae-Jung (since 1998) has also been devoted to supporting a successful World Cup. The government considers a successful World Cup a major part of its sport policy, and 45 per cent of the sports budget during its five-year term is being used to subsidise the World Cup (Ministry of Culture and Tourism, 1998). Furthermore, the government has supported 20–30 per cent of the total national fund for the ten new stadia, and most of the workers of the Korean Organising Committee for the World Cup (KOWOC) have been seconded from the central government bureaucracy. As the national soccer team's record has declined after 1998, even the Ministry of Culture and Tourism, which is in charge of the World Cup, created an 'Urgent Committee for the World Cup' (*JoongAng Ilbo*, 2000a).

In spite of the ardent support from the government for the World Cup itself, domestic soccer's popularity is not very great compared with other spectator sports. In 1997, while 3.9 million spectators attended professional baseball games with 504 games among 8 teams, just 1.2 million attended Korea League Soccer games with 179 games among 10 teams (Park, 1998, pp. 129–130). In the same year, average spectators were 7,744 at baseball games and 6,731 at soccer matches. According to statistics on the domestic sports market in 1995, the value of the professional soccer market was about $2 million, which was equivalent to 5 per cent of the entire sports market and much smaller than professional baseball's value, estimated at $5 million (Oh, 2000, p. 53). Although it has been over six years since the decision was made to host the World Cup, the grassroots for Korean soccer is still poor. For example, in 1999 there were 8,883 youth soccer teams in Japan, compared with only 212 teams in South Korea. Giving proof of the critical situation in Korean soccer, past head coaches of the national soccer team recently had an emergency meeting to urge reforms for Korean soccer (*JoongAng Ilbo*, 2000b).

Therefore, to fully understand the background to co-hosting the World Cup in Korea, we must look at factors outside soccer. Interest in capital investments in sports mega-events in South Korea has grown since the 1988 Olympic Games. Although sports such as baseball and basketball are popular in many countries, only soccer has followers worldwide. Due to the potentially enormous profitable gains to be made, big enterprises like Hyundai and Samsung have a natural interest in soccer and have taken a leading role in building the infrastructure for the 2002 World Cup. Hence the World Cup mediates between large economic groups and the government.

It is also important to describe the major ways that the Korean state makes use of the World Cup. The most compelling function of the World Cup is to promote the economic, political, and cultural hegemony of the government. The World Cup acts as a catalyst for popular harmony and system stability. As Kim Young-Sam's and Kim Dae-Jung's governments were worried about the absence of an ideology to funnel the energy of the people, the World Cup has provided a good opportunity to help shape a united ideological hegemony. This is similar to the appeal for political stability and social integration that the Fifth Republic government (1981–87) made in terms of the Olympic Games. Kim Dae-Jung's government has made use of the World Cup, in particular, through the ideology of unifying the people. The party in power, the Millennium Democratic Party, is hoping to use any social and economic benefits that may arise from the World Cup finals to win the next presidential election scheduled for the end of 2002.

The government's approach to the 2002 World Cup is, however, slightly different from that adopted towards the Seoul Olympic Games. While the government of the Fifth Republic made use of the Olympics as an undisguised tool for social integration and social stability (McBeth, 1988, p. 43), Kim Dae-Jung's government also uses the World Cup to promote hegemony in civil society. The World Cup helps to create and support an effective dominant culture because it conveys messages about norms, values, and dispositions that contribute to the ideological hegemony of the state.

In addition, the government policy regards the World Cup as a very effective tool to contribute to Korea's globalisation. According to the neo-liberalist rendering of the term, which was adopted by the Korean government, globalisation is the process whereby the principles of freedom and democracy in the political sphere and the principles of market liberalisation in the economic sphere are expanded and intensified (Lim, 1998). The optimistic view is that inequality between the various social groups, as well as inequality between states, will gradually be mitigated by the process.

Whilst foreign capital entered South Korea rapidly before and after the 1988 Olympic Games, it has been assumed that the equally worldwide sporting mega-event, the Football World Cup, would also lead to an acceleration of the opening of the Korean market in accord with the agreement reached with the World Trade Organization (WTO) in 1997. Through the World Cup, the principle of the market economy has not only been emphasised, but the globalisation policy, that sees Korea as a leading country of the world, has been promoted. Also, the co-hosting of the World Cup has been thought to contribute to the development of the information communication industry by introducing the most advanced Japanese information technology into South Korea. In these ways the World Cup contributes to economic globalisation.

The government's active support and involvement in the World Cup have led to other new initiatives. A special bill for administrative and financial support of the World Cup was established at the periodic National Assembly in 1996. The formation of the World Cup Countermeasure Committee in 2000 was further evidence of government support. In these and other ways it is clear that the Football World Cup finals has significance beyond being a simple sporting event and is being used as a tool that promotes and reproduces state hegemony.

The World Cup and civil society

Civil society 'comprises all those social relationships which are based on consent, as opposed to the relationships of coercion in political society' (Simon, 1977, p. 83). Although Gramsci refers to civil society as a 'hegemonic apparatus', civil society can be understood as the site of the class struggle where the domination of the capitalist class is continually challenged (Bates, 1975, p. 356).

Civil society, consent and hegemony correspond to one another, in opposition to political society, coercion and the state. But civil society and the state are not completely separate and independent of one another, and they do not wholly exclude one another (Bobbio, 1985, p. 25). Hence civil society is a sphere which may balance rule by means of military force, accomplished by ethical agreement and persuasion (or hegemonic dominance). The political system in South Korea was not democratised until 1988, and the hegemonic dominance in civil society has been gradually promoted during the 1990s. Civil society is a territory where, simultaneously, hegemonic dominance is achieved, and consumption, culture and leisure activities are performed. As the state uses mega-events, like the Football World Cup, within civil society, it has to be asked: what value does it have for its citizens?

The space of civil society in South Korea has expanded since the mid-1980s (Kim, 1993, p. 198). Labour unions were not allowed until 1987, the year democracy was obtained by the people. In addition, expansion of the space of civil society is based on social changes such as technological progress and the shortening of working hours. The expansion of civil society results in the increase of consumption, culture and leisure life. In other words, on the one side, discontent against the government and concerns about social reforms decrease; on the other side, interest in personal life and leisure increases (Kim, 1995). More people have participated in sports to heighten their quality of life. The massification of sports became the new public backbone for Korean society in the late twentieth century. People on the subway or the bus are commonly seen reading sports newspapers. Sport is a normal topic of conversation among colleagues, friends, or even between strangers. The average citizen usually watches sport on TV after work and at weekends (Ministry of Culture and Tourism, 1997).

This changed conception about leisure has contributed to the massification of sports in Korea. A survey on work and leisure, conducted by the Ministry of Culture and Sport (1995), showed that while the positive response to the statement that: 'labour is more important than leisure' decreased from 38.3 per cent in 1988 to 23.9 per cent in 1995, the response to the statement that: 'leisure is more important than labour', significantly increased from 4.3 per cent to 10.5 per cent during those same years. Yet, the expansion of leisure space in civil society promotes the de-politicisation of citizens, and the government has used the World Cup under these circumstances. In spite of the opposition party's insistence that the local government elections in 2002 should be held ahead of schedule in April (and not June), the President and the ruling party have not accepted this. It is felt that if the electorate have to cast their votes during the World Cup period, in June, the election outcome will be more favourable to the ruling party that has supported the mega-event. Unlike the Seoul Olympic Games, the World Cup is hosted on the basis of the total interest and support of civil society, as it particularly relies on the help of numerous volunteers.

Although the World Cup is employed as a means of hegemony for civil society, there exists at the same time a real opportunity to revitalise civil society. To examine the effects of the attraction of the World Cup affirmatively, from the viewpoint of civil society, is to consider it as an opportunity that expands mass sports as a part of welfare improvement.

Understood in this way, the tendency of pursuing quality of life and leisure has been rapidly increasing since the 1990s in Korean civil society. Citizens recognise the significance of more leisure time and an affluent lifestyle. Thus, it is inevitable that the government must provide a suitable policy to satisfy citizens' demands. Though there are various ways to fulfil the desire of the citizens in terms of quality of life, the expansion of sport involvement for citizens is a very useful policy. Sports involvement is the social practice that allows citizens to release tension and enjoy themselves.

As Kim Dae-Jung's government is aimed at constructing a productive welfare state, the establishment of a sport system based on grassroots opportunities for citizens is increasingly seen as a right, as well as one of the government's obligations. As Ingham and Lawson (1999, p. 1) argue: 'Mass sport participation may promote the health and enhancement of individuals, the well-being of families, the safety, security, and vibrancy of local neighbourhood communities, and some of the necessary conditions for strong democracy.' Sporting activities contribute to maintaining citizens' health. Sport also provides them with life satisfaction and pleasure. Therefore, it is natural that the government assumes the responsibility to expand grassroots sport to make good use of citizens' leisure time and to improve their fitness. And it is their right, as citizens, for welfare, that people acting in civil society demand the government support grassroots sports.

Nevertheless, until recently in Korea, sports policy has been heavily based on an elite-dominant paradigm. Elite sports and grassroots sports have suffered from a serious imbalance in the distribution of resources. On the basis of a sports promotion fund provided by the central government, during

1998–2002, the current presidential term, elite sports and grassroot sports expenditure amounted to 0.9 billion won and 0.5 billion won, respectively (Ahn, 2000, p. 729). In terms of performance, elite sport has maintained very high levels since the Seoul Olympic Games. In 1988 South Korean athletes achieved twelve gold medals and at the 1992 Barcelona Olympics they obtained the same. South Korea brought back seven gold medals from the 1996 Atlanta and eight gold medals from the Sydney Olympic Games in 2000. All national teams and athletes are accommodated at the Olympic Training Centre throughout the whole year, where the government financially supports them, and a pension is provided for any athlete who obtains a medal from an international competition.

On the other hand, the poor conditions of school sport and community sport facilities within civil society have often been criticised (Ahn, 2001; Park, 1999). Soccer, the most popular participation sport in Korea, has no grass field for the public. Also, the soccer club system has not yet been properly established. Only 5 per cent of schools throughout the country have gymnasiums, and the number of gymnasiums for citizens located in the community is only 288. In Japan, 20.8 per cent of sports facilities are publicly owned, while only 4 per cent of such facilities are publicly owned in Korea (*News Plus*, 1996). As a result of the limited sports facilities, just 32 per cent of Koreans regularly participate in sporting activities (Ministry of Culture and Tourism, 2000).

The World Cup is therefore a good opportunity to expand and promote grassroots sport and thus improve the quality of life for citizens. The development of grassroots sports is one of the central significant changes for civil society that the World Cup potentially will bring. Unfortunately, if the government sticks with the elite sport paradigm, which it looks likely to, it will tend to perpetuate the status quo. Yet without adequate government support, it cannot be imagined that public sport facilities will be expanded.

Conclusion

This chapter has analysed the 2002 World Cup from a Cultural Studies perspective on sport. Although the World Cup itself can be a hugely enjoyable event that allows citizens to feel pride, the World Cup is not free from ideological influences in South Korea. The World Cup contributes to reinforcing hegemonic definitions and values in South Korea. Specifically, the World Cup serves the political and economic interests of the government. Thus, the linkage between the World Cup and power, and the contradictory nature of such relationships, is manifested through the World Cup.

The political economy of the World Cup, like the political economy of other aspects of capitalistic society, shapes and moulds social relations that are marked by power and profit on the part of hegemonic groups – while not necessarily being beneficial to the majority of citizens. Unable to understand their potential to act as social change agents, the majority of citizens suffer from a kind of co-optation in the historical process. Without the concepts and explanations that would enable them to describe and understand the real conditions that restrict them, they lack the wherewithal for taking part in transforming their society. Nonetheless, members of civil society in South Korea should recognise the latent opportunity within the World Cup, and it is hoped that they can make the World Cup a turning point for the establishment of grassroots sports.

References

Ahn, Min-Seok (1990) 'The 1988 Seoul Summer Olympic Games: a critical commentary', unpublished dissertation, University of Illinois.

Ahn, Min-Seok (2000) 'Studying the managerial prospect of Seoul Olympic Sports Promotion Foundation', *Journal of KAHPERD*, 39, 1: 727–737.

Ahn, Min-Seok (2001) 'Toward grassroots sports', *KAHPERD Newsletter*, 77: 28–31.

Amsden, Anthony (1989) *Asia's Next Giant Step: South Korea and Late Industrialization,* New York: Oxford University Press.

Bates, Thomas (1975) 'Gramsci and the theory of hegemony', *Journal of the History of Ideas*, 36: 351–365.

Bello, White and Rosenfeld, Smith (1990) *Dragons in Distress: Asia's Miracle Economies in Crisis,* San Francisco: The Institute for Food and Development Policy.

Bobbio, Norberto (1985) 'Gramsci and the conception of civil society', in Chantal Mouffe (ed.) *Gramsci and Marxist Theory*, Boston: Routledge & Kegan Paul. pp. 21–27.

Clark, David (1988) *The Kwangju Uprising*, Boulder, CO: Westview Press.

Gramsci, Antonio (1971) *Selections from the Prison Notebooks*, London: Lawrence and Wishart.

Gruneau, Richard (1982) 'Sport and the debate on the state', in Richard Gruneau and Hart Cantelon (eds) *Sport, Culture and the Modern State*, Toronto: University of Toronto Press. pp. 1–38.

Hollands, Robert (1984) 'The role of cultural studies and social criticism in the sociological study of sport', *Quest*, 36: 66–79.

Ingham, Alan and Lawson, Hall (1999) 'Prolympism and globalization: knowledge for whom, by whom', unpublished keynote address at the German Association of Sport Sciences, Heidelberg.

JoongAng Ilbo (1995) 'Donating the World Cup's profit', 30 September, p. 4.

JoongAng Ilbo (2000a) 'Creating the urgent committee for the World Cup', 10 November, p. C2.

JoongAng Ilbo (2000b) 'Coming together, the past head coaches of the national soccer team', 15 November, p. C1.

Kim Mun-Gyum (1993) *Yeoga-wa sahoehak* [Sociology of leisure], Seoul: Haneul Publication.

Kim, Seog-Guk (1995) 'Gukga-wa sahoe byeonhwa' [The state and change in civil society], unpublished paper presented at Korean Sociological Association, Seoul.

Korea Times (1996) 'The President Kim's invitation for the World Cup', 4 April, p. 2.

Lie, John (1991) 'Democratisation and its discontents: origins of the present crisis in South Korea', *Monthly Review*, February, pp. 38–52.

Lim, Hyun-Chin (1998) *Gigusidae segye-ui byeonhwa-wa hanguk-ui baljeon* [The world change and Korean development], Seoul: Seoul National University Press.

McBeth, John (1988) 'Sporting Seoul awaits the five-ring circus', *Far Eastern Economic Review*, April, pp. 42–44.

Macintosh, Donald and Whitson, David (1990) *The Game Planners: Transforming Canada's Sport System*, Montreal: McGill-Queen's University Press.

Ministry of Culture and Sport, Korea (1995) *Yeoga siltae josa yeongu* [A survey on work and leisure], Seoul.

Ministry of Culture and Tourism, Korea (1997) *Gungminsaenghwalcheyuk siltae chamyeo josa* [A report on people's sport participation], Seoul.

Ministry of Culture and Tourism, Korea (1998) *Jje 2 cha gungminsaenghwalcheyuk jin-heung 5 geyeonkyehoek* [The second plan on people's sport promotion], Seoul.

Ministry of Culture and Tourism, Korea (2000) *Gungminsaenghwalcheyuk chamyeo siltae josa* [A report on people's sport participation], Seoul.

News Plus (1996) 'The serious situation of mass sports', 22 August, pp. 20–25.

Oh, Il-Yong (2000) 'The 2002 World Cup and Korean sport industry', unpublished paper presented at KAHPERD, Seoul.

Park, Myeog-Ki (1999) 'Some suggestions to develop school sports', *Sport Science*, 68: 8–16.

Park, Young-Ok (1998) *Hanguk sport saneop-eun yukseongbangan yeongu* [A study to promote Korean sport industry], Seoul: Korea Sport Science Institute.

Sage, George (1996) 'Patriotic images and capitalist profit: contradictions of professional team sport licensed merchandise', *Sociology of Sport Journal*, 13, 1: 1–11.

Sage, George (1998) *Power and Ideology in American Sport: A Critical Perspective*, Champaign, IL: Human Kinetics.

Schirmer, David (1991) 'Korea and the Philippines: a century of U.S. intervention', *Monthly Review*, May: 19–32.

Simon, Roger (1977) 'Gramsci's concept of hegemony', *Marxism Today*, March: 78–86.

Part IV

The 2002 World Cup as sports mega-event and sports media event

12 Building mega-events

Critical reflections on the 2002 World Cup infrastructure

Nogawa Haruo and Mamiya Toshio

Introduction: The World Cup is coming to town!

Ten venues in both Korea and Japan will help stage the matches played in the next FIFA World Cup finals tournament between 31 May and 30 June 2002. Many pros and cons about hosting and staging global sports mega-events, like the Olympic Games and the Football World Cup, have been aired in debates. Korea and Japan are also the only nations in the Asian continent so far to host the Summer Olympic Games. Eight of the ten venues in Japan have spent millions of yen to build shiny new public stadia in the name of this global football event. The Republic of Korea has also spent billions of won to build ten brand new soccer stadia for the 2002 World Cup. So, in total, eighteen new stadia will be constructed for the tournament and this is very unusual in the history of World Cup. At the time of writing this chapter (October 2001), seven stadia are still under construction. Total construction costs for the ten new and refurbished Japanese stadia are approximately US$2,881 million, while Korea has spent nearly US$1,513 million. All the stadia have been constructed according to FIFA's regulations and will accommodate 40,000 plus spectators.

In terms of urban and regional development, these countries have both experienced the merits and demerits of staging the Olympics. Some consider the major benefits for host cities to include: the promotion of sports culture; the development of the social infrastructure; the construction of superior sport facilities; the acceleration of internationalisation and globalisation; the enhancement of economic and non-economic impacts; and the enrichment of the image of the host city or cities. On the other hand, concerns have been expressed about negative aspects of sporting mega-events such as: the absence of a long-term operational plan for the new sport facilities; the burden of a long and heavy financial debt on local taxpayers; the potential destruction of the natural environment; and the acceptance of a homogenising globalisation process. In this chapter we focus on how the 2002 World Cup can be staged and operated effectively and successfully, but we cannot neglect or ignore the possible negative consequences of the event. What will soccer be like in Korea and Japan after the year 2002? What will regional development and revitalisation be like in the host cities after 2002? Are there any specific, long-term, plans in each host city or each host country regarding regional development? The answer to these questions seems to be negative in both countries. So difficulties do lie ahead.

Sport facility construction has been publicised as being part of a larger urban growth scheme that could provide real benefits to the 'city-as-a-whole'. Civic leaders have generally insisted that stadia and arenas could contribute to the city's quality of life by providing sports and entertainment for the citizens and spin-off benefits for the local economy. It is important to understand that the global sports mega-event boom is relatively recent. The 'global sport event provision process' is loaded with all the trappings of an urban growth machine. The World Cup tournament represents one of the foremost examples of the power of an 'urban regime' and 'regional regime' to direct a city towards 'growth' policies' despite the expressed wishes of the general population. The Football World Cup represents urban boosterism and metropolitan image crafting at the highest level, rather than simply regional boosterism (Chapin, 1996).

In terms of sports tourism, the tournament is an excellent opportunity for the venue cities and surrounding areas to promote both international and domestic tourism prior to and during the event. Some venue cities may need to provide more hotel accommodation and tourist attractions in order to take advantage of this opportunity. Regional development will last for much longer than just the period of the World Cup tournament if each venue city is able to display significant messages to attract tourists and television viewers. Host cities may tend to become near-sighted and expect an immediate payback and tangible profit from the World Cup tournament. But it is much more important to look at this occasion as a long-term project. For example, a great increase in decent soccer pitches is about to start all over Japan since the announcement of the location of official World Cup training sites. Numerous reasons explain the increased interest in the World Cup and subsequent public support. Elected officials and their constituents realise that sport events can generate attention, television exposure, and economic benefits to a community. Global sport events are more than just entertainment. They probably come to town only once in a lifetime. Global sport events promote tourism and provide employment and business opportunities. So tax-payers' money ought to be spent wisely and effectively. In order to develop the host city more attractively, the city is required to improve at least four things; the social infrastructure, sport facilities, tourist attractions, and hospitality.

World Cup Fever I: the race to become an official World Cup venue

As soon as FIFA made its final decision on the location of the 2002 tournament, in May 1996, fierce domestic competition began among fifteen cities in

Japan to become venues for World Cup matches. The fifteen cities knew five of them were eventually to be eliminated. These fifteen cities had agreed to join the Japan Bidding Committee for the 2002 FIFA World Cup and had put around US$3 million into the initial hosting campaign. These fifteen cities had held general assemblies to discuss the issues and consequences of bringing the tournament to their own city, including financial matters, stadium construction, and post-World Cup operation costs. Building soccer stadium facilities meant other services had to be neglected. In most of the cities the question of publicly financing a stadium had to be put to a vote and there were serious criticisms that insufficient explanation of these matters was provided, such as disclosing the fiscal budget to local residents. In other words, municipal leaders and assemblies have been accused of neglecting their duties with respect to accountability and disclosure of information. Similar criticisms have been heard from their Korean counterparts.

In late 1997, the Japan Preparatory Committee for the 2002 FIFA World Cup Korea/Japan had to make a decision on the basis of certain criteria, which were not initially openly divulged. The Committee announced that its selection of the ten venues was on the basis of: the maintenance of geographical balance; popularity of the game; density of population; and some political considerations. The latter were not fully revealed. Thus, the cities of Hiroshima, Kyoto, Toyota, Aomori, and Chiba were removed from the list of official venues. The elimination of Toyota, the home of the giant Japanese automobile company and main sponsor of the J.League's Nagoya Grampus Eight, stirred great debate since Toyota's archrival auto company, Nissan, the main sponsor of another J.League team, F. Marinos, qualified as a host venue in Yokohama. While Japan trimmed down from fifteen to ten venues, the number of Korean host sites grew from six to ten cities. For some observers a total of twenty venues appeared to be too many, a more reasonable number being about twelve sites. Ultimately, however, the official venues in Japan were decided as Sapporo, Miyagi, Ibaraki, Saitama, Yokohama, Niigata, Shizuoka, Osaka, Kobe, and Oita. The ten venue cities in Korea are Seoul, Busan, Daegu, Incheon, Gwangji, Daejeon, Ulsan, Suwon, Jeonji, and Seogwipo (see Table 12.1). The Korean venues are quite diverse in size – Seogwipo in Jeju (Cheju) Island, has a population of 85,737, while Seoul, the capital city, has 10 million inhabitants.

As far as a long-run scheme for the use of the sports facilities was concerned, very little had been proposed or developed in the two East Asian countries. This is the first time in the history of the World Cup that almost all the stadia are to be built for the tournament. At the time of the bidding only one stadium, Kashima in Ibaraki, Japan, already existed in either of the two hosting nations. How could the FIFA inspectors evaluate the venues and other operational and organisational matters adequately was one of the questions raised at the time. China, with a successful bid to host the 2008 Summer Olympic Games, may follow in the footsteps of Korea and Japan regarding the post-decision development of sports facilities. It would seem that in Asia,

Table 12.1 World Cup venues in Japan and Korea

Name of stadium	Inauguration	Construction cost (US$ million)	Capacity crowd	Surrounding population
Sapporo Dome 'Hiroba'*	June 2001	356.1	42,300	1,830,506
Miyagi Stadium*	March 2000	225	49,133	2,355,947
Ibaraki Prefeitural Kashima Soccer Stadium	April 1993	240**	41,800	2,987,169
Niigata Stadium 'Big Swan'*	March 2001	250	42,300	6,958,798
Saitama Stadium 2002	July 2001	304.1	63,700	3,452,006
International Stadium Yokohama*	October 1997	502.5	72,370	2,470,272
Shizuoka Stadium 'Ecopa'*	May 2001	250	51,349	3,771,527
Nagai Stadium*	May 1996	351.6**	50,000	2,604,775
Kobe Wing Stadium*	October 2001	193	42,000	1,500,292
Oita Stadium 'Big Eye'*	March 2001	209.1	43,000	1,221,128
Seoul World Cup Stadium	December 2001	166	64,677	10,373,234
Busan Sports Complex Main Stadium	July 2001	200	53,926	3,812,392
Daegu World Cup Stadium	May 2001	238	65,857	2,538,212
Incheon Munhak Stadium	December 2001	201	50,256	2,562,321
Gwangji World Cup Stadium	September 2001	126	42,880	1,375,212
Daejeon World Cup Stadium	September 2001	120	41,000	1,390,510
Ulsan Munsu Soccer Stadium	July 2001	123	43,512	1,047,793
Suwon World Cup Stadium	May 2001	121	43,138	951,253
Jeonju World Cup Stadium	September 2001	117	42,477	622,238
Seogwipo World Cup Stadium	December 2001	101	42,256	85,737

Notes
*   Multi-purpose stadium
** Renovation cost included.

staging a global sport event is synonymous with developing the social infra-structure and sport facilities almost from scratch. An obvious difference in stadium construction between Japan and Korea appears to be the degree of central government involvement. The Korean government appears to be firmly committed to the global mega-event much more than its Japanese counterpart.

As the tournament approaches, various monetary issues will come to the surface. The Japan Organising Committee for the 2002 FIFA World Cup Korea/Japan (JAWOC) announced a total revenue plan of US$505.8 million for the tournament in March 2001. The amount was US$22.5 million less than the original plan, however. JAWOC asked the ten venue cities to come up with another 100 million yen (US$833,333) each for the operation (*Yomiuri Shinbun*, 1 May 2001). Moreover, JAWOC revealed that it requested the ten venues to exempt a total of US$25 million from the stadium rental fees (*Yomiuri Shinbun*, 24 May 2001). To some it seems as if the ten venues have been exploited by both FIFA and JAWOC.

Table 12.1 reveals that all the new stadia in Korea are exclusively for the game of soccer while eight of the ten Japanese stadia are built as multi-sports facilities. Sapporo Dome in Hokkaido is uniquely able to accommodate both Japanese Major League baseball games and J.League matches. Three venues in Korea are home grounds for K-League teams whereas six stadia in Japan are the homes for J.League sides. Using modern high technology, most stadia have either a full or half dome to protect spectators from the elements. The stadia in Shizuoka, Miyagi, Gwangju, and Ulsan are also designed to provide barrier-free structures for physically handicapped people.

Let's spend the public money together! The World Cup as a 'growth machine'

The history of urban development in Japan has revealed many trends over the past four decades. Cities have attempted to foster economic development and build a better metropolitan image by holding international events such as the Tokyo Olympic Games, World Expositions, and the Sapporo and Nagano Winter Olympics. Municipal leaders and chambers of commerce have optimistically promised tremendous growth and development of fancy new sport facilities or convention centres that would promote tourism and a 'clean industry' image. Japan has experienced an incredible surge in the number of new sports facilities and theme parks that have been built in the past fifteen years. New arenas and stadia have been completed each year as cities have attempted to lure sports and cultural events as a means to economic development and revitalisation. Apart from economic development and local revitalisation, an important aspect of constructing new sport facilities is to provide sufficient facilities for local residents to enhance their quality of life and encourage health promotion through

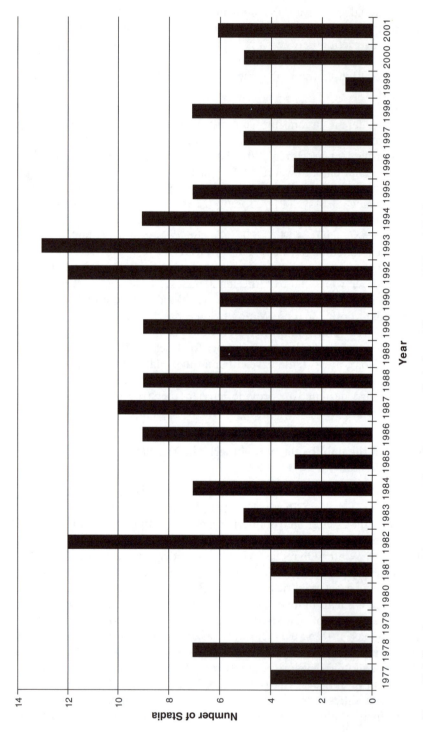

Figure 12.1 Brand new construction or renovation of soccer stadia in Japan (between 1977 and 2001).

sport/physical activity participation. In the last decade, an ever-growing increase in medical expenses, skyrocketing to US$250 billion, has become one of the most significant social issues and problems in Japan.

Within the last decade, major Japanese cities have witnessed the completion of new sports arenas and/or stadia to accommodate professional sport franchises. Figure 12.1 shows the number of brand new constructions and the renovation of soccer stadia. A total of sixty-eight soccer stadia have been built between 1992 and 2001 in Japan. Prior to 1992, most soccer pitches were contained within athletics stadia. In the wake of the launch of the J.League in 1993, a number of municipalities started to construct single-purpose stadia just for soccer. New stadia built in the last five years are considerably larger, more luxurious, multi-functional, and equipped with more high technology than ever before. Each stadium purports to serve both its principal tenants (the sports franchise) and its respective metropolitan area as an 'international class' or 'world class' facility providing both an important entertainment place and economic development tool (Chapin, 1996). Robertson (1995) has called this type of economic (re-)development tool, 'special activity generators'.

The past two decades have revealed two significant new special activity generators that have been taking Japan by storm: sports facilities and theme parks. A number of theme parks went bankrupt during the 1990s and have left severe financial troubles for some municipalities. While significant public investment in these facilities has been ongoing since the early 1970s, the incredible increase in the number of new sports facilities has resulted in significant attention from construction businesses. It is somewhat astonishing to discover the total number of newly constructed facilities since 1987. In total, 167 new sport facilities have been built in Japan since 1987. Of these, eighteen new public soccer stadia have been built to accommodate professional soccer teams. A total of US$3.55 billion public money was spent on these eighteen stadia. Eleven new baseball stadia have also been constructed to house professional baseball teams. Moreover, thirty-eight arenas and more than a dozen domed stadia, as well as a dozen aquatic centres have been constructed since 1987. The Japan Sports Facilities Publication (2000) estimated that over 2028 billion yen (equivalent to US$16.9 billion) was awarded to sports construction contracts for stadia and arenas in the past fifteen years. It is interesting to compare these figures with the US counterparts. Chapin (1996) indicated that over US$1.5 billion was awarded to sport construction contracts for stadia and arenas between 1986 and 1996. How big is this public investment in Japan? Of the US$16.9 billion spent, US$14.3 billion came from public investment (taxpayers' money). It must be noted that these figures represent direct public investment purely in sports facilities. They do not take into account indirect expenditure for infrastructure improvements, such as new highway interchanges and roads.

Soccer stadium debates

This urban development trend has generated substantial public debate in those cities that have constructed new sport facilities with substantial public investment. Ongoing heated debates have taken place in the World Cup venue cities about the prospects for post-tournament usage since these cities have spent an excessive amount of public yen on their stadia. The argument put forth by facility proponents is firmly rooted in the concept of the 'economic multiplier' (Baade and Dye, 1990). With respect to the supposed tangible benefits of urban growth strategies, construction of sport facilities has been likened to both job 'engines' and economic development 'magnets' (Schimmel, 2001). In short, pro-growth advocates argue that the economic benefits of a new facility will 'spin off' into new enterprises and increase local land values because of increased pedestrian traffic and subsequent tourism and various businesses in the area around the new stadium. Further, other less tangible economic benefits will be generated by the 'big time' image that a professional sport franchise and a world class facility present to the world (Chapin, 1996).

Stadium opponents, on the other hand, base their arguments less on perceived benefits and more upon various economic studies of actual sports facilities. Opponents of stadium development argue that the economic effects of these new stadia have been shown to be minimal and that public resources would be better spent elsewhere. Evidence suggests that the economic benefits that do accrue provide only low-wage, seasonal, jobs (Baade and Dye, 1990; Baade, 1996). Scholars in sport economics have refuted the claim that sport facilities and/or events generate economic benefits that spin off or multiply across various city segments. Sport sociology also provides evidence that the socio-spatial consequences of this type of urban growth have regressive effects on the local population (Schimmel, 2001). In addition, there are far fewer non-sport events that can utilise the stadia, primarily because stadia are significantly larger than other venues, such as arenas and few public events can attract stadium-sized crowds. The figures in Table 12.2 clearly support this criticism. Average attendance in the J.League in 2000 was close to 15,000. Both Saitama and Yokohama stadia can accommodate 60,000 plus spectators, but neither Urawa Red Diamonds nor Yokohama F. Marinos can fill anywhere near half their stadia. Kashima Antlers, one of the most consistent and popular J.League teams, expanded their stadium capacity from 15,870 to 41,800 for the World Cup tournament. They may be successful in attracting approximately 25,000 fans to the stadium if everything is going right on the pitch. Yet nearly 16,000 seats are likely to remain vacant. Furthermore, some studies have concluded that municipalities that finance new stadia have trouble capturing even these economic benefits. The economic effects spill over to other jurisdictions, thereby suggesting that a regional financing plan might be a better public investment strategy (Nunn and Rosentraub, 1995).

Table 12.2 Average attendance of home or would-be home professional J.League teams (Japan, 2000)

Name of stadium	Crowd capacity	Estimated annual income US$ million	Estimated annual balance US$ million	Home or would-be home pro team	Average attendance in 1999	Average attendance in 2000
Sapporo Dome 'Hiroba'*	42,300	19.1	0.83	Consadole Sapporo	10,986	12,910
Miyagi Stadium*	49,133	0.25	−2.83	Vegalta Sendai	7,470	8,885
Ibaraki Prefectural Kashima Soccer Stadium	41,800	2.25	Break even	Kashima Antlers	17,049	17,507
Niigata Stadium 'Big Swan'	42,300	Unknown	No estimate	Albirex Niigata**	4,211	4,007
Saitama Stadium 2002*	63,700	2.5	−3.30	Urawa Red Diamonds	21,276	16,923
International Stadium Yokohama	72,370	3.6	−5.00	Yokohama F. Marinos	20,095	16,644
Shizuoka Stadium 'Ecopa'*	51,349	Unknown	Deficit	Shimizu S-Pulse	12,883	12,422
Nagai Stadium	50,000	0.65	−5.10	Cerezo Osaka	10,216	13,548
Kobe Wing Stadium	42,000	1.7–2.5	Deficit	Vissel Kobe	7,691	7,512
Oita Stadium 'Big Eye'	43,000	0.41	−2.80	Oita Trinita**	3,886	4,818

Notes
* No J.League home teams
** J.League Division 2
Numbers compiled on the basis of different sources.

Construction and renovation of sport facilities are expensive undertakings. In order for a construction project to begin, funding must be sought from different sources, both public and private. However, the most common and probably easiest way to collect the funds is to issue bonds. The bonds are likely to be issued by either local authorities (cities or prefectures) or national authorities to underwrite the cost of sport facility construction. There are two types of bonds issued by local authorities: general obligation bonds or revenue bonds. General obligation bonds are used for sport facility construction. In fact, all the World Cup stadia in Japan have been constructed by receiving funding from local general bonds (city and prefecture). For example, the construction cost of the Niigata Stadium was US$250 million and consisted of 82.5 per cent prefecture budget and 17.5 per cent city sources. The construction cost of the Oita Stadium was approximately US$210 million. US$125 million of the total funds was collected from general obligation bonds of Oita Prefecture.

Despite the almost unanimous conclusion of these studies that public investment into sports facilities yields only minimal economic benefits, officials continue to push for new facilities and public yen continue to be spent on them. Why does this happen? In many cases these projects are trumpeted as successful not because of any objective assessment about their benefits to local residents, but because of the symbolic power of the edifices themselves (Schimmel, 2001).

It has been suggested by some authors that studies of these facilities fall short in identifying the total benefits of new sports stadia and arenas (Rosentraub, 1996). The economic focus of these studies cannot quantify the intangible benefits of these new facilities. For example, the psychological benefits of living in a 'major league' city cannot be summed in yen figures or in the number of jobs created. Further, the 'quality of life' benefits that are conferred by cultural and social facilities like museums, concert halls, and parks (many of which are subsidised publicly) also cannot be accurately quantified.

World Cup Fever II: the race to become an official World Cup training site

Cities and towns failing to become official World Cup venues got a second chance to be involved with the World Cup in the role of providing a training site for qualifying national football teams. JAWOC announced that any municipality was invited to bid to become an official World Cup training site in 1999. This instigated another period of urban growth machine politics. For local development and revitalisation, a total of eighty-three municipalities officially announced their participation in the competition to become one of the official training sites. All bidding cities and towns in Japan appeared to rely on the experience of the town of Aix-les-Bains in France. A border town near Switzerland, it became the training site for the Japanese national squad during the 1998 World Cup. An extraordinary amount of attention was paid to Aix-les-Bains when Japan participated in their first-ever World Cup finals tournament. More than eighty members of the mass media stayed in Aix-les-Bains to send almost minute-by-minute reports about the preparations of the national side back home. As a result a considerable number of Japanese travellers visited Aix-les-Bains during and after the tournament in 1998. The estimated economic impact was believed to exceed US$25 million to the town. Most bidding municipalities in Japan seem to have had the illusion of becoming the Japanese 'Aix-les-Bains'.

In order to file for a bid, each municipality had to fulfil the following requirements: (1) the possession of two or more well-maintained grass soccer pitches; (2) the provision of indoor training facilities; (3) the establishment of a blind fence all around the pitch to block out rival scouts and media during strategic practice sessions; (4) the existence of a decent hotel to accommodate a whole delegation near to the training facilities; and (5) accessibility to either a major airport or train station. Moreover, tight security for the team and delegation had to be available in close cooperation with JAWOC. In addition, usage of the facilities five days after the first match would be free of charge (JAWOC, 1999). On top of these requirements, participating teams were likely to want to negotiate specific deals and conditions with the official sites. In some cases this has already happened. For example, one South American national team has demanded everything be provided free of charge. In order to fulfil this requirement, each bidding municipality is likely to spend US$1.2 million without any financial support from central government. Many cities and towns therefore withdrew from the bidding process (*Yomiuri Shinbun*, 1 May 2001). Municipal officials and authorities realised that, while becoming an official training site could generate tremendous attention and media exposure, immediate economic benefits to the host community could not be guaranteed. In fact, most official training sites are likely to make a significant economic loss. Therefore, one by one, the original eighty-three municipalities began to drop out of the race.

Korean sites, on the other hand, are a different story. The Korean government decided to grant 3,000 million won to the twenty-one candidate cities for supplying training facilities (*Yomiuri Shinbun*, 12 May 2001). Differences in the degree of commitment and involvement between the two central governments are quite clear in terms of constructing stadia and developing the fundamental infrastructure for the official training sites. Although bidding municipalities sought to get the right to accommodate qualifying countries prior to the tournament, becoming an official site could not assure them which of the qualifiers they would accommodate. It has been left to the qualifying country to decide where to stay and train. Final arrangements were clear until after the draw for the tournament that took place on 1 December 2001 in Busan, Korea.

A few municipalities were able to make a contract with some national teams prior to the draw. The city of Ibusuki in Kagoshima Prefecture has been selected as the training site of the defending champions, France.

Romania has chosen Furukawa Town in Gifu Prefecture if they qualify. Fukushima is in a good position to take advantage of this tournament since it is located in between Miyagi Prefecture and the Kantō region, which includes three World Cup finals venues in Ibaraki, Saitama, and Yokohama. Fukushima is not only situated within a distance of a little over one hour from Tokyo and Sendai by 'bullet train' (*shinkansen*), but also owns one of the best soccer training facilities, fourteen grass pitches, and good accommodation with a quiet atmosphere, in the J-Village. There will be at least sixteen qualifying teams which need to find their training site in Japan one month prior to the tournament or even earlier. It goes without saying that each qualifying team will look for a decent training site and Fukushima will definitely become one of the most sought after. Shizuoka, another training site venue, is also in an excellent position to offer several training sites for qualified teams. Known as a 'soccer prefecture', Shizuoka is a goldmine of young soccer talent and the home of two J.League teams, Jubilo Iwata and Shimizu S-Pulse. A Shizuoka spokesman has announced that Shizuoka would build a national soccer-training centre in the very near future. Shizuoka is located between the Tokyo and Osaka metropolitan districts. Land transportation, including bullet train and toll highway, is well developed there, whereas the so-called 'soccer town' of Kashima in Ibaraki, the home of the J.League's Antlers, is located in a more inconvenient place.

Ironically, this development appears to be promoting the spread of decent grass soccer facilities throughout Japan. In the 1970s and 1980s, very few well-conditioned grass soccer pitches were available in Japan so that most players had to practise and play the game on a muddy ground until the early 1990s. The number of grass soccer pitches increased after the J.League was inaugurated. Now, a second wave of increase in well-conditioned soccer fields all over Japan is likely to happen because of the official World Cup training site competition. This may be a good thing for the promotion of soccer, but many questions still remain, such as 'Who will be responsible for maintenance?', 'How many pitches are enough?' and 'Do we over-emphasise or over-promote the game of soccer?'

Back to reality: facing the financial trauma

To say the least, those host cities in Japan driven by the 'civic pride' that the 'FIFA World Cup' status endows, are expected to face very severe financial difficulties after this global event. Most Japanese stadia have been constructed as multi-sports and multi-purpose facilities whereas the Korean counterparts have been built strictly for the game of soccer. The Japanese stadia have been built to accommodate future national sport festivals including track and field and other sports. The national sport festival takes place annually in a different prefecture. The Shizuoka Stadium, 'Ecopa', will be the main venue for the 2003 festival, while the Oita Stadium, 'Big Eye', will host it in 2008, and the Niigata Stadium, 'Big Swan', is the venue in 2009.

Six out of the ten new stadia are the home grounds of J.League Division One and Two teams. The rest are planned to become the supplemental home grounds for either Division One or Two J.League teams after the tournament. Some common problems among these stadia include the fact that the rental price of the stadium is much higher than that of existing smaller stadia. It is rare to get a packed crowd at a J.League match, especially for the Division Two games; so even J.League teams tend to stay away from these fancy new stadia (see Table 12.2). Another problem for public stadia is that management is carried out by public corporations with very little marketing experience. The majority of the public stadia and arenas in Japan are operated by public corporations and their management has been severely criticised to be very insufficient (Mamiya and Nogawa, 2001). In a survey conducted by Mamiya and Nogawa (2001), it was found that the management of most stadia and arenas had very little intention of attracting various events or starting their own programmes to increase operating revenues. Another shortcoming is strict government regulations on use of the stadium in terms of naming rights, permanent advertisements, and other potential revenue-earning streams. While private sport stadia and arenas are allowed to post a number of permanent commercial advertisements to help secure their financial position, public sport facilities have had many problems and will face severe assessment from the public in the very near future.

Table 12.2 clearly indicates that most World Cup stadia estimate their annual balance sheet will be in heavy deficit. For example, Saitama Prefecture has poured approximately US$735 million of taxpayers' money into their new luxurious stadium, the Saitama Stadium, yet is staging just one of the semifinals in the World Cup. But the revenue streams for the Saitama Stadium are also very limited since this stadium will not house any professional sport franchise and because of strict governmental restrictions on stadium sponsorship (signage and naming rights) as previously mentioned. So citizens of Saitama Prefecture will likely pay US$2.5 million of annual operation deficit on top of the construction costs each year after this tournament.

Saitama Stadium is not alone. Sapporo Dome, expecting a little short of US$1 million in its annual balance, has to find more than US$20 million to maintain its mobile dome each year. Whilst an initial annual budget estimate was somewhere around US$16 million, it has kept on rising to US$20 million. Although the management team of the Sapporo Dome has worked hard to fill their schedule with baseball games, music concerts, exhibitions and shows, in addition to J.League matches, more than US$4 million is unofficially estimated to be the annual short-fall for their operation. Both Yokohama and Nagai Stadia have officially disclosed that their deficits are likely to exceed US$5 million each year. Miyagi Stadium is even worse than the rest because the location of the stadium is so inconvenient that Vegalta Sendai, the local J.League team, will not use the facilities. At the first world congress of sociology of sport in Seoul, held between 20 July and 24 July 2001, several Korean sport sociologists have indicated that some of the Korean stadia will have very similar problems. During the congress, quite a few Korean scholars showed their serious concerns about the post-tournament usage of the new stadia and condemned the negligence of their government for a long-term, sound financial plan. Nevertheless, in typical Asian manner with a smile, none of them has made an overt criticism on this matter.

As far as the post-usage plans are concerned, no cities or prefectures in either Japan or Korea have any significant or realistic plans to use the new stadia after the tournament. Regardless of location and amount of money, all the new stadia are likely to become big financial burdens on their municipality. For the cities, prefectures, stadium authorities, and other representatives of the public sector, this issue will soon become increasingly problematic. Venue cities in particular will face hard choices because most have stable or declining tax revenue and increasing municipal government costs (Masteralexis *et al.*, 1998). Covering the deficit of sport facilities means other services may need to be neglected. If nothing is done soon, it is as if people keep on pouring water into a bucket with holes. No matter how much water they put in, they will never fill it up. So there are two options if they continue to pour the water: either to fix the holes or discard the bucket. Thus, very critical attention will need to be paid to the use of public subsidies for operating the World Cup stadia in the midst of the long-running recession in Japan, and the attempt to recover from the 1997 financial crisis in Korea.

A rehearsal and post-World Cup usage: the future of soccer stadia in Japan and Korea

The FIFA Confederations Cup tournament was held in Japan and Korea from 30 May to 10 June 2001. The event was seen as a rehearsal for the 2002 tournament and aimed to promote enthusiasm for the World Cup. Both JAWOC and KOWOC needed to find out how to run a tournament as smoothly as possible. The security system at the stadium, the transportation system, ticket and accreditation systems, broadcasting, media control, the volunteer system, and stadium conditions were all closely examined. Measures for dealing with hooliganism and riots were also an ongoing consideration. A total of sixteen games were played at seven venue cities, three in Korea and four in Japan. No serious major shortcomings were found at any venue regarding the condition of the pitches. Nevertheless, one obvious problem at several venues was found in transportation methods since some of the stadia were constructed at inconvenient locations. As far as the Japanese venues were concerned, temporary shuttle bus or train systems will be operated during the World Cup tournament. Unlike Europe and South America, hooligans and riots are not the main target of the security system in Korea and Japan. However, the security system at each venue has become a much more important matter since the terrorist attack on the World Trade Center on 11 September 2001. JAWOC alone has increased their security budget from US$18.3 million to US$23.1 million in order to tighten the security system by adding more security guards and better metal detectors (*Tōkyō Shinbun*, 10 October 2001).

In order to expand soccer culture in both host countries, the versatility of the World Cup stadia is crucial for the citizens and visitors to use these facilities after the World Cup 2002. Regarding the usage of the stadium post-World Cup 2002, Koreans seem to be heading towards the establishment of multi-cultural entertainment facilities while Japanese counterparts head for the development of multi-sport parks. On the basis of an analysis of the Internet homepages of each venue in October 2001, the ten venues in Japan have developed very little concrete usage plans for after the tournament. Korean venues, in contrast, appear to have clear post-World Cup usage plans. For instance, the Seoul World Cup Stadium plans to establish versatile state-of-the-art sports and leisure facilities. The following facilities have been constructed for use after the World Cup: 53,071 square metres of diverse modern space including multiplex movie theatres, sport centres, large discount stores, and restaurants; seventy-five units of membership business rooms; and a versatile stage for events. The Korean cities of Ulsan and Daejeon have somewhat similar plans for their stadia to serve as multipurpose sports and leisure complexes equipped with commercial and cultural facilities. On the Japanese side, the stadia in Niigata, Shizuoka, Miyagi, and Oita will develop into total sport facilities by adding sport medicine centres and health promotion centres adjacent to each of the stadia.

The World Cup stadia have to generate sufficient funds to meet both the annual operating costs of the facilities and the annual debt payments. But how can these stadia find funding after the World Cup 2002? With regard to financial sources for the World Cup stadia, there are various sources available in both countries. Both countries will allocate a certain portion of revenues from 'sin taxes', raised on public gambling and alcohol consumption. A Japanese version of football pools, the *Toto* lottery, was formally introduced in March 2001. Japanese government forecasts the total revenue of the *Toto* to be US$667 million in 2001, but relatively low dividends (payback prize money) and irregularity of the *Toto* have caused a sharp decline in *Toto* buyers. On their original plan (as of November 2001), of US$667 million, US$46 million will be allocated to sports bodies like basketball associations and soccer associations at local and national level. Another US$46 million will be allocated to promote sports in municipalities all over Japan. JAWOC expects to receive US$25 million out of this US$46 million for its operation next year. Moreover, approximately US$58 million from the *Toto* will be allocated to JAWOC for sure (*Yomiuri Shinbun*, 4 September 2001). The World Cup stadia are likely to receive somewhere around US$2 million from the *Toto*. Although JAWOC expects to get much more allocation of the *Toto*, a number of municipalities and other sports associations are strongly opposed to the allocation of the *Toto* because financial resources for sports promotion such as sport promotion funds and corporate sponsorships have become so limited in the last ten years. The primary aim to start the *Toto* was to help local sport organisations and community sport clubs to operate, not for the 2002 World Cup and the stadia.

The Korean government has seriously taken into consideration starting their own version of football *Toto* next year. The Korean government will also establish a World Cup legacy programme to support the stadia, not only through facility finance, but also sport and cultural programmes. Japan, on the other hand, may lift some restrictions caused by urban park regulations. Deregulation of sport facilities in a public park will allow the World Cup stadia to be able to control revenue streams by inserting stadium sponsorship (signage and naming rights). Unlike American public sport facilities, Japanese public stadia and arenas have never been allowed to obtain permanent or long-term advertisements to cover their annual operation costs and to make debt payments.

The vast majority of public sport facilities have been in large deficit for their operational budgets each year in Japan. The World Cup stadia will be no exception if nothing is changed. It goes without saying that most public sport facilities have been managed by public corporations. It is inevitable that the fees to use these facilities ought to be minimal for local residents. How could these facilities survive? The answer is simple; all the deficits have been covered by public funds so far. In fact, this social system has resulted in all facilities owing approximately 75 per cent of their fiscal budget to public subsidy, that is taxpayers' money. Under the management of public corporations, these facilities cannot be operated without public financial support. Since the public benefits justifying stadium construction and operation remained, but the costs have been going up, the discussion of how to finance stadia and arenas has shifted from public methods to private methods in the last few years. Despite the fact that the majority of these shiny new stadia are forecasted to face severe financial difficulties after this sporting mega-event (see Table 12.2), none of the venue cities has developed any specific or realistic financial schemes to rescue their new stadia. As mentioned above, de-regulation of the current laws will solve some existing problems but not everything. Changing the management system from public to private management will reduce some deficit. Public corporations in various social sectors have been criticised very severely recently due to their lack of effective management and productivity. It is widely thought that more efficient management, including marketing expertise, will be extremely important for future stadium and arena operation.

Thus, the 2002 World Cup finals will be a turning point for Japanese sport professions to establish sound management systems in order to operate public sports facilities better. Unless the World Cup stadia are able to generate sufficient funds to meet the annual operating costs of their own facilities, their existence will become heavy burdens to local citizens and leave a negative heritage of the 2002 World Cup.

References

Baade, Robert A. (1996) 'Professional sports as catalysts for metropolitan economic development', *Journal of Urban Affairs*, 18, 1: 1–17.

Baade, Robert A. and Dye, Richard F. (1990) 'The impact of stadiums and professional sports on metropolitan area development', *Growth and Change*, Spring: 1–14.

Chapin, Timothy S. (1996) 'A new era of professional sports in the Northwest: facility location as an economic development strategy in Seattle, Portland, and Vancouver', paper presented at 'Sport in the City' Conference, University of Memphis, November 1996.

Japan Sports Facilities Publication (2000) *Supōtsu shisetsu nenkan* [Japan sports facilities yearbook 2000], Tokyo: Japan Sports Facilities Publishing.

The Japan Organizing Committee for the 2002 FIFA World Cup Korea/Japan (1999): *JAWOC Newsletter,* 13 (January, 1999).

Mamiya Toshio and Nogawa Haruo (2001) 'Ōgata sutājiam arina unei no yukue' [Directions of large stadium and arena management], *Gekkan Taiiku Shisetsu*, 374: 57–65.

Masteralexis, Lisa Pike, Barr, Carol and Hums, Mary (1998) *Principles and Practice of Sport Management*. Maryland: Aspen Publishers.

Nogawa Haruo and Mamiya Toshio (2001) 'Sociology of sports stadiums,' *Proceedings of First World Congress of Sociology of Sport*, Seoul, Korea, pp. 201–208.

Nunn, Samuel and Rosentraub, Mark S. (1995) *Sports Wars: Suburbs and Center Cities in a Zero Sum Game*, Indiana University: Center for Urban Policy and the Environment.

Robertson, Kent A. (1995) 'Downtown redevelopment strategies in the United States: an end of the century assessment', *Journal of the American Planning Association*, 61, 4: 429.

Rosentraub, Mark S. (1996) 'Does the emperor have new clothes? A reply to Robert A. Baade', *Journal of Urban Affairs*, 18, 1: 23–31.

Schimmel, Kimberley S. (2001) '"Globalization" and "Americanisation"'. Past and ongoing debates in the sociology of sport', discussion notes for Japan Society of Sport Sociology Symposium, University of Tsukuba, 28 March.

Internet sources

Korean sources

The analysis of Korean venues is based on information available to the public via the Internet. All pages were accessed between 1 October and 11 October 2001. For the same and more information, look at:

<http://smg.metro.seoul.kr:8000/venues/stadium/index.cfm>
<http://210.96.95.35/db-data/2002/j-2002.htm>
<http://2002.gjcity.net/ENG/e-frame.htm>
<http://www.metro.taejon.kr/english/etc/e01/index02.htm>
<http://www.worldcup.daegu.kr/eng/>

Japanese sources

Some Japanese venues have been accessed via the Internet for the purpose of this study:
<http://www.pref.oita.jp/10200/english/stadium/index.html>
<http://www.yokohama.jp/me/w-cup/english/stadium/stadium.html>
<http://www2.shizuokanet.ne.jp/worldcup/location/ecopa01.html>
<http://www.2002saitama.com/stm.html>

13 The World Cup and television football

John Horne and Wolfram Manzenreiter

Introduction

Since the 1970s the World Cup finals have arguably been turned into the showcase of an international media–business–sport alliance at the core of virtually all processes involved with the production of the World Cup. Before the advent of regular mass television broadcasting sport had been connected to new developments in other forms of mass communication. From 1900 onwards sport was linked with new developments in press and journalism. By the 1930s radio had shown its capacity to enable a nationwide audience to imagine they were present at 'live' events. Also in the 1930s these broadcasts were supplemented by newsreel films of major sporting occasions shown at cinemas. The Berlin Olympics in 1936 was broadcast 'live' to the world by radio and televised, via a local cable system, within the host city. It is television, however, which has helped to transform the nature, scale of, and research interest in, major sport event cycles such as the Olympic Games and the Football World Cup (Roche, 2000, pp.159ff.).

From its beginning, efforts were made to capture the World Cup in motion. The 1934 finals, played in Italy, were filmed and shown in cinemas within 48 hours. Televised football was transmitted during the 1936 Berlin Olympics. Technological developments, and especially the introduction of satellite broadcasts, have enabled live action to be captured since the 1960s on an increasingly global scale. Other technical refinements, such as video recording, action replay, slow motion and colour photography, have all added to the appeal of live and recorded sport, enjoyed by ever increasing audiences. 'Television football', like media sport more generally, nowadays is both an economic commodity and a vehicle for the diffusion of meaningful discourses about identity and the nation. From the late 1980s, neo-liberal politics promoted the deregulation of media markets and communication technologies, which have turned into major agents of the global cultural economy. Sport mega-events, such as the FIFA World Cup, are characteristic examples of the complex of mediatised markets, where multinational producers flatter worldwide consumers. Operating within the global flow of cultural signs and meanings promoted by television, the football tournament contributes to the reproduction and development of the contemporary trans-cultural sphere, or mediascape.

A century earlier, the media were crucial in the formation of national cultural economies. Sport had played a considerable part in this process, as scholars have noted with reference to various, mostly Western, cases. Sport coverage began with short notices in regional papers on events of clearly focused local interest and spread gradually from reporting on regional tournaments to the analysis and interpretation of sport events on a national scale. Constructing a new meta-language of personal pronouns ('us' and 'them', 'we' and 'others'), national newspapers expanded the horizon of collective identity of their readers who were turned into modern subjects. Ever since the creation of markets and the birth of consumer culture met with the development of modern sport, the relationship between the media and sport has remained pivotal and conjunctural.

Japan is no exception to the rule. In fact, the mass media, in hand with the modern transport industry, emerged as the chief promoter of sport, while the government's body politics concentrated on physical education and the docile bodies of labourers and soldiers. Already in the first decades of the twentieth century, newspapers sponsored all kind of sports events – baseball, rowing, marathon races, skiing – which were often performed in front of huge audiences. Railway companies not only transported the spectators to the events, they often also owned the sport venues and were employers of the athletes. From the beginning, a substantial part of public sport in Japan was inextricably linked to the commercial interests of its main sponsors. Since the 1920s, the state increasingly became aware of the mass appeal of sport and the symbolic power embodied in national sport tournaments and international competitions. The Tokyo Olympics, scheduled for 1940 and intended to coincide with commemorations of 2000 years of imperial rule, yet cancelled due to the outbreak of the Pacific War, were planned as a public ritual, a celebration of national achievement and for the enforcement of national solidarity (Sakaue, 1998).

In his seminal work on 'mega-events', Roche (2000) explored the way world exhibitions and the Olympic Games were transformed into media events for the benefit of the millions who were not in the same place as the 'live action'. Such mediatised events, and the space they are attached to, attain the power to transform ordinary places into special 'host city' sites. These are of particular importance for the collective memory of the host nation that is thus able to demarcate junctures or periods of transgression (ibid., p. 224). As Tomlinson (1996, p. 586) remarks, each Games provides a case study of 'event management, civic boosterism, national pride, cultural identity and media sport'.

That the World Cup is a huge media event hardly needs stating. On the one hand, the resources made available for the communications systems, the enormous media centres, and the amounts paid by national broadcasting systems to televise the event provide ample evidence for this. In the case of the

Olympic Games, TV rights account for approximately one-third of the total income, followed by sponsorship, ticketing and merchandising in that order of magnitude (Roche, 2000, p. 168). In the case of the 1990 World Cup, sales of television rights were estimated to amount to US$65.7 million (41 per cent), sales of tickets to US$54.8 million (34 per cent) and sales of advertising rights to US$40.2 million (25 per cent). These numbers hardly reflect the current position as the world TV rights (excluding the US) for the 2002 and 2006 finals were sold for US$1.97 billion, a six-fold increase on the US$310 million paid by the European Broadcasting Union (EBU), a consortium representing the interests and financial power of Europe's public broadcasters, for the three tournaments held in the 1990s.

On the other hand, there is the enormous effort made in terms of producing memorable opening and closing ceremonies that are as much for worldwide media consumption as for the local live spectators (Tomlinson, 1996). In addition, the timing of heats and finals in Olympic events and the kick-off times of key games in the World Cup finals now routinely take into account the 'world clock', and more especially the peak viewing times of audiences watching in the advanced economies of Western Europe and North America. By making the Olympics and the World Cup global media events, drawing estimates of accumulated audiences that well exceed the total world population, television underpins virtually all the other sources of income. Even though it is necessary to be sceptical about such estimates of television viewers for 'global television', as there are no reliable statistical bases by which to assess them, and approximately 71 per cent of television sets belong to 23 per cent of the world's total population (Spa *et al.*, 1995, p. 212) the cumulative audience figure is highly relevant to advertising and sponsors.

Constructing the game

Studies of media involvement in sports mega-events have usually looked at the triad of production, audience reception, and content. While the first is concerned with political economy, the second deals with the meaning of media sports, and the third with representations and ideologies. We shall briefly outline each of these features of televised football and the World Cup with particular reference to recent research in and about Japan.

For France'98 the International Media Centre (IMC, or in French, CIM) was set up in the Porte de Versailles in Paris from 1 June to 13 July. It covered 34,000 square metres, the equivalent of approximately six football pitches. The IMC combined three operations under one (very large) roof: the main press centre (MPC), the international broadcasting centre (IBC) and the main accreditation centre (MAC) for the press and journalists. The IBC was home to TVRS 98, the host broadcaster of the 1998 competition and 175 rights-holding radio and television companies. They would produce 5,760 hours of TV broadcasting for an estimated 37 billion accumulated TV viewers (revised upward after the event). The IMC used 200 kilometres of cabling,

120 tonnes of air-conditioning conduits and provided 3,000 TV sets. The IMC would use 14 Mw of power, equivalent to that required for a small town with a population of 40,000. It was estimated that 150,000 meals would be served for the 3,500 journalists expected on average per day (all information from *CIM Guide*, France'98).

Clearly following that would be difficult for all except the most advanced industrial and information societies. In 2002 each Local Organising Committee (LOC) is responsible for arranging its own media facilities, infrastructure and services. In order to reach the global television audience the World Cup will be serviced by two International Media Centres (IMCs), one in Korea and one in Japan. The Korean IMC is in the COEX exhibition centre in Seoul, which at 37,000 square metres, actually offers a larger area than the IMC in Paris. The Japanese IMC is in the Pacifico Yokohama Exhibition Hall and is a little over half the area (20,000 square metres). It is possible for additional private office space to be hired at each IMC. In addition, at each of the ten stadia in the two countries there will be a Stadium Media Centre (SMC). The price of enjoying the creature comforts that journalists covering the World Cup have come to expect will not come cheap – it will cost an additional US$4,300 in Seoul, and US$5,455 in Yokohama, to rent a 20 square metre unit of private space in the MPC. And 20 square metres of office space will cost an additional US$2,880 at Korean stadium SMCs and US$3,636 at Japanese stadium SMCs (all information from KOWOC and JAWOC *Press Rate Cards*, June and August 2001).

'For the good of the game' is the FIFA motto. After the scandals in 2001 which rocked FIFA and World Cup football, some commentators have considered a more accurate motto might now be 'For the good of the greedy'. Underlying the problems that emerged for FIFA President Sepp Blatter in May 2001 regarding the collapse of Switzerland-based International Sports Media and Marketing AG (ISSM) and its affiliate International Sport and Leisure Marketing (ISL) was the issue of television rights for the 2002 and 2006 World Cups.

Television rights are at the centre of the new political economy of world sport (Sugden and Tomlinson, 1998, pp. 83–97). In 1996 FIFA sold the world television rights (except for the USA) for the World Cups in 2002 and 2006 to the ISL marketing company and KirchMedia, acting jointly. ISL/KirchMedia were therefore set the task of handling rights and securing arrangements with all the broadcasters in the rest of the world for the televising of the 2002 and 2006 World Cups. The price paid was US$2.2 billion (or £1.45 billion: £650 million for 2002 and £800 million for 2006) and was six times more than for all three World Cups in the 1990s (Herman and McChesney, 1997, p. 77). In 1987 a consortium of European broadcasters had secured the rights for the 1990, 1994 and 1998 World Cups for a total of £141 million. This meant, for example, that the British Broadcasting Corporation (BBC) and Independent Television (ITV), the two main terrestrial channels in Britain, paid about £5 million for the right to televise the 1998 World Cup, while French TV paid approximately 50 million francs. With the ISL/Kirch deal, and other changes in the financing of professional football, some business commentators felt that the influx of 'corporate cash' meant that European soccer changed more in the year 1996 'than in the previous hundred' (*Business Week*, 23 September 1996, p. 66).

The global media market is dominated by ten or so vertically integrated media conglomerates. KirchMedia, run by Leo Kirch, is a second-tier media firm behind the likes of the major players, such as News Corporation, Time Warner, Viacom, Sony and Bertelsmann, but it has equity joint ventures, equity interests and long-term exclusive strategic alliances with most of them (Herman and McChesney, 1997, pp. 70–105). The company has sought to capitalise on commercial and pay TV and fill regional or niche markets. For example, while Rupert Murdoch's News Corporation has a minority stake in Premiere, one of Kirch's pay TV channels, with 2 million subscribers in Germany, Kirch has a majority stake in SLEC, a company which owns the rights to televising Formula One motor racing for the next 100 years. Kirch also launched DFL, Germany's first digital satellite service, and signed exclusive deals with all the major Hollywood film studios in 1996. Securing the non-USA rights to the two World Cups in the same year fitted well with this strategy. It led several commentators, however, to warn that France'98 might be the last free-to-air World Cup, since Kirch would need to recoup the vast sums of money paid in securing the rights. In 2000 it became increasingly clear that Kirch was holding out for a much larger sum from British broadcasters than ever before. A stand-off in negotiations – in which Kirch was reported to have asked for £170 million for 2002 only and the BBC and ITV were only prepared to offer £55 million was announced early in 2001. Then the news about the financial collapse of ISSM/ISL began to change the situation.

The idea of selling exclusivity of marketing rights to a limited number of partners began in Britain in the 1970s with Patrick Nally and his associate, Peter West, as the media agency WestNally. In the early 1980s the idea was taken up by Horst Dassler, son of the founder of Adidas, and at the time chief executive of the company. With the blessing of the then FIFA President João Havelange, Dassler established the agency ISL Marketing in 1982. ISL was 51 per cent owned by Adidas (Dassler) and 49 per cent owned by the largest Japanese advertising agency, Dentsū. It was clearly a means of maintaining Adidas's position as the leader in the sportswear market. Klaus Hempel was appointed as the ISL President. Later in the 1980s ISL linked up with the International Olympic Committee (IOC), presided over by Juan Antonio Samaranch. It was ISL that established TOP, or 'The Olympic Programme', in which a few select corporations were able to claim official Olympic partner status. In 1987 Dassler died and the influence of Adidas in the world sportswear market declined as Nike, Reebok, Umbro and other companies challenged on a number of fronts. In 1991 Hempel and Jürgen Lenz left ISL to establish a rival marketing agency called TEAM (initially 'The Event and Marketing' AG, then 'Television Event and Media Marketing' AG). While

TEAM has provided services for the European Football Union (UEFA) in establishing sponsors for the European Club Championship (or 'European Cup') and then the expanded UEFA Champions League, ISL has acted for FIFA and UEFA during Euro'96 held in England. The problem for ISL was that its parent company, ISSM had begun to lose influence in football and sought to act for other sports. Different reports suggest it paid either £160 or £800 million to the ATP tennis tour for a ten-year deal. ISMM also signed a deal with CART motor racing in the USA, the International Amateur Athletics Federation and the International Basketball Federation. It increasingly became over-stretched and in April 2001 filed for bankruptcy in Switzerland with debts of £350 million (US$500 million).

FIFA required reassurance about its involvement with ISL. Less than half of the money owed to FIFA for television rights had been paid by May 2001. FIFA also discovered that the US$60 million (£43 million) supposedly paid by O Globo TV for rights to the 2002 World Cup in Brazil could not be traced. Reacting to the financial situation of its agency, FIFA cancelled the Second World Club Championship scheduled for Spain in the summer of 2001. At the time of writing, it is thought that FIFA might lose US$60 million as a result of the bankruptcy of ISSM/ISL. Things could have been worse, as Sepp Blatter, the FIFA President, admitted in mid-2001 but the ISL collapse will cast a long and lasting shadow over his term in office. The first collateral damage was the World Club Championship, another Blatter initiative that has not gone unchallenged. Whether the 'dead duck' competition that FIFA said it wanted to reschedule in 2003, will be revived, is still questioned by football insiders since, as a correspondent in *The Financial Times* stated, 'None of the big media markets want to touch it with a barge-pole' (Garrahan, 2001).

The mess of unsolved legal issues and the immense capital losses prevented even big players from considering stepping into the ring, besides the fact that the Kirch group was waiting behind the curtain to act on an option to purchase the ISL rights. FIFA came out after some weeks with its own marketing subsidiary, managed by former ISL managers. The long-term implications of the ISSM/ISL collapse for the 2002 World Cup are not yet fully apparent, but the delayed start to ticket sales was finally resolved, as was the installation of the information technology system to be used during the tournament.

Further discussion of the problematic nature of the relationship between FIFA and UEFA – the leading organisations in world and European football – is dealt with briefly elsewhere in this collection and in most detail in Sugden and Tomlinson (1998). Suggestions that the large sports agency founded by Mark McCormack, International Management Group (IMG), offered FIFA £1 billion for the 2002 and 2006 World Cup television rights a year before ISL/Kirch made their much smaller offer adds further to the intrigue. In Japan, Dentsū acquired the broadcasting rights for the national team in spring 2001, although private broadcasters were said to have delivered a higher bid. For an unspecified amount – insiders believe 6 billion yen in addition to the current 10 billion yen sponsoring contract – Dentsū is now in charge of the broadcasting rights for the next six years – with the lucrative exception of the World Cup finals. The point is that whereas it used to be said of boxing that it was a beautiful sport but a lousy business, the same might now be said to apply to the 'beautiful game' of football (Tanaka, 2001).

The new political economy of world sport now includes television, sponsors and marketing agencies, in addition to the international associations and federations of sport, as parties in a 'golden triangle' or as McCormack once famously put it, an 'unholy alliance' (see Whannel, 1986). Not all parties are as well placed in it as others. Following the collapse of ISSM/ISL Kirch took out its options to purchase the entire rest of the world and US television rights for the 2002 and 2006 World Cup finals. It then resold rights to broadcasters in eighteen European countries, most of Africa, Japan, Korea and the smaller Asian market. South American rights realised US$860 million – from TV Globo (Brazil) and DirecTV (covering Argentina, Chile, Colombia, Mexico, Uruguay and Venezuela). It has also sold separate Spanish-language and English-language rights to the USA. In Britain, with the 1996 Broadcasting Act requiring that all World Cup matches should be available on terrestrial television, the two major free-to-air broadcasters eventually agreed to sign their largest sports rights agreement ever. The BBC and ITV agreed to pay £160 million in October 2001. However, both parties have claimed the deal a success. The sum agreed was very close to that originally asked for by Kirch. Yet the agreement covered both television and radio transmissions for the next two World Cups in 2002 and 2006. Although the timing of events for Western European audiences is not good in 2002 – matches are likely to kick off at 7 a.m., 9 a.m. or 12 noon in Britain, for example – the 2006 finals that start in Munich in June 2006 are perfect for European television. So although the two broadcasters have paid nearly forty times more than previously for a World Cup in television cost terms, the deal is not unreasonable. The companies have bought 128 football matches, at approximately £1.25 million for two hours of programming. Compared with the costs in Britain for costume drama (£1 million per hour), and detective series (£600–700,000 per hour) the price is not excessive when the low origination costs of football tournaments are taken into account. In addition to TV and marketing rights, Kirch also inherited the role of mounting the broadcasting relay for 2002. This will be conducted by a 100 per cent subsidiary of Kirch, Host Broadcasting Services (HBS). In turn, Japan Telecom will provide the system linking the two International Broadcasting Centres (IBCs) in Seoul and Yokohama and the ten Stadium Broadcasting Centres (SBCs) in each country.

Audience reception

If the success of a sport, or a sport event, depends on the way it is capable of attracting television viewers, precise knowledge about potential target groups and the way interest is generated among core and new audiences is imperative for the media corporations. Highly specialised market research institutions in Japan such as the Tokyo-based Video Research Institute or the research departments within large advertising companies, such as Dentsū, carefully monitor trends in audience ratings, the social stratification of sport viewers, and the particular behaviour, tastes and dislikes of viewers.

Sports programming has become an increasingly important item on the agenda of media broadcasters because of its potential for high added value. While sports programmes are relatively cheap to produce, they can reach large audiences. Among the all-time best ten audience figures in Japan six are sport-related. In fact, virtually all of these programmes stem from the earlier days of television, when competition between broadcasters, or between television and alternative leisure activities, was considerably less. These highlights include coverage of sports mega-events like the Summer Olympics in Tokyo (1964, 66.8 per cent) and Munich (1972, 58.7 per cent), and historic events like the wrestling fights of Rikidōsan against 'The Destroyer' in 1963 (64.0 per cent) and the World Bantamweight title bout between Masahiko 'Fighting' Harada and Eder Jofre in 1966 (63.7 per cent). In the past two decades, only two programmes were able to reach similar audience ratings, and the latest contribution was during the 1998 World Cup when Japan played against Croatia. During the same tournament, the number of Japanese viewers watching the match against Argentina was equally impressive (60.5 per cent).

Consideration of these statistics reveals three striking features. First, the standing of televised football in Japan has been relatively low, compared with other major sports. In 2000, seventeen sport programmes were ranked among the top thirty, but most of them were related to the Sydney Olympics (including four matches involving the Olympic football team). On a domestic level, only the traditional market leaders baseball, sumo and the classic Hakone road relay race (*ekiden*) reached the top. Second, neither revenues from advertising nor broadcasting rights have been able to turn professional football into a vital business, and this probably will continue for some time (see Table 13.1). Critical voices among the media mounted when television rates were first announced in 1993. Nationwide transmission rights were sold for 10 million yen per game, while matches in the region of Tokyo went for 5 million yen, all other regional rights for 3 million. After the surprising success of the first year the fees for nationwide transmission were doubled. Compared with Europe, however, the economic value of television football remained very moderate, as only 4.1 per cent of club revenues were generated from television fees in the mid-1990s. In comparison, sponsoring companies provided about half of the income, and about 35 per cent was cashed in at the ticket gates (Kanbara, 2001, p. 31). A number of structural as well as historical reasons are responsible for the comparatively low fees for broadcasting rights, including the large number of corporate-sponsored sports events and the opaque assessment criteria used by broadcasting companies.

Third, public interest in professional football has shown a considerable

Table 13.1 J-League club team average income distribution (million yen)

Income from	1993	1994	1995	1996	1997	1998	1999	2000	2001 (estimate)
							(Division 1 only – J1)		
Admission fees	840	1,481	1,530	886	580	533	456	393	572
Allocation funds	601	679	475	346	275	237	241	230	205
Prize money	48	24	36	59	48	43	41	33	12
Merchandising	251	253	138	88	32	20	13	7	10
TV Rights	54	172	138	87	134	114	137	103	131
Start money	248	229	183	112	70	60	50	88	52
Average attendance	17,976	19,598	16,922	13,353	10,131	11,982	11,658	11,065	17,454 (first stage)*
Home games	18	22	26	15	16	17	15	15	15
J.League Teams	10	12	14	16	17	18	16	16	16

Sources on income distribution from the J.League Newsletters No. 56 (August 1999), No. 64 (November 2000) and No. 73 (June 2001).
All other data are from the *J.League Yearbook 2001* (Nihon Puro Sakkā Kyōkai, 2001) or from other information distributed by the J.League via the official website http://www.j-league.or.jp.

* *Hōchi Shinbun*, 23 July 2001.

decline in recent years (see Table 13.1). The decline in spectators cheering the teams on in Japan's stadia has been accompanied by a similar tendency among television viewers. Audience rates climbed as high as 30 per cent and more during the initial years of the J.League but went down after 1995 to a minimum of 7–10 per cent during daytime broadcasting and a maximum of 15 per cent in the evening. The nationwide broadcasters pulled out one after the other. At present most matches are only available from local broadcaster services, while nationwide games are banned from prime time (Okada, 2000). Even the professional baseball league has recently had to face a steady decline in television popularity. The average viewer rating for Japan's long-time most successful media sport content, Yomiuri Giants' matches, was 15.1 percent across all networks by August 2001, about three percentage points lower than the year before, and the lowest ratings since 1965 when the Giants won the first of their nine straight championships.

There are several reasons for the decrease in baseball ratings, including the recent progress of Japanese athletes in US Major League Baseball (MLB). Since Ichirō moved from Blue Wave Kōbe to his new club, the Seattle Mariners, attention has shifted to the 'real thing' in the MLB. When Red Sox pitcher Hideo Nomo faced Mariner outfielder Ichiro Suzuki in May 2001, even though it was shown at midday, an estimated 20 million Japanese fans tuned in to see the live broadcast (Zielenziger, 2001). Nonetheless, Tokyo Giants' games remain an important element for commercial television networks in Japan since a 15 per cent viewer rating is equivalent to a major hit drama series. Viewer surveys have shown that the Giants are especially popular among the male-3 (M3; 50 years of age and older) category of viewers, and which currently is the fastest growing category of television viewer in Japan.

This kind of information indicating more subtle nuances of viewer behaviour is of particular importance for the marketing departments. The 1998 World Cup viewing rates referred to above actually indicate the number of households tuned in but do not provide detailed insight into age, sex, or the educational background of individuals, which are of crucial importance for the sales staff of advertising around sports programmes. With a few exceptions, sport usually attracts a predominantly male audience which most commercially driven media organisations otherwise find difficult to reach. While this was true in Japan as well as in the West, recently gender divides started to narrow. In former TV viewing behaviour, women tended to have few contacts with sports, but since the Nagano Olympics 1998 this tendency has been considerably modified as a result of new programming, convenient viewing times, and the increasingly dramatic nature of the events (spectacularisation). These tendencies were evident in a survey Japan's former national television broadcaster conducted during the Sydney Olympics in summer 2000 (Endō, 2001). It actually confirmed a change in consumer behaviour that was already visible during the 1998 World Cup when the matches of the Japanese national team were followed by an average of about 40 per cent and

58 per cent of all Japanese tuned in at least once during a game. The most outstanding commitment to football was evident among M2 (35–49-year-old men) and F2 (women of the same age). All other age groups, with the exception of young children who were excluded from viewing due to the late night broadcasting time, showed a similar degree of interest which tended to fade away during the second half of the match (Kamimura, 1998).

While the long-term trends in audience reception look like being good news for advertisers in Japan, research into the effectiveness of World Cup advertisements suggests some reasons to be less optimistic. Various unaided recall tests, in which subjects have been asked to recall brand names that were displayed on signs at the edge of the pitch, have shown poor results. Most participants did not remember any of the corporate names, although these were on display throughout the matches. In addition, the average viewer could not recognise any clear difference between Official supplier and Official sponsor – which amounts to a financial difference of US$20 million on the part of the companies involved (Nufer, 1998). It is interesting to note that FIFA, having already cut down the 1994 number of ninety to forty-five in 1998, reduced the field again to fifteen Official Partners in 2002.

Content

In addition to the analysis of costs of producing sports mega-events and the composition of audiences, research has looked at the imagery and symbolism contained in the mediated events (Tomlinson, 1996). The difference in viewing interest between domestic and international football games in Japan clearly indicates that high viewing rates do not just depend on the nature of the sport on the screen. Hence consideration of the actual content, and different means of representing sports, must be taken into account before the attraction of sport mega-events can be adequately understood.

Even before the finals themselves, the qualifying games provide plenty of opportunities for the construction of competitive nationalisms. 'What a bummer!' was the headline on the front page of the Scottish edition of the *News of the World* Sunday newspaper on 2 September 2001, accompanied by a colour photograph of a Scottish supporter lifting his kilt to reveal his backside. It was the day after Scotland had drawn 0–0 with Croatia, while England had beaten Germany 5–1, in World Cup qualifying games. No paper south of the border in England covered the story in this way. Moorhouse (1991) has suggested that sport acquires an over-determined significance in relations between dominant and subordinate nations. While his article focused on the rivalries between the four 'home nations' (England and the 'submerged' nations of Scotland, Wales and (Northern) Ireland) we have seen elsewhere in this book – see the chapter by McCormack especially – how the sports field is often associated with other more serious issues. In the case of the 2002 World Cup, these have mainly derived from the treatment of Koreans by Japanese in the colonial period, in both Japan, but especially Korea.

New technologies have been pivotal for the packaging of sport events in the midst of market upheavals where particular sport events not only vie with each other but also have to persist in competition with other media products. Therefore, broadcasting corporations are constantly on the look-out for new products and strategies to enhance their customer base. Diversification, customisation and localisation are basic strategies adopted by media content sellers all over the world. Researchers who have specifically looked at television football have focused on problems and issues involved with representing the game on the small screen. Football as a team game on a large pitch does not fit neatly on the screen – at best only a third of the playing surface is visible at any one time. This argument was one of the major objections raised against the introduction of football as an economically viable endeavour in Japan before the J.League was actually launched in 1993.

How can mass audiences appreciate football if television staff are not sufficiently skilled in representing the particular sport at its best? Lack of football knowledge by commentators and the technical staff added a communication problem to the financial ones. Kanbara (2001), for example, has criticised Japanese broadcasters for their continuing lack of expertise even years after the launch of the J.League. In comparison with the international feed of action from the 1998 World Cup finals, the match images transmitted by two uni-lateral camera machines and two Hi-Vision mobiles for Japan's public and private broadcasters consisted of a considerably higher number of close-up shots, zoom-ins on popular players, and overall a much greater focus on the Japanese team. That the amount of long shots and representations of the team as a unit were greater, and the number of action replays were much smaller, than the international feed, Kanbara argues was rooted in the Japanese media's general obsession with star players and general lack of knowledge about how to fit replays into a game broadcast live (Kanbara, 2001, pp. 103–104). While the findings appear hardly surprising, and rather good business sense for the Japanese market, Kanbara suggests that the result is a product of the semi-public national broadcaster, NHK, capitalising on nationalistic feelings. Instead of blunt quota fishing, he argues that NHK should be more aware of its public service mission, aim at educating the viewer into the game of football, and stop competing with the private broadcasters (2001, p. 114).

The quantitative preference for seeing their own squad on the screen is of course not a phenomenon peculiar to the Japanese. As Geraghty *et al.* (1986, pp. 21–28) have argued, since the 1960s various common conventions about styles of coverage of international football matches have developed. While in the 1966 World Cup finals in England close-up shots amounted to around 13 per cent of the total, the share of close-ups in sport coverage in general has increased considerably since then. Different camera angles permit identification with personalities and 'star' individuals to be established during the normal coverage of football on television. A camera, or even a single transmission channel, may be used to focus on a single star player throughout a match (as happened to the Japanese star player, Nakata Hidetoshi). In British broadcasts Geraghty *et al.* (1986, p. 35) and others have argued that such techniques are altered during World Cup transmissions and identification is built up more firmly with national teams. Interestingly this was not the case with Japanese broadcasts during the last World Cup finals. A number of writers have pointed out that the globalisation of culture does not equate with its homogenisation. In fact, at the level of the nation–state there is a 'repatriation' of difference in terms of goods sold, and the slogans, signs and styles which help to distinguish one national (or sub-national) group from another (Miller *et al.*, 2001, p. 85). It will be interesting to investigate if this difference in representation in Japanese television coverage of football is still evident during the 2002 World Cup.

Next to lack of expertise and outright nationalism, two additional Japanese conventions in broadcasting which affect the consumption of sport are the comparatively slow rate of cuts and the preference for close-up shots. Freelance football commentator Kurashiki (2000, pp. 51–52) has shown how most of the basic principles of camera work and narrative development in Japanese sports broadcasting are a product of the dominance of live baseball coverage. Baseball has constituted a quarter of all media sport in Japan over the past thirty years, and, in contrast to association football, is a much more static game. Structured by its own particular rhythm of action and pauses, it lends itself better to a certain dramaturgy of extended close-ups that mirror the emotions, hopes, and despair of individual players, and to advertising. Such conventions are hard to break with. Hence on commercial television channels in Japan advertisers were granted advertising segments during football matches.

Broadcasting data in Japan, and elsewhere, has shown that the number of sport programming hours has been increasing steadily. Japanese television companies have seized the opportunities in various ways. Commercial satellite broadcasting started in Japan in 1989 but it was only in 1992 that satellite television put an end to the growth dynamics of terrestrial broadcasting. In anticipation of the 1998 Winter Olympics, NHK started to shift the main bulk of its sport programming from its general channel towards its satellite channel in March 1995, thereby pushing the number of subscribers to more than 5 million. In 1997, with the launch of the Japan Sky Broadcasting Company – a joint venture between Rupert Murdoch's News Corporation and Softbank Corporation – exclusive, live, English Football Association Premier League games from BSkyB, Murdoch's British satellite television company, were made available to Japanese subscribers. The internationalisation of sport in Japan in the 1990s meant first of all that the domestic media covered international sports – US Major League Baseball, NBA Basketball, NFL Football and European Champions League soccer – as much as, and often in competition with, or in preference to, domestic sports competitions. After NHK announced that it planned to broadcast 150 Seattle Mariners' games by satellite subscriptions to the service grew by nearly 50,000 in April

2001. NHK's associate director, Nagato Kōichirō, stated 'We're expecting MLB programming to be the killer content that leads to the diffusion of satellite services' (*Nikkei Weekly*, 7 July 2001, p. 8).

Since 1998 the renamed SKY PerfecTV! has competed with other companies seeking to be in at the launch of digital television in Japan, because, amongst other possibilities, digital TV promises an even bigger expansion of sports channels offering live matches and time-delayed recordings (i.e. 'as if live') from the major European and South American association and rugby football leagues. After the 1998 World Cup, interest in television football has increased, and competition between broadcasting corporations has provided the Japanese television audience with the largest selection of foreign football leagues to select from worldwide (Kanbara, 2001, p. 30). SKY PerfecTV! has also attempted to enlarge its subscriber base by broadcasting matches from Italy's Serie A, where Nakata was based after 1998. The investment for the Japanese broadcasting rights for three seasons amounted to 6 billion yen, since then, an average of 60,000 new subscribers per month have joined SKY PerfecTV!.

Japanese TV companies have attempted to expand their interests while foreign companies, such as Time Warner, Disney ESPN, TCI and News Corporation have teamed up with them. Murdoch also became the first foreign investor to overcome the prohibitions on foreign ownership of Japanese broadcasting. Some commentators compared Murdoch's acquisition of a 21.4 per cent stake in TV Asahi in December 1996 to the advance of Commander Perry's 'Black ships' in 1853, a powerful metaphor referring to the enforced rupture separating feudal from modern Japan. He subsequently sold it back when it became clear that he could not place any News Corporation executives on the Asahi board (Bell and McNeill, 1999, p. 776). In England Murdoch's attempt to purchase the premier football club Manchester United in the same year was rebuffed by a combination of the British government's Mergers and Monopolies Commission, a successful pressure group campaign by United fans opposed to the deal, and popular opinion. By controlling both the content and the distribution routes of programming, media companies such as Kirch and News Corporation are following a simple yet highly effective corporate strategy that aims at cutting costs by eliminating third parties and maximising control over the production and consumption of sports. Yet such strategies are not without their risks. In six years of operating in Japan, Murdoch's SKY PerfecTV! has still not made a profit and the costs of securing exclusive coverage of the 2002 Football World Cup finals he obtained in August, 2001 for 14 billion yen, will ensure that it does not do so for several years. This is especially the case since the Japan Consortium, a group of public and private broadcasters, paid 6 billion yen for the rights to terrestrial broadcasting of forty World Cup matches, including all matches involving the Japanese team, the semi-finals and the final. What they are not going to offer is the particular service of the digital broadcaster. In March 2001, SKY PerfecTV! announced it was to open ten dedicated channels for World Cup coverage. Customers could choose from live channels with different camera angles (team A, B, etc.), reruns, highlights, commentaries and background information. The catch with this 'free' service of course was that people who wanted it would have to subscribe to the company and have the SkyPerfecTV! special set-top box and satellite dish installed.

The Internet and the World Cup

The broadcasting rights issue discussed earlier evolved out of the shock that hit Europe when the Kirch Group outbid the European Broadcasting Union, a consortium representing the interests and financial power of Europe's public broadcasters, in 1996. Suddenly the truth nobody wanted to recognise was on display: national and international sports events, contrary to public opinion, were no longer a public good. When Kirch representatives offered the broadcasting rights to national markets in 2000 and 2001, public reaction was halfway between criticism and despair. After a two-week deadlock between the sport rights agency and public broadcasters in Germany, which also saw the intervention of German Chancellor Gerhard Schröder, the public broadcasters finally secured the rights for 2002 and 2006. Of course the 2006 tournament will be hosted by Germany and is therefore particularly attractive to them. As a result of the deal, the private broadcasting corporations that are affiliated with the Kirch Group will receive additional rights to broadcast other sports 'mega-events' until 2008, including the Olympic Games and the European Soccer Championship to be held in 2004 in Portugal (FAZ, 6 March 2001). Other countries were not that well equipped for the tough negotiations. The 2002 World Cup will not be seen in Switzerland. In Britain, negotiations were particularly demanding as free viewing of the World Cup was legally protected, yet this was, from the Kirch perspective, a major market distortion.

Property issues, national markets and global rights were also at the heart of the debate on the future role of the Internet in the World Cup. Referring to the 'extension to sport of the rules of neo-liberal economics', during France'98, Pierre Bourdieu has suggested that television was the 'Trojan Horse for the entry of commercial logic into sport' (1999, pp. 16–17). Similarly, television broadcasters and media managers seemed to regard the Internet as the Trojan Horse for the entry of anarchy into their well-ordered house of mutual respect and prosperity. Representatives of the new media did not get accreditation during the Sydney Olympics, precisely because Internet rights could not be allocated for national markets. The IOC and its rights proprietor, NBC, were afraid of the damage that the streaming media might inflict on the interests of their own customers. The 1998 World Cup was the first chance to witness the significant commercial impact of the new medium on a sport mega-event – even if the influence was distorted by a 'media anomaly' since all media rights were negotiated a decade earlier and long ahead of the commercial spread of the Internet. ISL set up a World Cup site in 1997 which counted more than one billion hits by mid-tournament, and on one day it achieved a record of 73 million hits (McKeever, 1999).

Although the official tournament site (www.FIFAworldcup.com) vanished with ISL, the Internet became even more central to the marketing policy of FIFA, its affiliates and uncountable free riders. In September 2001, two global players found each other. FIFA Marketing signed a contract with the Internet portal Yahoo! as the 15th and final official sponsor of the 2002 World Cup. According to FIFA sources, the agreement centres on the establishment and management of the official website of the FIFA World Cup, a six-language data bank with ample chances for premium services and e-shops. Details of the deal were not made public but a volume of sales worth at least US$20 million has been predicted. Soon after the agreement was publicly announced, South Korean providers that stored content featuring World Cup logos received a warning letter from Yahoo! that insisted on its exclusive rights. However, FIFA regulations can be somewhat ambiguous in Korea where the concept of intellectual property, especially that of online content, is not firmly established (Ryu, 2001). While the country was certainly hit by a first and maybe second round of ambush marketing in the summer of 2001, the Korean Government declared its eagerness to crack down on copyright violations of trademarks associated with FIFA's official sponsors.

Conclusion

As mediated events, baseball, soccer, and other sports, have been used most prominently and effectively as a 'battering ram' by Rupert Murdoch as part of commercial strategies of consolidation and horizontal integration. Murdoch's News Corporation devoted more energy to dominating global television sport in the 1990s than any of the other leading media corporations. Hence 'Murdochisation' has now been added to the list of nouns derived from the names of global brands or entrepreneurial personalities which offer a way of re-labelling old-fashioned economic terms such as consolidation, vertical and horizontal integration, diversification and monopolisation (see Cashmore, 2000, pp. 292–293). As this chapter has shown, considerable power lies in the control of networks, or more precisely as we are referring to the media in network society, power lies in the hands of individuals or conglomerates that can connect networks and act as intermediaries between them (Castells, 1996). It would appear that different forms of the mass media, but at the moment especially television, have increasingly been able to dictate what they want from sport. Even if they do not interfere directly with the rules of the game – and they have done in a number of well-documented cases – their agency has transformed the sport. What caused the heightened media interest in sports programming in the past twenty years was not simply greater free time or the sudden growth of widespread interest in sport. Increasing commercial pressures on television companies, the cost benefits of sport *vis-à-vis* other TV shows – drama, documentaries, etc. – and the development of new, and competing, media – video, cable, satellite, digital, Internet, mobile phones – have all been responsible for the search for a relatively low-cost means of attracting or maintaining audiences. Yet tastes in sport and leisure, as in foodstuffs and other cultural activities, are slow to change and continuities prevail. Assessing the meaning of sports mega-events and their sociological functions, Roche (2000) and Hirose (n.d.) have developed similar arguments. Just as modern competitive sport and large-scale sport events were developed in line with the logic of modernity, sports mega-events and global sport culture are central to late modern societies. As media events, the Football World Cup provides cultural resources for reflecting upon identity and enacting agency, and more 'generally, for constructing a meaningful social life in relation to a changing societal environment that has the potential to destabilise and threaten these things' (Roche, 2000, p. 225).

References

Bell, Desmond and McNeill, David (1999) 'Multimedia and the crisis economy in Japan', in *Media, Culture and Society*, 21, 6: 759–785.

Bourdieu, Pierre (1999) 'The State, economics and sport', in Dauncey, Hugh and Hare, Geoff (eds) *France and the 1998 World Cup*, London: Frank Cass, pp. 15–21.

Cashmore, Ellis (2000) *Sports Culture: An A-Z Guide*, London: Routledge

Castells, Manuel (1996) *The Rise of the Network Society*, Oxford: Blackwell.

Endō Naoko (2001) 'How the Japanese viewed the last Olympics of the century, the 2000 Sydney Olympic Games: from the survey report on viewers' impressions of the Games', *Broadcasting Culture and Research*, No. 16. Online at <http://www.nhk.or.jp/bunken/BCRI-fr/h16-rl.html> (Accessed 20 October 2001)

FAZ /Frankfurter Allgemeine Zeitung/ (2001) 'Public broadcasters secure coverage of soccer World Cups', Frankfurter Allgemeine Zeitung, 6 March 2001.

Garrahan, Matthew (2001) 'Fifa drops world club event', *Financial Times*, 18 May 2001.

Geraghty, Christine, Simpson, Philip and Whannel, Garry (1986) 'Tunnel vision', in Tomlinson, Alan and Whannel, Garry (eds) *Off the Ball: The Football World Cup*, London: Pluto Press.

Herman, Edward and McChesney, Robert (1997) *The Global Media*, London: Cassell.

Hirose Ichirō (n.d.) 'Kindai (modan) to supōtsu' [Modernity and sport], first published in *Gekkan Nyū Media*. Online at <http://home.att.ne.jp/blue/supportista/series/hirose/hirose_modern1.tml> (Accessed 7 November 2001)

Kamimura Shūichi (1998) 'Wārudo kappu Nihon sen wa kō mirareta' [Audience interest in Japanese matches during the 1998 World Cup], *Bunken Nyūsurettā*, 1, July 1998.

Kanbara Naoyuki (2001) *Media supōtsu no shiten: giji kankyō no naka no supōtsu to hito* [The perspective of media sports: people and sport in a simulated environment], Tokyo: Gakubunsha.

Kurashiki Yasuo (2000) 'Jikkyō anaunsā no manazashi to chiizuke' [View and position of live announcers], in Seikyūsha Henshūbu (ed.): *Sonna supōtsu chūkei wa, iranai*, Tokyo: Seikyūsha, pp. 45–64. Online at <http://www.nhk.or.jp/bunken/NL-file/n001-5.html> (Accessed 20 October 2001)

McKeever, Lucy (1999) 'Reporting the World Cup: old and new media', in Dauncey, Hugh and Hare, Geoff (eds), *France and the 1998 World Cup: The National Impact of a World Sporting Event*, London: Frank Cass, pp. 161–183.

Miller, Toby *et al.* (2001) Sport and Globalization. London: Sage.

Moorhouse, H.F. (Bert) (1991) 'On the periphery: Scotland, Scottish football and the new Europe', in Williams, John and Wagg, Stephen (eds) *British Football and Social Change: Getting into Europe*, Leicester: Leicester University Press, pp. 201–219.

Nufer, Gerd (1998) *Event Sponsoring. Am Beispiel der Fußball-Weltmeisterschaft 1998 in Frankreich*, Online at <http://www.uni-tuebingen.de/uni/w04/DiskBeitraege/a5a.pdf.> (Accessed 25 October 2001.)

Okada Takuya (2000), *J. riigu no mesasu atarashii supōtsu bunka sōzō. Kigyō kara shimin e. Urawa rezzu no rei o chūshin ni* [The creation of the new sport culture the J.League is aiming at], Class paper prepared for the industrial management course at the Faculty of Economics, Meiji University.

Roche, Maurice (2000) *Mega Events and Modernity*, London: Routledge.

Ryu Jin (2001), 'Dispute hits Yahoo!'s exclusive marketing rights', *Korea Times*, 5 October.

Sakaue Yasuhiro (1998) *Kenchiku sōchi to shite no supōtsu. Teikoku Nippon no kokka senryaku* [Sport as power apparatus: sport strategies of Imperial Japan], Tokyo: Kōdansha.

Spa, Miquel de Moragas, Rivenburgh, Nancy and Larson, James (1995) *Television in the Olympics*, Luton: John Libbey.

Sugden, John and Tomlinson, Alan (1998) *FIFA and the Contest for World Football*, Cambridge: Polity Press.

Tanaka Manabu (2001) '2002 nen sakkā wārudo kappu zen shiai muryō hōsō o Sukapā ga happyō' [SKY PerfecTV! announces showing all World Cup games for free], *Hōsō Kenkyū to Chōsa*, 2001: 5, 79.

Tomlinson, Alan (1996) 'Olympic spectacle: opening ceremonies and some paradoxes of globalization', *Media, Culture and Society,* 18, 4: 583–602.

Whannel, Garry (1986) ''The Unholy Alliance': notes on television and the re-making of British sport 1965–1985', *Leisure Studies*, 5, 1: 22–37.

Zielenziger, Michael (2001) 'Japanese baseball resistant to change', *The Seattle Times*, 5 May.

Index